# PERSPECTIVES
## ON CRIME AND JUSTICE

*Joseph A. Schafer,*
*Series Editor*

# Q POLICING

# POLICING

## LGBTQ+ EXPERIENCES, PERSPECTIVES, AND PASSIONS

### EDITED BY RODDRICK COLVIN, ANGELA DWYER, AND SULAIMON GIWA

Southern Illinois University Press
Carbondale

Southern Illinois University Press
www.siupress.com

First printed [insert month] 2024.

*Cover illustration*: Police officers take part in the annual gay pride march in central London on July 6, 2019. Ink Drop/Alamy stock photo (cropped).

ISBN 978-0-8093-3957-0 (cloth)
ISBN 978-0-8093-3956-3 (paperback)
ISBN 978-0-8093-3958-7 (ebook)
This book has been catalogued with the Library of Congress.

Printed on recycled paper ♻

Southern Illinois University System

# Contents

# *Illustrations*

Q POLICING

# INTRODUCTION

Roddrick Colvin, Angela Dwyer, and Sulaimon Giwa

Many communities can claim fraught relations with the police, yet few communities have experienced such a complex and confusing relationship as the one between the police and lesbian, gay, bisexual, transgender, and queer (LGBTQ+) communities. Recent history is replete with contradictory interactions, approaches, and policies, often resulting in targeted discrimination, harassment, and violence against LGBTQ+ community members and spaces.

On one side of the ledger, we see incidents of police harassment through raids that sparked famous protests like the Compton Cafeteria riot in San Francisco in 1966; the Toronto bathhouse raids, "Operation Soap," in 1981; the 21 Club raid in Belfast in 1982; and the Puppy Palace raids in Melbourne in 1994 (Radulova, 2014). We see shoddy police investigations like the one into the still-unresolved death of Marsha P. Johnson in 1992; the murder of transgender man Brandon Teena in 1993; and the shooting deaths at Pulse nightclub in 2016.

On the other side of the ledger are positive actions and interactions, including the creation of LGBTQ+ police associations like the Gay Officers Action League in 1993; the founding of community-based LGBTQ+ policing units like the Gay and Lesbian Liaison Unit in Washington, DC, in 2000;

1

the hiring of India's first transgender police officer, Prithika Yashini, in 2017; participation by police officers in Pride parades around the world; recruitment efforts to employ more LGBTQ+ police officers (for example, in the United Kingdom, New Zealand, and Los Angeles); and formal apologies for past police wrongdoings (for example, the New York Police Department's 2019 apology for the Stonewall raid and the New South Wales Police Force's 2016 apology for its arrest of 53 people during the first Sydney Mardi Gras in 1978).

Recently, some LGBTQ+ communities have accused police services of "pink-washing." In this context, pink-washing is the strategy of supporting and promoting LGBTQ+ rights and protections as evidence of openness, legitimacy, and accountability while continuing to discriminate, harass, and perpetuate violence on LGBTQ+ communities (Blackmer, 2019). LGBTQ+ community members point to higher disappearance and murder rates for transgender people, disparate frequencies of traffic stops, the use of force and excessive force against people of color, and a persistent and corrosive organizational culture in police departments marked by heteronormativity and misogyny—all as evidence of continued policing malady. As a result, police officers and police departments are being disinvited from participating in community-based events like Pride parades. In some cases, officers have been banned from recruiting at universities due to discriminatory practices in policing (Mello & Arredondo, 2020).

Police officers and services evoke strong emotions and differing perspectives within LGBTQ+ communities. To some, they remain guardians who have become partners in community and public safety. To others, they are the physical manifestation of state-sanctioned oppression and abuse (Giwa et al., 2021). It is within this context that we developed *Q Policing*. In this edited volume, we brought together a diverse group of scholars and community leaders, including academics, former police officers, social workers, and community activists, to ponder the varied and complicated relationships that LGBTQ+ communities have with police and other law enforcement. This volume expands the conversation through a variety of voices, sources of data, and methodologies. Central to this expansive approach is an intentional focus on race, age, sex, gender, and other characteristics and identities that help explain and contextualize people's lived experiences. As such, this book is one of the first to try to bring about a more systematic study and understanding of LGBTQ+ identities in relation to policing, both on police forces and in society.

## How This Book Is Organized

We divided the book in three parts. Part 1, "Intersections with Cultural Diversity," contains chapters on the intersections of race/ethnicity, sexual orientation, gender identity, and policing. These chapters explore the differences and similarities in the lives of LGBTQ+ people. Their experiences are distinctive yet strikingly similar, particularly regarding the police's hostile treatment of community members.

In chapter one, Babu and Blount-Hill acknowledge that most of the research literature on LGBTQ+ communities and police relations has focused on the Global North. Their focus on India reminds us of the importance of decentering the Western narrative about LGBTQ+ people and their experiences and invites us to seek knowledge through a more global approach.

In chapter two, Martin, Badio, Marlow, and Abreu ask us to consider the intersection of ethnicity, sexual orientation, and gender expression with law enforcement. The authors highlight immigration policy as an additional consideration when considering the experiences of some Latinx LGBTQ+ individuals and communities. The authors make a case for law-enforcement-free spaces. These spaces could help promote collective healing and well-being in communities exposed to police violence and abuse.

In chapter three, DeGagne explains how white supremacy and poor cultural competencies can put Two-Spirit (a third or different gender identity for LGBTQ+ Native American/Indigenous persons who eschew the Western notion of binary categories for sex and gender) and other LGBTQ+ community members at additional and unnecessary risk for harassment and violence.

As a whole, the chapters of part 1 shed light on the multifaceted nature of encounters between police and members of LGBTQ+ communities. They show how negative interactions with police exacerbate the loss of trust in the criminal processing system (Mallory et al., 2015; Wolff & Cokely, 2007). They also highlight the important role that race and ethnicity play in shaping our understanding of community and policing.

Part 2 of the book, "Intersections with Marginalities," explores the experiences and perspectives of LGBTQ+ people through lenses other than race and ethnicity. The authors in part 2 highlight the experiences of individuals who are marginalized for their social construction as transgender, unhoused, southern, or fetish-interested. The chapters investigate the intersectionality of identities to understand better how these other factors change perceptions of or experiences with police.

In chapter four, Osborn explores how being visibly transgender or non-binary can make one more vulnerable to harassment, discrimination, or violence during police encounters. Osborn notes that many transgender and nonbinary people feel pressure to "perform" cisgender normativity and heteronormativity to avoid attracting negative attention from police and others. The data suggest that transgender people are less likely to call the police for fear of being mistreated by them (Williams et al., 2015).

The organizational structure of policing can influence attitudes toward LGBTQ+ homeless youth, the topic of chapter five. McCandless applies Bolman and Deal's (2017) four-frame model of organizational dynamics to explain how structure, human resources, politics, and symbolism can affect LGBTQ+ homeless youth's experiences and perceptions of police.

Recent reforms to reduce bias in police treatment of LGBTQ+ people is a positive step toward a new relationship between the police and members of the LGBTQ+ community, but the positive outcomes are not shared by everyone. This is true in many states of the U.S. South, where LGBTQ+ rights are still being fought for and where hate crime laws against discrimination based on sexual orientation and gender identity are virtually nonexistent. In chapter six, Sellers explores how contradictions between state and local laws, such as hate crime laws or gender marker policies, have created patchwork variability across the southern United States.

Arguably, the epitome of a marginalized intersectional community is the queer kinkster community (those who engage in bondage, discipline, sadism, and masochism, or BDSM) within the larger LGBTQ+ community. Queer kinksters risk being labeled doubly deviant because of their sexuality and unconventional sexual practices (Haviv, 2016). In chapter seven, Turley argues that police forces' inability to distinguish between consent and abuse exposes consenting adults to unnecessary criminal interventions. When sexual violations do occur during consensual BDSM activities, the aggrieved party is unlikely to report it to police for fear of being outed as a member of the BDSM community, of having the case dismissed or being blamed for the assault, or of being viewed as a sex object because of their interest in BDSM.

Finally, part 3, "Intersections in Uniform," presents the perspectives of LGBTQ+ people inside police services. In addition to chapters on gay men and lesbian police officers, this part includes chapters on the experiences of often-overlooked genderqueer and transgender officers. While LGBTQ+ police officers may be thought to enjoy privileges that other LGBTQ+ people do not have, they too experience harassment, discrimination, isolation, and even violence at work. These chapters highlight how social and cultural components of policing create an environment on the job that marginalizes and excludes non-heteronormative and non-cisgender-normative identities.

LGBTQ+ police officers who are trying to make policing safer for LGBTQ+ community members may be marginalized and excluded by their own colleagues. According to Panter, in chapter eight, nowhere are marginalization and exclusion more keenly demonstrated than in the experiences of transgender police officers. Whether affirming their gender when in service or when recruited as a transgender person, these officers may have some of the most challenging experiences with police colleagues. Hypermasculine police culture conduces to negative experiences for transgender officers who do not align themselves with binary cisgender expectations for femininity and masculinity.

In recent decades, many police organizations have changed to support gay and lesbian police officers better. Evidence suggests that these officers are better supported in their workplaces than are their transgender colleagues (Mennicke et al., 2018). However, as Moton discusses in chapter nine, lesbian police officers still experience a range of discriminations related to their sexuality, and these discriminations parallel and collide with the sexism that attends their being women. Although female police officers tend to use force less and make crime victims feel more supported when reporting crime, they continue to be denied promotion to leadership positions, leaving no doubt that hypermasculinity heavily influences their experiences.

Interestingly, while we might assume that gay male officers share the dividends with other male officers in hypermasculine police organizations, this is not necessarily the case. Some recent evidence suggests that gay male officers are faring better than they did in the past. They are being recruited to police forces more often and are promoted and provided with training and development opportunities more so than previously (Colvin, 2020). However, in chapter ten, Rumens explains that gay male officers continue to navigate significant challenges in heteronormative masculine police culture that deems them overly feminine and unfit to do police work. They also must navigate uncertainties in disclosing their sexuality versus engaging in behaviors that align them with heteronormative masculinity. More importantly, Rumens asserts that we know little about how intersecting vulnerabilities of cultural diversity, age, and disability influence their experiences.

One strategy that police organizations use to address the vulnerabilities of LGBTQ+ communities is to establish police liaison programs, where LGBTQ+ police officers, as well as heterosexual and cisgender allied officers, volunteer for special training to support LGBTQ+ people when they are victims or perpetrators of crime. Even so, as Meyer, Elias, and Moore explain in chapter eleven, LGBTQ+ community members are still reluctant to engage with liaison officers because of their past negative policing experiences. Still, these programs have the potential to bend and queer the power differentials of police and policed, a much-needed shift in dynamics if vulnerable LGBTQ+ people are to be better supported by police.

Strategies like liaison officer programs would likely overlook the experiences of those officers and civilians who identify as nonbinary or genderqueer. These strategies often adopt "siloed" approaches to addressing LGBTQ+ identities, meaning that they focus on one group in ways that omit other members of the community. The sex-segregated characteristics of police organizations suggest a similarly siloed approach: policing has always been sex-segregated, so officers who do not neatly fit within binary sex are marginalized. They can also be overlooked in criminological research simply because their experiences are subsumed under the LGBTQ+ umbrella, with too few genderqueer officers being interviewed to warrant their own analysis and discussion. As such, Dwyer, Rouse, and Panter, in chapter twelve, explore the experiences of genderqueer police officers working in police organizations. While their experiences are mostly unknown, the authors use what is known about policing and LGBTQ+ communities to speculate on the state of genderqueer persons in policing.

The chapters in part 3 highlight the need for further research, specifically inquiry into the intersectional experiences of genderqueer, transgender, lesbian, and gay police officers. For example, transgender officers are seemingly comfortable coming forward and speaking about their experiences with researchers, but most of these officers have been white and middle class. Lesbian officers are still expected to align their presentation of gender with heteronormative femininity, and we currently do not understand how race intersects with that presentation. Gay male officers are doing better in the workplace, but police culture is still holding them back, and we have little idea of how older gay male officers experience police service. These examples of unknowns suggest areas ripe for further study. Such research can enhance our understanding of barriers and opportunities for LGBTQ+ people interested in careers in police services.

## Common Language

While contributions to the volume represent, by design, diverse perspectives, methodologies, and conclusions, we decided on some common definitions and terminology to facilitate conversations among chapters. Readers will find consistency across chapters where intersectionality, criminal processing systems, and sex as distinct from gender were central to the research.

*Intersectionality*

According to Sirma Bilge (2013), intersectionality is a theoretical framework for understanding how multiple social identities such as race, gender, sexual orientation, socioeconomic status, and disability intersect at the micro-level of individual experience to reflect interlocking systems of privilege and oppression (in the form of racism, sexism, heterosexism, and classism) at the macro-level of social structure. Intersectionality is rooted in Black feminist scholarship. Although feminist legal scholar Kimberlé Crenshaw coined the term *intersectionality* in the 1990s to describe the exclusion of Black women from white feminist discourse (which equated women with white) and antiracist discourse (which equated Black with men), the framework has evolved to incorporate a multitude of social constructions that can influence a person's lived experiences in society. It has also become a vehicle for acknowledging that all individuals are multidimensional and complex, with contradictory values, beliefs, and perspectives. Through this framework, we can explore how one lesbian of color might embrace a profession in law enforcement as a noble endeavor while another may reject it outright. Contributors to this volume took different perspectives on police and law enforcement informed by an intersectional framework. Such an approach yielded a diversity of analyses, results, and conclusions about the state of policing in queer communities.

*Criminal Processing Systems versus Criminal Justice Systems*

Where appropriate, contributors used the phrase *criminal processing system* in place of *criminal justice system*. This language was selected to convey the lack of justice in criminal legal systems around the world. The volume's editors, from the United States, Australia, and Canada, can all point to disparities in their respective countries as examples. In the United States, according to the National Association for the Advancement of Colored People (2021), although Black people make up 13.4% of the population, they make up 22% of fatal police shootings and 47% of wrongful conviction exonerations. In Canada, the Office of the Correctional Investigator (n.d.) found that the percentage of Indigenous inmates in federal institutions rose to 28% in 2017–2018, while Indigenous people represented only 4.1% of the Canadian population in 2019. The Australian Law Reform Commission (2018) found that while Aboriginal and Torres Strait Islander adults made up around 2% of the national population, they constituted 27% of the national prison population. These criminal "justice" disparities are not only related to race or ethnicity. According to Hereth (2022), individuals who identify as lesbian, gay, bisexual, transgender, or queer, or who hold other marginalized sexual orientations or gender identities, are overrepresented in the criminal processing system around the world. So, while there are divergent perspectives on police and law enforcement, the contributors agree that the system does not promote justice equitably. Instead, it punishes those we label "criminal" rather than healing and transforming their communities (Dwyer & Colvin, 2022).

*Sex, Gender, and Gender Identity*

It is common to confuse or conflate sex, gender, and gender identity (Newman, 2023). Sex is a label—male or female—assigned by a doctor at birth based on the genitals that one is born with and the chromosomes one has. Sex is what gets designated on a birth certificate, and sex as assigned at birth influences society's expectations about one's behavior. Gender is more complex, as it is a social and legal status and carries societal expectations for behaviors, characteristics, and thoughts. Each culture has standards for how people should behave according to their gender. Gender identity is how one feels inside and expresses gender through clothing, behavior, and appearance. In most situations for many people, social expectations about gender and one's personal gender identity are in alignment.

To reduce confusion, we asked authors not to refer to *biological sex* and instead to use the phrase *assigned male at birth* or *assigned female at birth*. This usage acknowledges that someone (often a doctor) decides sex for someone else. The assignment of biological sex may or may not align with what later happens with a person's body, how they feel, or how they identify. In cases where there is misalignment between gender and sex, the authors generally used the words *transgender, genderqueer, gender nonconforming*, or *nonbinary*. While numerous concepts try to capture sex and gender diversity today, these are currently the most common and inclusive ones. We acknowledge, though, that both language and identities are fluid.

## Conclusion

The expansive work presented across the chapters of this collection delves deeply into the nuanced, complex, and multifaceted relationship between LGBTQ+ communities and police services, offering an invaluable perspective from different corners of the world and distinctive intersections of identity. At its core, this collection underscores the undeniable importance of reevaluating current policing methods, practices, and organizational cultures to address the historical and ongoing challenges faced by LGBTQ+ individuals, both inside and outside police organizations.

The chapters of part 1 emphasize the significance of broadening our analytic lens to consider other contexts worldwide, specifically in places like India. They also highlight the profound implications of intersections among race, ethnicity, sexual orientation, and gender expression in their collective impact on community-police relations. This first set of chapters lays a foundation for understanding the diversity of identities and experiences of LGBTQ+ communities, as well as their distinctive strengths and vulnerabilities.

The chapters of part 2 elaborate on some of the strengths and vulnerabilities already explored. They describe how specific groups, including young unhoused persons and nonbinary individuals, face heightened risks arising from society's entrenchment in cisgender-normative and heteronormative expectations. Furthermore, issues like the organizational dynamics of policing, disparities in policy reforms, and the paradoxical experiences of queer kinksters delineate the intricacies of how systemic structures often fail LGBTQ+ persons and communities.

The perspective of LGBTQ+ individuals who serve on police forces, presented in part 3, stands as a call to action. While policing institutions are sworn to serve and protect, these chapters show how they often discriminate against their own members. The experiences of genderqueer, transgender, lesbian, and gay officers underscore the need for organizational reform and a shift away from ingrained hypermasculine police culture. Furthermore, although initiatives like police liaison programs attempt to bridge the gap between LGBTQ+ communities and police, their efficacy appears to be limited by a legacy of mistrust and misaligned organizational priorities.

The chapters of this book, taken together, argue for a fundamental paradigm shift in policing culture, practices, and policies to better serve and protect LGBTQ+ communities. While recent strides have been made in certain areas, there is still a long road ahead. The diverse identities under the LGBTQ+

umbrella bring unique challenges that must be addressed comprehensively. Future studies in this domain can illuminate a more inclusive path toward equality and justice for all members of LGBTQ+ communities, both on the police force and in the broader society. Only through dedicated effort can we hope to bridge the chasm of mistrust and to build a more inclusive, protective, and equitable future.

PART 1

# Intersections with Cultural Diversity

# 1. INCLUSIVE CRIMINOLOGY

## A Note on Queer Experiences of Police in India

Dhanya Babu and Kwan-Lamar Blount-Hill

Like other authors in this book, we begin with the following question: How do queer people experience police? Before we answer, we must first consider the idea of police.

Police officers are charged with enforcing norms, or "collective expectations for the proper behavior of actors within a given identity" (Katzenstein, 1996, p. 5), in other words, behaviors and practices expected by the typical person within a social environment. Police officers enforce two kinds of norms. First, they enforce laws. Laws are governments' attempts to codify norms—what is expected—and enforce them using state power (Goodman, 2001; Taylor, 1896). Police are also moral agents. Morals are norms "imbued with an ethical significance" (Hazard, 1995, p. 451); they carry expectations about "right" versus "wrong" behaviors, often based on a principle that one should not cause harm (Krettenauer & Lefebvre, 2021). When we say police are moral agents, we are saying that they are symbols of, and enforce norms about, what is right and what is wrong (Herbert, 2006; Moton et al., 2020). Police are moral agents, but morals are culturally determined and vary across time and place. Understanding what police officers enforce requires an understanding of moral orders that are specific to the places where they operate.

The same holds true for understanding how they enforce and also against whom they enforce. In fact, across different societal settings, the *police* as a term might be defined differently. If one defines police as officials of a government with the power to investigate legal infractions, impose punishments, and initiate prosecution—as we do—then these may be figures in a national organization or a subnational one, with a general or specific jurisdiction, authorized to use varying degrees of force and at the helm at various stages of a criminal processing system's prosecution and punishment mechanisms. Enforcement might involve the application of law, moral judgment, or neighborhood or personal preference. Whom the police enforce these normative codes against might include criminals but might also include mere "deviants" (norm violators) or, in some locales, the general public, the press, or those with opposing political views.

Simply by noting international variation, we have scrambled the definitions we tried to clarify. If the broader project of queer theory is postmodernist disruption of rigid categories of "what is" in favor of a shifting sense of "what might be" (Stein & Plummer, 1994), then an international scope helps us to show how queer the most basic of concepts become—in fact, how queer even the notion of "police" can become.

In this chapter we center voices of those who might be called "queer" in an Indian social context to shed light on how their stories of encounters with police should both elicit concern, support, and political action toward their protection and cause you to recognize how understanding their experience can enrich and deepen understanding of your own. Queer describes people who identify with non-normative sexuality or gender, encompassing a spectrum of identities and behaviors including, but not limited to, lesbian, gay, bisexual, transgender, and intersex, along with hijras and kothis, sexual and gender communities in Indian culture that may not fit into Westernized categories. Queer also refers to the unstable, shifting, and difficult to delineate nature of sexual and/or gendered being and, in so doing, highlights the instability of a social life that authorities seek to control through strict labels and rigid norms. Decentering the West in the study of queer experience necessitates a fluidity of thought that assists in developing a more meaningful queer theory. Moreover, it is part of a larger modern project of creating a more expansive, more inclusive criminology that does not exclude sex and sexuality from its inquiry nor the Global South and East from its concern (Blount-Hill et al., 2022).

## Queer Identity in India

Western accounts of the queering of social theory position defiance of binary sex and gender categories as arising from a convergence of lesbian and gay studies with radical feminist critiques of gender and sexuality (Marcus, 2005). Eastern cultures may trace their understandings of how sex and sexuality blend and innovate to even earlier roots. While heteronormative, sex-normative, and cisnormative practices have always been the cultural norm in India, there is ample literary evidence of nonprescriptive queer discourses that preceded colonial times (Vanita & Kidwai, 2002). Such discourses resulted from the country's complex history of cultural assimilation of successive invaders and colonizers. India underwent changes in attitude toward queer identity and sexuality from the Vedic period (1750–500 B.C.E.) to the colonial era (1858–1947). This historical context is essential for understanding queer-police interactions in India.

Queer identities and relationships have carried less social stigma at times in India's past than they do today. Early Hindu laws (such as the *Manusmriti*) prohibited homosexual acts. Still, sacred texts in Hinduism, such as the *Mahabharata* and *Ramayana*, had numerous examples of queer attachment and introduced several characters that defied the gender binary, including the warrior and transman Shikhandi. And the *Kamasutra* described and prescribed queer sexual practices, as did many temple sculptures and carvings preceding the second century C.E. (Vanita & Kidwai, 2002).

Beginning in 1757, the colonial British dictated India's social, cultural, and judicial architecture. This included sexual norms animated by Victorian moral standards (Hinchy, 2019). Communities of hijras, visibly genderqueer people in public spaces, posed a significant threat to Western morality and European ideas of gender and sexuality (Reddy, 2010). Colonial Britain introduced the Criminal Tribes Act in 1871 to criminalize gender-nonconforming people, among others (Commuri, 2017). According to this law, hijras were an obscene public nuisance, rumored to kidnap and castrate children, and were mandated to register as gender-nonconforming people (Hinchy, 2019).

The British introduced a legal prohibition on sodomy in India in 1860. The law permitted up to life imprisonment for any who engaged in "carnal intercourse against the order of nature with any man, woman or animal," according to Indian Penal Code §377. Even once India became an independent nation in 1947, this remained the law. IPC §377 helped sustain a legal and moral norm of queerphobic attitudes in India, legitimizing discrimination and harassment of LGBTQ+ people by moral agents like police (Narrain, 2004). Only after decades of community-based advocacy and pressure from activist movements did the Supreme Court of India rule section 377 unconstitutional on September 6, 2018 (Navtej Johar v. Union of India, 2018).

## Policing Expressions and Performance of Queer Identity

Research literature on queer experiences with police in India is scant. A keyword search (of the terms *law enforcement, LGBT, queer, hijra, transgender, India, South Asia*) in relevant academic databases produces few relevant results. We do know that sexual and gender minorities experience Indian policing in ways that reflect intersecting attributes of identity and that many face considerable violence and discrimination in their lives, both in public and private spaces. Some of the most visible and pervasive forms of discrimination against queer persons in India are perpetuated through the criminal processing system, especially by the police (International Commission of Jurists, 2018). Two major themes emerge from the research about queer experiences with police in India: (i) the use of both neutral and explicitly gendered laws to arrest queer persons and (ii) police violence against queer persons. We also see an activist movement arising from within queer communities in India that is exposing discriminatory practices in the criminal processing system.

Until it was struck down in 2018, section 377 enabled queerphobic police violence. Few people were formally charged under this section, but police widely used it to intimidate, threaten, blackmail, and extort money from queer people in India (Joseph, 2005; People's Union for Civil Liberties–Karnataka, 2001). Section 377 was also frequently used to assist the families of queer persons that sought to forcefully separate gay couples (Fernandez & Gomathy, 2005), and it served as a barrier for queer people to report crimes against them to the police for fear of self-disclosure.

In addition to the queer-specific IPC §377, many other seemingly neutral laws were used by the police to target and arrest people with non-normative gender and sexual identities (Banerjie, 2019). Police frequently used laws like the Immoral Traffic Prevention Act of 1956 and nuisance and anti-beggary laws to arrest, harass, and extort money from queer people (Banerjie, 2019; International Commission of Jurists, 2018). In 2014, the Supreme Court of India recognized that one of the most common issues faced by transgender communities in India was police abuse and harassment (NALSA v. Union of India, 2014).

This was especially true for members of the hijra community, who often engage in begging and sex work (Jain & Rhoten, 2020). An infamous case of this discrimination occurred in November 2014, when the Karnataka police detained 167 transgender persons, citing 1975 anti-beggary laws, which permit police to relocate anyone found begging to a beggars' home. These transgender people, including many from the hijra community, were later forcefully relocated to a 158-acre "beggars' rehabilitation colony," a settlement instituted during the colonial period to keep beggars away from the central city (Banerjie, 2019; International Commission of Jurists, 2018).

Laws like the Meghalaya Police Act, the Kerala Police Act, and others that empower officers to regulate public nuisance and riotous behavior are disproportionately enforced against queer people for occupying public space. Jain et al. (2020) conducted interviews with self-identified transgender women and hijra persons in Delhi. The interviewees described widespread, targeted police harassment in public spaces, especially at night. One of the interviewees told of two police officers who had questioned her for merely sitting on a public bench as she awaited the arrival of friends. During her questioning, the police slapped her and accused her of soliciting sex work, and later they threatened to sexually assault her in the police station if she did not leave the premises right away.

Other laws more explicitly criminalize transgender persons and are used by police against those perceived to be queer. The Karnataka Police Act and the Telangana Eunuchs Act 1329 F criminalize transgender identities and communities in multiple ways. These laws permit police and state authorities to keep records of people perceived to be "eunuchs" and arrest those found dancing or singing or cross-dressing in public (Banerjie, 2019; International Commission of Jurists, 2018). Vagueness in these laws only enhances already substantial police power, as officers may interpret and enforce them as they see fit (Jain & Tronic, 2019). Police officers are enculturated into heteronormative and cisnormative systems; their individual interpretation and enforcement of vaguely defined laws often results in the criminalization, regulation, and condemnation of any queer expressions (Dwyer, 2011a).

In addition to the discriminatory use of laws or enforcement of patently anti-queer legal codes, ample evidence demonstrates that police use overt violence on people they perceive to be queer (Banerjie, 2019; Jain et al., 2020; Nataraj, 2017). Queer people have reported sexual assault, extortion, and torture by police on the streets or in detention. A report submitted by the International Commission of Jurists in 2018, based on 150 interviews with queer people from nine cities, exposed several forms of violence against them. Queer persons, especially transgender women (including hijras), had been asked to strip off their clothes in police stations and were then sexually victimized by the officers, including rape and sexual torture. One of the interviewees said that when she reported to the police that seven men were chasing her, the police offered to protect her from the attackers in exchange for sex.

In 2016, Tara, a 28-year-old transgender woman, was found near a police station in Chennai with her body almost entirely covered with burns; she later succumbed to her injuries at a hospital. In her last statement, Tara told her friend that the police had confiscated her scooter and keys and then harassed her when she went to the police station demanding to have them back. She was told to "go die; no one will mourn your death" (Mathew, 2016). Tara responded by immolating herself. Unfortunately, fatal incidents of transphobic violence by the police are not uncommon in India. In her autobiography, Revathy (2010) described being stripped naked in front of other prisoners at a police station and being struck in the genitalia by an officer: "He repeatedly struck at that point with his lathi [police baton] and said, 'So, can it go in there? Or is it a field one can't enter? How do you have sex then?'" (p. 206).

## India on the International (Criminological) Stage

To date, the bulk of criminological scholarship on the queer experience with police has been done in the Global North and West. This body of work finds that heteronormative, cisnormative, and sex-normative stereotypes and patriarchal structures within social institutions encourage abusive behavior toward queer people (Carpenter & Marshall, 2017; Dwyer, 2015; Mallory et al., 2015).

Angela Dwyer (2008) focuses her attention on queer embodiment, primarily among young people. Dwyer argues that queer bodies can be "read" almost as living texts that enact ways of "doing sexuality" that contradict heteronormativity. In so doing, these bodies invite police gaze and police regulation. Moreover, policing of queer bodies is justified by reference to risk, both being at risk of victimization and being risky and crime-involved (Dwyer, 2014a). Queer encounters with police serve as stages of spectacle, whereon police engage in teaching what is allowable and what is to be suppressed, especially in public space (Dwyer, 2015). It is often unclear whether the discrimination Dwyer observes is due to her subjects' queerness, age, or the intersection of the two. The intersection of multiple oppressed identities has complicated the study of queer oppression in other research (e.g., race and sexuality in Meyer, 2020).

The research on India suggests that sexual and gender discrimination occurs irrespective of age and despite largely homogenous ethnic membership, although India's caste dynamic may affect how queer persons experience oppression. Nevertheless, the phenomena observed by Dwyer are resonant in an Indian context. For instance, hijra serve as a "spectacular" display of non-heteronormativity, non-cisnormativity, non-sex-normativity and are both noticed and heavily regulated for it by police. They are assumed to embody riskiness and are presumed dangerous to children and to be purveyors of illicit sex; their treatment serves to demonstrate the boundaries of norms of appropriate behavior, especially regarding the performance of gender, sexuality, and sex.

Indian queer experience with police mirrors Western themes of discriminatory enforcement and forms of anti-queer violence by police. In her work in Australia, Dwyer (2014a) found that LGBT young people especially experienced discrimination and abuse from police when they expressed their sexual or gender identity overtly. A 2015 U.S. transgender survey revealed that more than half of transgender persons who interacted with the police had experienced harassment, abuse, or other forms of mistreatment (James et al., 2016). Farr (2016) used data from the National Coalition of Anti-Violence Programs in the United States to show that the rate of police violence against LGBTQI people was positively correlated with the rate of LGBTQI people reporting violent crimes to police—a chilling result suggesting that to become known to police as queer (victim or not) is to become a target for their bigotry. An assessment of the 25 largest police departments in the United States conducted by the National Center for Transgender Equality (2019) found that transgender people were often treated with bias and abuse in policing and in the criminal processing system.

The Indian context also complicates the picture of queer-police interaction reported in Western research literature. India has only recently repealed the legal tools that allowed police, as enforcers of legal norms, to discriminate against queer people. It is still not clear to what extent these legal changes have altered officers' views as enforcers of publicly endorsed moral norms. We are not aware of claims that the Indian public has abandoned prior-held values opposed to sexual diversity, especially as a more conservative national

Hinduism takes hold culturally and politically (Banerjie, 2019). And, unlike past periods in the West, widespread homophobia and transphobia exist in a present-day global milieu of social liberalism that demands protections for individual freedoms (e.g., Shah, 2009). The interaction between countervailing national and international norms toward sexuality, sex, and gender identity makes India a unique place to study queer-police interaction.

Culturally, Indians continue to exhibit familial collectivism (Krishna, 2014) supported by a social structure that makes upward mobility difficult for those without privilege or networks with social capital (Krishna, 2013; Kumar et al., 2002). Given the social and economic exclusion of members of queer communities in much of the country, how will queer communities in India find pathways to acceptance by the groups that can curtail police actions, like their counterparts have in the West? Ongoing and successful queer rights movements in India are now being documented (Kumar, 2017), but little work addresses how these strides have influenced Indian police work. This situation is further complicated by class and caste division, wherein queer elites may exist wholly separated from the genderqueer communities most often encountering police (Kumar, 2020; Tellis, 2012). How do police-queer relations develop for queer communities that lack social, economic, and political clout?

There are yet more basic questions still to answer: What does the embodiment of queer identity look like in India? Are its movements, garments, color schemes, and communicative affects different from or the same as those observed by scholars of Western queer communities? Can they be as easily or more easily "read" by police officers? Western gay rights advanced in a historical period in which several social lines were also blurred—or, perhaps, queered—including gender and racial divides. In a country where strict hierarchies persist, can a queering of sexuality, sex, and gender take root in India?

## India Moving Forward

In November 2019, the Indian government passed the Transgender Persons (Protection of Rights) Act, which prohibits discrimination in employment, education, and property rights based on gender identity. Yet the bill protects only transgender people who are registered with the government and have valid proof of gender confirmation surgery. The bill also prohibits people from engaging in begging and sex work, two typical sources of income for

India's hijra community (Saria, 2019). As in most parts of the world, decriminalizing queerness alone is not enough to create safer conditions for queer communities. Additionally, when forming laws to protect the rights of queer communities, it seems imperative that lawmakers consult these communities in advance. Otherwise, ostensibly inclusive policies, such as the Transgender Persons (Protection of Rights) Act (2019), might lead to further discrimination or criminalization of queer communities.

The research literature shows that even seemingly neutral laws provide police officers with immense power to enforce both legal and moral norms in discriminatory and unfair ways against the performance of queer identity. Although this literature documents police organizations' strivings to move beyond queerphobic attitudes, countries in the Global South and East have struggled with (or sometimes merely accepted) slow progress in removing homophobia from the criminal processing system—often, we should note, a remnant of past colonial rule (Ahmed, 2017).

Rare but hopeful signs exist in the form of, for example, recruitment programs in Indian states such as Chhattisgarh and Odisha, where transgender people are eligible to apply for sub-inspector and constable positions in the state police department (Barik, 2021). Many prior victims of police brutality were among the first 40 applicants. In a further show of support for a fully representative police workforce, the government in Chhattisgarh provided transgender applicants from poverty-stricken families with special education, food, and lodging to prepare for the police qualification tests (Mishra, 2021). Before this recruitment effort, there had been only two transgender persons on a police force—one in Tamil Nadu and one in Rajasthan. Chhattisgarh became the first state in India to recruit a cohort of 13 transgender police officers into the constable rank. Nonetheless, there is still much more to do.

Queer theorists—specifically queer criminologists and queer legal theorists—have undertaken to expose how law and legal enforcement regimes identify and oppress queer identity while constructing and reifying cisheteronormativity (Ball, 2019; Woods, 2014). It is essential to reevaluate the discriminatory nature and disproportionate effect of institutional and social structures on historically oppressed communities. Queer criminologists can play a significant role in bringing to light the experiences of queer persons in criminal processing systems (Dwyer & Panfil, 2017). Yet Ball and Dwyer (2018) point out that queer criminologists often overlook differences in policing models between the Global North and South when recommending universalized solutions to building better police-queer relationships. If queer criminology continues to be defined by Western experiences alone, it will be challenging to ensure its goal of inclusion. Decolonizing queer criminology can be done only by making visible queer experiences outside the Global North (Giwa et al., 2020; Moosavi, 2019). We must refrain from applying criminological knowledge sourced from the West as a prescription for injustices that queer people face in other parts of the world. Moreover, ensuring that queer criminological work is accessible outside academic spaces will help inform a wider audience who can benefit from it.

## Conclusion

Scholars of sexuality in Asia have noted the clumsiness of applying Western concepts of sex, gender, and sexuality (Jackson, 2000). We have not argued for specific parameters of queer identity in this chapter. Instead, we have contended that simply decentering the Global North and Western focus of scholarship on queer-police interactions serves to queer these inquiries by revealing, at once, overlaps and asymmetries in queer experience across national and regional contexts. Police officers around the globe have the power to investigate violations of law, arrest the violators, and initiate formal processes of penalty. Defining police as law enforcers and moral agents provides a universally transferable notion of police only in its broadest interpretation. How much more complicated it is to try to universalize notions of sex and sexuality. Inclusive criminology cannot fulfill its explanatory mission by contorting non-Western phenomena to fit Western ideas. Truly inclusive criminology—inclusive queer criminology—necessitates studying queer experience in all its contexts, including contextualized inquiries of queer encounters with police.

## 2. LATINX LGBTQ+ COMMUNITIES AND LAW ENFORCEMENT PERSONNEL
### Oppression, Violence, and Reform

Julio A. Martin, Koree S. Badio, Tyson Marlow, and Roberto L. Abreu

Few relationships are as contentious as the one between law enforcement and the communities they serve, particularly for marginalized members of those communities. The acting out of brutality, marginalization, and discrimination upon minoritized communities by law enforcement personnel has been a long-standing sociopolitical issue that has everything to do with the United States' legacy of asserting and sustaining white supremacy with a system that maintains the dominance of white, cisgender, heterosexual men and that has served as the foundation for colonialism and other systems of oppression (such as heterosexism and cis-sexism) (Beliso–De Jesús, 2020; Grzanka et al., 2019). Minoritized communities—such as LGBTQ+ communities, immigrants of color, and BIPOC (Black, Indigenous, and people of color) communities—are and have been especially vulnerable to brutal policing (Brown, 2019; Mallory et al., 2015; Padrón, 2015).

Many scholars have discussed the role of race, ethnicity, sexual orientation, gender identity, or immigration status in policing and police bias, but few have discussed the experiences of policing within Latinx LGBTQ+ communities in the United States. This chapter discusses historical events that have shaped the relationships between U.S. law enforcement personnel and LGBTQ+ communities. We introduce theoretical concepts for understanding the experiences of Latinx LGBTQ+ people in the context of policing. We also provide recommendations for improving relationships between law enforcement personnel and LGBTQ+ people of color, and specifically Latinx LGBTQ+ people.

Latinx LGBTQ+ communities often encounter law enforcement personnel other than police officers. Therefore, we use this term, abbreviated LEP, to capture the different categories of policing agencies regularly encountered by Latinx people, including officers at immigration detention centers, border patrols, and government officials who are likely to affect the present and future of Latinx LGBTQ+ immigrants in the United States.

We also reference the scholarly understanding of cultural, economic, and political white supremacy and white nationalism as systems that sustain white people's dominance in all sectors of society, leading to racial segregation and, thus, racial disparities. The interacting systems of white supremacy, white nationalism, and policing are essential to understanding interactions between LGBTQ+ communities and LEP, and underlie our analysis.

Moreover, we use the term Latinx to indicate inclusivity of gender diversity and heterogenous Latinx communities. Our use of Latinx allows for the inclusion of those who do not identify as male or female as well as those who do not speak Spanish. Scharrón–del Río and Aja (2015) argue that one of the principal acts of imperialism and colonization of Latinx people is the erasure of non-Spanish native languages and dialects. We also use LatCrit theory (Valdes, 2005; discussed under Theoretical Considerations below) as a critical lens for understanding Latinx people in the context of colonization.

## Disclosure of the Authors' Positionalities

Given the intersectional nature of this chapter, it is important to contextualize how the authors' intersectional identities provided the lenses through which we approached and presented the information in this chapter. The team includes a PhD student in counseling psychology (Martin) who identifies as a first-generation Latinx (Cuban descent) gay, queer, cisgender man; a PhD student in counseling psychology (Badio) who identifies as a second-generation cisgender, heterosexual, Afro-Caribbean American (West African descent) woman; a postbaccalaureate student (Marlow) who identifies as a Latinx (Puerto Rican descent) heterosexual, cisgender man; and an assistant professor of counseling psychology (Abreu) who identifies as a first-generation Latinx (Cuban descent) gay, queer, cisgender man. The authors acknowledge that, as cisgender people, we do not have the experiences of the transgender communities mentioned in this chapter. Furthermore, even though we are Latinx and other people of color, our experiences might be different from the experiences of the people we discuss. Our goal in disclosing our intersecting identities as they relate to the content of this chapter is to be transparent and to use both our oppressed and our privileged identities to amplify the voices and experiences of the communities we discuss.

## Theoretical Considerations

Intersectionality is of utmost importance when discussing Latinx LGBTQ+ people's perceptions of LEP. Drawing from intersectional theoretical concepts that underlie the experiences of Black women within the legal system (Crenshaw, 1989), we posit that legal institutions are weaponized to promote oppression and violence toward people who hold multiple marginalized identities. LatCrit is a theoretical framework developed by legal scholars to apply when discussing the experiences of Latinx LGBTQ+ people in the United States (Valdes, 2005). LatCrit aims to understand the intersection of race and ethnicity in the context of a legal system that dates to colonialism. Through this lens, we can understand how concepts such as "Hispanics" were put in place to erase Latinx communities' heterogeneity, which includes diversities of skin tone and gender identities. LatCrit provides a critical lens that brings to light injustices that go unseen because they have become an "acceptable" part of the culture. The primary LatCrit principle guiding this chapter is recognizing and naming the laws and policies that were designed to erase the impact of systems of oppression on Latinx LGBTQ+ communities.

We can use intersectionality and LatCrit to understand how LEP engage with Latinx LGBTQ+ people and communities at the intersection of white supremacy, xenophobia, sexism, and cis-sexism (Abreu, Gonzalez, Capielo Rosario, Lindley, et al., 2021). These systems use oppressive narratives, such as viewing LGBTQ+ people as highly sexualized objects, to give LEP license to discriminate against these communities and cause harm and fear. These narratives often lead LEP to see LGBTQ+ Latinx people as unworthy of humanhood. For instance, this narrative is pervasive for immigrant Latinx LGBTQ+ people seeking asylum in the United States after fleeing their countries of origin to escape harassment and violence resulting from homophobia and transphobia. Throughout this chapter, our goal is to provide examples of negative perceptions, bigotry, and violence from LEP toward Latinx LGBTQ+

people positioned within systems that are invested in maintaining white supremacy at all costs.

## History of Policing Tactics and Violence toward BIPOC and LGBTQ+ People

Structural and institutional discrimination and violence often influence policing tactics toward marginalized communities (Robinson, 2020a). Structural discrimination within U.S. policing systems has systematically disenfranchised BIPOC and LGBTQ+ people (Machado & Lugo, 2021). The social system of policing was established to enforce slave ownership (Brown, 2019), and structural racism, discrimination, and violence continue to play a significant role in police bias and violence toward members of BIPOC communities. For instance, Latinx people in the United States are often misperceived by police to be drug lords, criminals, and prone to violence, while simultaneously being exposed to anti-immigration policies that threaten their physical and mental health (Cross et al., 2022; Groenke, 2019).

Throughout the history of the United States, LGBTQ+ communities have been subjected to routine and systematic acts of violence for simply existing and expressing their authentic selves. Therefore, when analyzing police-LGBTQ+ relations, it would be negligent not to acknowledge the historical institutional roots of discriminatory and oppressive policing practices toward LGBTQ+ communities, as well as to acknowledge that these practices reflect widespread cisnormative and heteronormative social structures that have shaped the political and social ideologies of the United States.

Up until the late 1960s, same-sex/same-gender/queer relations were widely illegal across the United States, and being openly LGBTQ+ could result in physical punishment and incarceration (History.com Editors, 2017). Despite this brutalization and harassment, LGBTQ+ communities have a rich history of resistance, activism, and collective action. The country has seen many protests, marches, demonstrations, and other acts of civil unrest at various establishments in response to police and societal violence. One of the first acts of rebellion against police brutality by LGBTQ+ people was in 1966 at an LGBTQ+ gathering space in San Francisco, California, where transgender women of color ignited the Compton Cafeteria riot. This riot not only made LGBTQ+ rights part of the civil rights movement, but it also exemplified the power of LGBTQ+ people coming together to reject police violence and societal oppression (Stryker, 2017).

Compton Cafeteria served as the meeting place for Vanguard, a transgender/drag/gay organization that began bringing LGBTQ+ people together. With the rise of the civil rights movement and the publication of such titles as *The Transexual Phenomenon* (Benjamin, 1966), Vanguard's members became motivated to fight for their right to freedom of expression. The moment to stand up against police violence arrived in August 1966 when a riot broke out at Compton Cafeteria after a police officer grabbed a transgender woman. This riot is one of the first known riots of LGBTQ+ people protesting police violence; it paved the way for many changes in the San Francisco area and around the nation.

In 1969, the famous Stonewall uprising—a violent clash between LGBTQ+ bar patrons and the New York City Police Department—was fueled by the oppressive and discriminatory nature of LEP, including warrantless arrests, sexual harassment, and the use of physical violence (Colvin, 2012). In the act of resistance and revolt, many of the bar patrons fought back and protested the violation of their rights to assembly and to explore personal freedom (Gillespie, 2008). Although much progress has been made since Stonewall, LGBTQ+ communities continue to be victimized and over-policed by LEP (Mallory et al., 2015). The fight against police brutality and general discrimination continues even to this day, with many LGBTQ+ people drawing inspiration from their revolutionary community ancestors.

Sylvia Rivera, a self-identified drag queen born in New York City to Latinx parents, left her home at the age of 10 and began fighting for the rights of gay people and drag queens by the time she was 18 years old. Sylvia and Marsha P. Johnson, along with other young LGBTQ+ activists in the early 1970s, cofounded Street Transvestite Action Revolutionaries, which offered services to LGBTQ+ homeless young people and fought to pass the Sexual Orientation Non-Discrimination Act in New York, a law to prohibit discrimination in the workplace based on sexual orientation. Sylvia and Marsha both endured violence and discrimination at the hands of LEP. However, they found strength within LGBTQ+ communities to fight for their rights and the rights of LGBTQ+ people. This continued fight is salient today for intersectional groups within LGBTQ+ communities such as Latinx LGBTQ+ persons (Groenke, 2019).

Although policing and law enforcement practices have changed over time, the negative perceptions of LEP in Latinx LGBTQ+ communities generally have not. For example, the National Transgender Discrimination Survey (NTDS) reported that about 46% of 6,450 transgender people did not feel comfortable seeking help from LEP, and of 54% that had interactions with police, 22% reported experiencing harassment (Grant et al., 2011). This is not surprising given the targeting of BIPOC and LGBTQ+ communities through criminalization and the overrepresentation of these groups in criminal processing systems, which is one of the many policing problems these groups face today. Given the fraught historical relationship between police and LGBTQ+ communities, their interactions are particularly important to the public interest.

## Policing Latinx LGBTQ+ Bodies

To understand Latinx LGBTQ+ perceptions of LEP institutions, it is important to take into consideration several dimensions, including personal experiences, perceived bias, institutional discrimination and violence, and dominant historical narratives of violence against LGBTQ+ people who hold intersecting identities. For example, in the NTDS report, researchers found disproportionate rates of harassment by LEP toward transgender people of color compared to their white counterparts; 22% of white respondents reported harassment, compared to the following reporting by population: 23% Latinx, 29% Asian, and 38% Black (Grant et al., 2011). This finding has been corroborated by other studies. For example, in one study of 220 Latinx transgender women living in Los Angeles, California, 58% reported being stopped by LEP without their having violated any law, and 33% of these participants reported being stopped by LEP three to five times in the same year (Woods et al., 2013).

This type of experience is even worse for Latinx LGBTQ+ asylum-seeking people who are escaping anti-LGBTQ+ violence in their country of origin (Randazzo, 2005). These people fled their homeland only to face further discrimination, harassment, profiling, and state-sponsored homophobic and transphobic attitudes at the hands of U.S. LEP (e.g., Abreu, Gonzalez, Capielo Rosario, Lindley, et al., 2021; Cerezo, 2016). In a sample of immigrant Latinx LGBTQ+ women, discrimination in the United States was associated with adverse mental health outcomes such as depression, post-traumatic stress disorder, and substance abuse (Cerezo, 2016). In addition, a report of experiences by immigrant Latinx transgender women noted that all participants experienced anti-LGBTQ+ violence crossing the United States–Mexico border (Borges, 2018). In a 2021 study of 30 immigrant Latinx transgender people held at a detention center in the United States, all participants reported abusive and dehumanizing treatment by detention personnel (Minero et al., 2022), and 57% of participants reported being held in solitary confinement as a form of torture. Because immigration centers are typically the first experience of U.S. LEP for immigrant Latinx LGBTQ+ communities, they set the expectation for future interactions with LEP in the country. The continual fear and threat of deportation for undocumented Latinx LGBTQ+ people at the hands of LEP agencies leads to perceptions of LEP by the Latinx and immigrant LGBTQ+ population that are understandably unfavorable. These early negative experiences may contribute to future lack of crime reporting by these communities once living in the United States (Abreu Gonzalez, Capielo Rosario, Lindley, et al., 2021).

Negative experiences of policing also affect naturalized and Latinx people born in the United States who are profiled as non-natives or undocumented immigrants. For example, due to discrimination in finding employment, Latinx transgender women often have no choice but to engage in sex work for food and shelter (Abreu et al., 2023; Cerezo, 2016). This outcome is even more likely for immigrant Latinx transgender women who are undocumented and face greater struggles in finding employment. These intersectional experiences of oppression often result in Latinx transgender women living in poverty. For example, the National Center for Transgender Equality and the National LGBTQ Task Force found that 28% of Latinx transgender people reported having a household income of less than $10,000 a year (Padrón, 2015).

Given the discriminatory and criminalizing approach of LEP toward people of color, Latinx transgender women are often victims of LEP mistreatment. In a study of Latinx transgender women living in Los Angeles, 71% of the sample reported being arrested at least once, with 64% reporting unjust treatment in the custody of LEP (Woods et al., 2013). Furthermore, 65% of this sample experienced verbal harassment, 22% reported sexual assault, and 21% reported physical assault by LEP. Not only do Latinx LGBTQ+ people lack support and protection from LEP, but they also are often the victims of violent encounters, such as physical or sexual assault (Devylder et al., 2020; Panfil, 2018a). A study by Woods et al. (2013) found that 15% of Black transgender and 9% of Latinx transgender participants reported being physically assaulted by police officers, while 7% of Black and 8% of Latinx participants reported being sexually assaulted by police officers. Research also shows that Latinx transgender women are often stopped and frisked by police under the presumption they are performing sex work, a phenomenon known as "walking while trans" (Padrón, 2015). Furthermore, Latinx LGBTQ+

people can rarely question the reason for their arrest, given that questioning charges often leads to experiencing further violence at the hands of police (Stotzer, 2014).

These negative interactions with LEP and intolerance toward Latinx LGBTQ+ bodies by LEP lead to mistrust and negative perceptions from these communities. Research shows that among LGBTQ+ people there is a general mistrust toward law enforcement and policing institutions (Borges, 2018). This mistrust is also true for Latinx LGBTQ+ people, who are exposed to systemic racism, xenophobia, and discriminatory policies based on their racial and ethnic identity as well as their sexual and gender identity. Using intersectionality to understand and explain negative police perceptions among Latinx LGBTQ+ people can allow us to draw conclusions and formulate culturally mindful, liberatory recommendations moving forward.

## Latinx LGBTQ+ Perceptions of Law Enforcement Personnel

Not only have LEP assaults on Latinx LGBTQ+ people been traumatizing for these communities, but they also have created an overall negative perception of law enforcement agencies as untrustworthy institutions. This is not surprising, as research demonstrates that people from historically marginalized groups experience more negative perceptions of LEP compared to people that experience more sociopolitical privilege (Taylor et al., 2020). These negative attitudes include questioning the legitimacy and usefulness of police and other LEP. For example, many LGBTQ+ people are hesitant to rely on police to protect them from individual experiences of discrimination and oppression, and they do not trust that police and other LEP will protect them from systemic oppression. For example, Dario et al. (2019) found that LGBTQ+ participants were more likely than heterosexual participants to report unfavorable perceptions of police legitimacy. This has led many LGBTQ+ people to feel uncomfortable reporting crimes against them and unable to view LEP institutions as a protective force (Miles-Johnson, 2013b). Instead, the idea of calling LEP is perceived by LGBTQ+ people to be an invitation for discrimination and ridicule. In fact, many members of LGBTQ+ communities do not see police or the work they do as legitimate (e.g., Giwa & Jackman, 2020) and have historically created their own ways of protecting one another through pride and activism (e.g., Abreu, Gonzalez, Capielo Rosario, Lindley, et al., 2021; Abreu, Gonzalez, Capielo Rosario, Lockett, et al., 2021).

The distrust of LEP is incredibly problematic for Latinx LGBTQ+ communities, whose members are often victims of crimes. For example, in a report of 101 Latinx transgender women, 61% reported being sexually assaulted and 78% reported being insulted or beaten because of their intersecting identities, but 80% of these Latinx transgender women did not report these crimes to police for fear of being ridiculed and laughed at by LEP (Padrón, 2015). There is no doubt that the ongoing discrimination and violence by LEP toward Latinx transgender women are a violation of human rights and an example of systemic and institutional discrimination against people of color. For Latinx transgender communities, who already face a volatile and dangerous relationship with LEP, these issues compound and multiply into an incredible source of distress and traumatic experience. According to the NTDS, 46% of 6,450 transgender respondents reported that they felt uncomfortable seeking help from police and only 35% reported that they felt comfortable seeking out LEP (Grant et al., 2011; Woods et al., 2013).

## Recommendations

The literature reviewed in this chapter illustrates the critical need to build communities where Latinx LGBTQ+ people, especially those who are most marginalized (e.g., darker skin, undocumented), can thrive instead of merely surviving. This section contains our recommendations, at a systemic and community level, for decentering the involvement of LEP within Latinx LGBTQ+ communities and empowering Latinx LGBTQ+ people. These recommendations include (a) reallocating LEP funds, (b) eliminating unnecessary LEP presence (c) examining immigration centers, (d) providing medical, legal, and psychological assistance, and (e) policing and reporting by Latinx LGBTQ+ communities.

### *Reallocating LEP Funds*

Several models have been proposed to dismantle and restructure forces of institutional oppression such as LEP. Movements to abolish the police have been gaining momentum as violence against Black communities and other people of color have been on full display in recent years. Although the phrase *abolish the police* has been interpreted to mean the complete removal of police and LEP institutions, and, in fact, some do call for the complete removal of these institutions, several courses of action can be considered under this slogan.

For instance, a justice reinvestment model advocates for reallocating funds to create community-centered initiatives guided by community organizers, mental health providers, and other leaders within specific communities. According to an Urban Institute analysis of 2020 data from the U.S. Census Bureau, state and local governments spent $123 billion on police, of which 97% went to salaries and benefits (State and Local Backgrounders, 2020).

We propose that a portion of these funds be reallocated to Latinx LGBTQ+ communities to build self-reliant safety patrolling and community account-ability models. The reallocation of police funds toward these community investments can provide the financial support Latinx LGBTQ+ communities need to create safe spaces. For example, the establishment of accountability systems led by Latinx LGBTQ+ persons would ensure the adequate processing of crimes within and against these communities. To our knowledge, there is no current documentation of specific ways in which LGBTQ+ communities come together to report and address crimes against them, but there is exten-sive evidence of the ability of LGBTQ+ communities, especially BIPOC LGBTQ+ people, to organize and fight crimes against BIPOC and LGBTQ+ people. In addition to the previously discussed Vanguard and Street Transvestite Action Revolutionaries, there is the work of Ray Navarro. In the 1990s, Navarro, a Chicano, cofounded the Latino Caucus of the organization AIDS Coalition to Unleash Power, or ACT UP, in New York City to fight against HIV and AIDS in Latinx LGBTQ+ communities. Another example of community organiza-tion in Latinx LGBTQ+ communities is the YES Institute in Miami, Florida, which began as a personal project and is now a leading force in community efforts for LGBTQ+ suicide prevention. More recently, the Say Gay movement, formed in 2022, has brought together Latinx LGBTQ+ people from all over the country to fight against anti-LGBTQ+ bills in Florida, a state with one of the largest populations of Latinx people. A justice reinvestment model of LEP funds can provide Latinx LGBTQ+ people with the resources needed to organize systems to address crimes against their communities.

*Eliminating Unnecessary LEP Presence and Surveillance*

Historically, LEP presence in places where LGBTQ+ people gather and live represents surveillance and control to these communities. Redefining LEP presence in Latinx LGBTQ+ lives is an overdue move toward eradicating sys-temic oppression within these communities. For instance, the presence of LEP at LGBTQ+ events such as Pride parades dishonors the long and intricate struggle for LGBTQ+ rights in the United States, particularly the struggles of older LGBTQ+ people who fought tirelessly against LEP abuse to have the right to be their authentic selves. In fact, there is some movement across the country toward banning police presence at Pride events. For example, New York City Pride organizers banned the New York City Police Department from participating in the event until at least June 2025. This decision acknowledges both that Pride events originated from a need to fight police brutality against LGBTQ+ people and that recent abuse and violence perpetrated by LEP has been directed at other marginalized communities (e.g., Black and Brown people). In essence, the presence of LEP at LGBTQ+ events is seen as a way that LEP enact oppressive power and continue to surveil LGBTQ+ communities. Therefore, redefining LEP presence in LGBTQ+ spaces is critical to forming new relationships with Latinx LGBTQ+ communities. A possible way to achieve this might be planning Pride events where local LEP can provide funding and other forms of support while removing themselves from a space that was created for LGBTQ+ people to be free and authentic without the gaze of cis-heteronormativity.

*Examining Immigration Centers*

There is an immediate need to examine the practices of immigration centers working with Latinx LGBTQ+ communities. Immigration centers, like prisons in the United States, often serve to normalize power and enact massive elimination of minority groups (Cisneros, 2016). Massive elimination has been theorized as a racist and discriminatory approach to removing marginalized groups through imprisonment, detention, or deportation. Immigration detention centers act as oppressive prison-like systems that capture and hold as many as 500,000 immigrants each year. Latinx LGBTQ+ people often flee persecution in their home country due to their sexual and gender identity and seek asylum in the United States. This process is arduous, and immigrants are usually held at detention centers for an average of 102.4 days while their case is being processed (Human Rights Watch, 2016). The number of immigrants and the length of their detention are concerning because detention centers often fail to report deaths in custody. In 2010, the *New York Times* and the American Civil Liberties Union published a report that indicated a failure to report thousands of deaths in detention centers (Bernstein, 2010). Given that immigrant Latinx LGBTQ+ people often lack familial networks in the United States, many of their deaths or disappearances go unrecorded. Using repurposed funds from LEP could aid in establishing U.S. agencies that properly house Latinx LGBTQ+ people seeking asylum. These agencies could assist with legal representation to ensure the processing of asylum requests, a critical need given that only 3% of Latinx transgender asylum requests are processed (United We Dream, 2019).

### Providing Medical, Legal, and Psychological Assistance

Another critical next step in eradicating LEP discrimination and violence against Latinx LGBTQ+ communities is meeting their vital need for medical, legal, and psychological assistance, especially for new immigrants. Given the complex trauma endured by Latinx LGBTQ+ communities, it is critical to have in place interdisciplinary systems that provide needed services (e.g., psychological, legal, medical). For example, funds could be used to support immigrant Latinx LGBTQ+ people in obtaining legal services to expedite proper documentation in the United States and psychological services in their native language to heal from trauma experienced in detention centers. These services would support a healthy transition and opportunities for Latinx LGBTQ+ communities to thrive by using culturally mindful strategies instead of LEP violence.

### Policing and Reporting by Latinx LGBTQ+ Communities

Latinx LGBTQ+ communities currently do not feel safe and supported by LEP, and individuals often fail to report crimes against their person. Given the high rates of victimization in Latinx LGBTQ+ communities, a crime reporting system created by and for members of these communities would provide a safe way of reporting hate crimes. Training could be provided for community policing to equip Latinx LGBTQ+ people with the resources needed to protect one another when they experience violent crimes. One example of a community model that prevents LEP violence is Crisis Assistance Helping Out on the Streets (CAHOOTS), a first-responders' system in Eugene, Oregon. CAHOOTS is a clinic of unarmed crisis-trained professionals who respond to 911 calls related to mental health or drug-related emergencies. CAHOOTS is funded through police departments and takes only 2% of their annual budget (Gerety, 2020). Programs where 911 calls from LGBTQ+ people are answered by those trained to assist LGBTQ+ people are critically needed to ensure the protection of LGBTQ+ people and the adequate processing of crimes against their communities' members.

In addition, technology could be used to help achieve this goal. For example, allocations from LEP funds could be used to create a mobile application that allows Latinx LGBTQ+ people in danger to call for help or alert other

Latinx LGBTQ+ people in the area. Additionally, the mobile application could be used by Latinx LGBTQ+ people to report crimes against them and their communities in a safe and culturally sensitive manner (e.g., by using the native language of the person reporting). We recommend that such an app not be monitored by LEP institutions. Instead, this system of protection would be led by Latinx LGBTQ+ community members invested in providing protection from violence and ensuring appropriate processing of crime reporting.

## Conclusion

This chapter provided an overview of the historical and current effects of mistreatment, harassment, and violence at the hands of LEP toward Latinx LGBTQ+ people. Using the theoretical frameworks of intersectionality and LatCrit, we conceptualized from a systemic view the experiences of oppression, bigotry, and violence of Latinx LGBTQ+ people committed by LEP. We explored current policing structures and models that impede proper training for and processing of crimes against members of Latinx LGBTQ+ communities. In addition, the chapter covered how Latinx LGBTQ+ individuals have found ways to form social-justice-oriented movements that provide liberation from LEP violence. Despite systemic oppression by LEP, Latinx LGBTQ+ members are resisting, finding communities, and building spaces that promote collective well-being. Latinx LGBTQ+ communities are in need of spaces that provide safety and support from existing LEP structures in the United States.

Other countries have considered justice reinvestment models to create police stations specific to the needs of marginalized people (Carrington et al., 2020). In Argentina, police stations called Comisarías de la Mujer (CMFs) respond to gender-based violence in the city of Buenos Aires. By the year 2018 (two years after their inception), 128 station units had responded to over 257,000 complaints of domestic violence and 7,000 complaints of sexual assault. CMFs are operated by their own command structure and report to their selected commissioner, in a move away from traditional policing models. Other Latin American countries—such as Bolivia, Ecuador, Nicaragua, Peru, and Uruguay—have adopted variations of the CMF model (Jubb et al., 2010). As we see it, the recommendations proposed in this chapter are not only feasible but have also proven to be successful in other countries. Our proposed courses of action would create safe spaces that redefine the purpose of LEP for Latinx LGBTQ+ communities, ultimately increasing their crime reporting and decreasing crimes against them.

Another critical issue in policing systems of the United States concerns immigration centers that process Latinx LGBTQ+ asylum-seeking immigrants. Our chapter outlined the experiences of Latinx LGBTQ+ people who met with violence while seeking protection from crimes against them in their country of origin. Once in the United States, they are typically denied asylum and thus are forced to face the inhumane options of staying and enduring further oppression and violence or returning to their country of origin and the suffering that had propelled them to migrate to the United States in the first place. Those who remain in the United States are forced to live in poverty and oftentimes engage in undesirable and inhumane work for survival, leading to violent interactions with police. As explored in this chapter, a reinvestment model could use LEP funds to provide appropriate housing and processing of Latinx LGBTQ+ asylum seekers. The reallocated funds would ensure properly humane psychological attention to these communities, whose members have escaped persecution and endured unmeasurable trauma. Additionally, redirected funds would staff and train LEP to use trauma-informed models that do not perpetuate harm against these communities.

LEP have the potential of playing a role in eradicating violence against Latinx LGBTQ+ communities. Although this currently may seem like an unattainable goal given the oppressive history and current relationship between LEP and Latinx LGBTQ+ communities, there are concrete, realistic steps that can be taken toward making this a reality. LEP models that attend to the needs of Latinx LGBTQ+ people can open a space where these communities feel safe, visible, and empowered. If LEP choose to make this a reality, we have the potential to redefine what police and policing mean to Latinx LGBTQ+ communities in the United States.

# 3. DEFENDING QUEER SPACE AGAINST WHITE SUPREMACISTS AND POLICE IN HAMILTON

Alexa DeGagne

In 2019, organizers for Pride Hamilton warned the city police of Hamilton (Ontario, Canada) that a group of white supremacists and homo/transphobic street preachers were planning to disrupt the annual Pride festival in Gage Park. Pride Hamilton, like many Pride organizations across the country, had been debating whether police should be present at Pride events and in queer spaces. That year, Pride Hamilton barred police from wearing their uniforms when marching in the parade and denied the department's request to have a recruitment booth at the Pride festival in Gage Park, acknowledging that police presence in the space could be unsafe for racialized and marginalized Two-Spirit, queer, and transgender community members.

As Pride Hamilton had warned, the group of white supremacists and homo/transphobic preachers entered Gage Park during the 2019 Pride festival and began yelling transphobic and homophobic slurs and taunts at Pride attendees. Two-Spirit, queer, and transgender activists—later called Pride Defenders—lifted a large black banner to block out the far-right protesters, shoring up queer and transgender public space. The far-right protesters re-acted by shoving, kicking, and punching the Pride Defenders, many of whom sustained injuries from the altercation. Despite the Hamilton police being warned of this potential violence, they were slow to react to the escalating tensions and excused their inaction on not being invited to participate in Pride events. The far-right protesters eventually left the park after dozens of community members joined the Pride Defenders in holding up the black banner and pushing back the attackers. Most of the initial arrests related to the event were of members of Two-Spirit, queer, and transgender communities, as opposed to the far-right protesters (Bergman, 2020). The police, accordingly, were seen as sympathetic to the far-right protesters for enabling their encroachment on queer space and neglecting to protect festivalgoers from their abuse.

The story of the Pride Defenders at Gage Park disrupted carceral narratives in which Two-Spirit, queer, and transgender communities are united with police services against discriminatory, hateful, and violent forces. To the contrary, the events at Gage Park brought into sharp relief the fact that police protection of marginalized people remained conditional. According to Hamilton police, they would have provided protection at the festival had they been given access to the queer space and to the associated pink-washing of appearing to be an ally to Two-Spirit, queer, and transgender communities. Many in attendance at Gage Park rejected these conditions and carried on a long tradition of Two-Spirit, queer, and transgender people providing their own defense of their queered space.

For this chapter, I analyzed eight semi-structured, open-ended interviews,[1] which I conducted with Two-Spirit, queer, and transgender people who were involved in the events at Gage Park,[2] including Pride Hamilton organizers, the Pride Defenders, members of anarchist groups, and activists.[3] The interviewees discussed the conditions that precipitated the events at Gage Park, including police targeting of Two-Spirit, queer, and transgender people and spaces, the loss of queer spaces through gentrification, and the rise of far-right protests at Pride events and city hall. They recounted the moments of fear and moving solidarity they had experienced at Gage Park. I share their stories as a testament to the collective power of Two-Spirit, queer, and transgender communities to resist the ongoing expansion of carceral forces into queer spaces.

## No Uniforms, No Recruitment Booths

Two-Spirit, queer, and transgender community members had long debated whether police, in any form, should be allowed in Two-Spirit, queer, and transgender spaces in Hamilton.[4] Many of them pointed to two past flash points between Two-Spirit, queer, and transgender communities and the police. In 1997, Hamilton police initiated Project Rosebud, an undercover operation targeting men having sex with men at the Royal Botanical Gardens, and arrested 20 people. The names and addresses of those who were charged were published in the *Hamilton Spectator* (Pike & Rollings, 2016, p. 2), a tactic of public shaming common in other Canadian municipalities, which leads to immeasurable danger and damage for those outed and to anger and distrust toward the police among Two-Spirit, queer, and transgender communities. In 2004, a task force—which included Hamilton police—targeted three businesses known to serve gay communities. Among the targets was the Warehouse Spa and Bath. Police raided it, claiming that they were responding to hygiene and bylaw violations, and charged two people with committing indecent acts in the spa. Community suspicions that police were targeting gay spaces and hook-up spots were confirmed when the Hamilton police admitted they had launched the raid after surveilling a gay cruising website (Bergman, 2020; Bradley, 2021).

People from the Tower, a social space for anarchists in Hamilton, connected these historical events of police harassment to current police relations. "This isn't just a matter of the past," they wrote in a social media post about bathhouse raids in Toronto, Montreal, New York, and Hamilton; "beyond such momentous occasions, every day in hundreds of both big and small ways, the police enact violence against queers and those they care about" (The Tower, 2019). Indeed, the report *Mapping the Void: Two-Spirit and LGBTQ+ Experiences in Hamilton* found that one-third of Two-Spirit and LGBTQ+ survey participants had experienced unfair treatment by police officers, with transgender participants reporting being most likely (at 44.6%) to be treated unjustly by the police (Mills et al., 2019, p. 37).

Chevranna Abdi, a 26-year-old Black transgender woman, died in 2003 after Hamilton police officers dragged her, face-down, down seven flights of stairs in her apartment building. She stopped breathing once they reached the lobby and later died in police custody. The Special Investigations Unit ruled her death an accident due to cocaine poisoning. Media outlets outed and deadnamed Chevranna Abdi and focused on her drug use and sex work. "Abdi's treatment by police, as well as by media," Robyn Maynard (2017) wrote, "cannot be seen as separate from her identity as a Black transgender woman—this fact helps render invisible the responsibility of the police for the violence used against her. Black transgender women often live at the intersection of both societal demonization of Black women and a societal hostility toward transgender persons" (p. 124). Although Project Rosebud and the Warehouse Spa and Bath raid were understood as targeted police attacks against the gay community, the death of Abdi garnered far less attention and outrage, revealing the anti-Black racism and transphobia of the mainstream white gay community (Giwa & Greensmith, 2012). On this point, Maynard (2017) said, "I wish to honor the full value of the life of Chevranna Abdi [ . . . ] Even in death, Abdi was ridiculed by the media and ignored by the larger LGBTQI and Black communities. In short, it is urgent that all Black lives are seen as valuable and all Black suffering is acknowledged" (p. 14). When considering if and how to engage with police, and whether to permit police in Two-Spirit, queer, and transgender space, communities needed to acknowledge how anti-Black racism and settler colonialism condition police treatment of Two-Spirit, queer, and transgender people.

Pride Hamilton's relationship with police was important because the organization was one of the few remaining Two-Spirit, queer, and transgender organizations in the city. Such organizations and spaces had been displaced and had disappeared in large part due to the gentrification of Hamilton, brought on by an inflow of gay and straight people who were priced out of Toronto but could afford property in Hamilton. Safety, in these neoliberal times, came from police protection of newly acquired private property through police cleanup and displacement of marginalized and houseless people (Doan & Higgins, 2011; Kennelly, 2015; Nash & Gorman-Murray, 2014). Police targeted sex work and queer public sex hook-up spots (Interview B4), all of which pointed to heteronormative practices of courting real estate investors by presenting spaces voided of Two-Spirit, queer, and transgender life, communities, and sex. Thus, safety for some came at the expense of queer public life. During this period, the LGBTQ+ community center shut down. A queer, white, transgender woman and anarchist I spoke to lamented the inevitable loss of all of Hamilton's gay bars (Interview B4), a phenomenon happening across Canada and the United States, for which gentrification is to blame as much as the hook-up app Grindr. Still, the specific causes and detrimental effects of the rapid loss of almost all of Hamilton's Two-Spirit, queer, and transgender public spaces should not be overlooked.

Many of the Hamilton activists I interviewed, in addition to HG Watson (2020) of *Xtra* online magazine, drew connections between the lack of Two-Spirit, queer, and transgender spaces in Hamilton and Two-Spirit, queer, and transgender people feeling unsafe in public spaces and experiencing discrimination and violence. Authors of the *Mapping the Void* report found that about half of Two-Spirit and LGBTQ+ people in Hamilton had experienced discrimination in outdoor public spaces (sidewalks, public transit, parks, etc.) (Mills et. al., 2019, p. 35). "Compared to white cis and transgender people within the Greater Hamilton population," the report stated, "racialized cisgender and transgender people felt considerably less safe at home, in indoor and outdoor public spaces and in restaurants" (p. 34).

In this context of harassment and criminalization by Hamilton police, discrimination and violence in public spaces, and the loss of queer public spaces, community members (including an Indigenous, Two-Spirit, and cis femme anarchist) argued that Pride Hamilton needed to take a firm anti-police stance (Interview B6). For a decade, police and military recruitment booths and uniforms had been barred from Pride Hamilton events (Bradley, 2021). In 2019, Hamilton police applied for a booth with the intention of recruiting Two-Spirit and LGBTQ+ people to work for the police service. Pride Hamilton denied their application in part because it did not have time to consult with communities on whether people wanted uniformed police officers at Pride Hamilton spaces or events. Pride Hamilton acting-president Terri Wallis further justified the decision, saying, "we want Pride to be a time when people can come together and feel safe, and feel comfortable, and be proud, and just celebrate who we are [ . . . ] We want that to be a very friendly, very open, very safe and secure environment. And we feel that if the police were present, that wouldn't happen" (Polewski, 2019).

The police and Two-Spirit, queer, and transgender communities disagreed about how the police were expected to become involved in the Pride Hamilton events at Gage Park in 2019. Pride Hamilton maintained that although it did not permit uniformed police or a police recruitment booth within the festival area, it did warn Hamilton police of potential violence from far-right protesters and expected Hamilton police officers to be at the perimeter of the park, ready to intercede and thwart the anticipated violence of members of the yellow vest movement,[5] white supremacists, and homo/transphobic street preachers (Polewski, 2019).

White supremacist and homo/transphobic activists, and later yellow vest members, had previously held protests, disrupted Pride events in Hamilton and surrounding communities, and held influence at city hall, all with seeming impunity (Watson, 2020). Homo/transphobic street preachers had begun targeting Pride events in small towns in Ontario, including 2018 Pride events in Dunnville, south of Hamilton. The street preachers chanted and proselytized for six hours, by some accounts, condemning Dunnville Pride attendees for engaging in sodomy and pedophilia, the latter being a shop-worn and wearing accusation against gay and transgender people (North Shore, 2019). Two-Spirit, queer, and transgender people and activists from Hamilton who had attended Dunnville Pride shared with me that they experienced fear, anger, and exhaustion as they defended the Pride space by drowning out the street preachers through chanting, drumming, and playing music (Interview B1). The police negotiated with the Pride event organizers and with the street preachers, who agreed to leave if they could have 5–10 minutes to address the crowd. "The police actually escorted the preachers on stage" at Dunnville Pride, said a white, queer, transgender woman and anarchist, "and everybody who was there just turned their backs on them while they talked about how homosexuality makes you go to hell and it's the same as abusing children. And then they left peacefully, under police escort" (Interview B4). To gain police protection, Two-Spirit, queer, and transgender communities were made to cede their queer public space to homo/transphobic street preachers. According to the North Shore (2019),[6] Pride Hamilton should have known that the presence of the police, in any form, would not guarantee safety or protection against the known harm of far-right protesters and would render Two-Spirit, queer, and transgender community members vulnerable to police abuse.

## Opening Scenes at Gage Park

Two-Spirit, queer, and transgender communities' fears intensified through 2018 as the same preachers disrupted Hamilton Pride and as white supremacists and the burgeoning yellow vest movement began holding hate-propagating anti-immigration protests every Saturday at Hamilton's city hall. Consequently, many community members arrived at Gage Park on June 15, 2019, bracing for protest and violence by white supremacists, homo/transphobic street preachers, and yellow vest members.

Yet even before these protesters arrived, the space and event were unsafe for Indigenous peoples because of the actions and partnerships of Pride Hamilton. An Anishnaabe Ojokwe activist and lawyer was asked to open the 2019 Pride Hamilton events and called out the organizers for their "hypocrisy":

My words exactly were "You can't ask an Indigenous person to open up your celebration and then come to me and present me with a bottled Nestlé water knowing that only 35 kilometers away the largest Indigenous community in Canada, Six Nations, has an ongoing legal battle with Nestlé and that with over 140 Indigenous communities not having access to clean water."

It was just disrespectful from the beginning, and I pointed that out from the beginning. Then I get in front of hundreds of people and look to my left and see your major sponsor is TD Canada Trust, who is also a major contributor to pipelines and oil lines that are being forced to Indigenous communities. It was just hypocrisy and disrespectful left, right, and center, and I made sure that I pointed that out. (Interview B2)

Pride Hamilton's continued affiliation with Nestlé and TD Canada Trust enabled the corporations to pink-wash their ongoing seizure of Indigenous lands and resources. As an Indigenous, Two-Spirit, cis femme anarchist described (Interview B6), local police and Royal Canadian Mounted Police inflict colonial violence and violate Indigenous sovereignty to facilitate these corporations' movement into and exploitation of Indigenous lands and resources, thereby harming Indigenous peoples' lives and communities (Crosby & Monaghan, 2018; Greensmith & Giwa, 2013). Thus, even though uniformed police were formally denied access to the Pride space and events in Hamilton, the impact of the police endured through the corporate organizations that were welcomed.

Moreover, the exclusion of uniformed police from Gage Park did not guarantee that Pride Hamilton attendees would not be directly harmed by police. After formally opening the Pride events, Interviewee B2 was contacted by a few of their family members who were on their way to join them at the Pride events. Their family had seen the white supremacists and anti-gay street preachers heading toward Gage Park, and a mother in the group told them, "My children are not feeling comfortable because they see the haters coming to Pride, so we're not going to be coming" (Interview B2). Once the Anishnaabe Ojokwe activist and lawyer saw protesters approach the park, carrying signs and chanting, they quickly left as well, not out of fear of the protesters, they said, but the police:

With any kind of foreign governance system such as elected officials at city [hall], as well as policing structures, there's this level of trust that is not there, and so that's already a harm done walking into these situations. And the continued fear of that kind of brutal force that gets used against us as an Indigenous person, and then you couple that and marry it with being Two-Spirit or Indigenous queer, and it becomes even more horrific to even think about what that would look like.

When I realized that there was going to be violence happening at Pride, I knew instinctively I needed to get out of there because the first people who are going to be targeted [by the police], based on my experience, are going to be Indigenous people and people of color.

[ . . . ]

I got the hell out there for my own safety, not from the haters, but from the police. (Interview B2)

Even though police were not invited to the Pride Hamilton events, the interviewee anticipated that the police would react to any violence that erupted, would come into the queer space, and would target Indigenous people, Black people, and people of color. Neither the private security company hired by Pride Hamilton nor the Two-Spirit, queer, and transgender activists and anarchists' plans to defend the space would have kept the police out, so Interviewee B2, their family, and other racialized Two-Spirit, queer, and transgender people left the park as the protesters arrived.

## The Black Banner

Some 30 to 40 far-right protesters—consisting of homo/transphobic street evangelists, white supremacists (Soldiers of Odin, Proud Boys, and the Canadian Nationalist Party), and members of the yellow vest movement—marched to Gage Park, in what the Hamilton Pride Board described as "a measurable escalation from last year's protest" (Bergman, 2020). "[W]ith massive signs decrying people's 'sins' in hand," reported the Tower (2019), the protestors "screamed insults, specifically focused in on LGBTQ young people and racialized people, aggressively harassed individuals, made jokes about rape, and threatened physical violence." Many of the festivalgoers were some distance from the edge of the park and did not immediately notice the commotion. A queer white woman, who was volunteering for Pride Hamilton, watched the mounting tension and could "feel the electricity in the air." She said, "In the area where it was taking place, there were a lot of trees, so I felt very claustrophobic and very trapped and very helpless" (Interview B3). The climate of this queer space was being transformed. Back in 2018 she had been annoyed at the protesters, but in 2019 she was scared because they were "so aggressive."

Following the 2018 protests at Dunnville Pride and Pride Hamilton, community members had gathered and strategized about how they could respond differently in 2019. At a town hall held by Pride Hamilton, "a bunch of us stood up and said we can fix this problem, we can get creative, we can block our site, we can be more prepared," recalled an Indigenous, Two-Spirit, cis femme anarchist, "and we came with a bunch of ideas of how to do it without the police" (Interview B6). Someone there proposed getting the city to build a wall or fence around the event space at Gage Park. This idea was supported by some, but others argued that Gage Park was too big to enclose with a wall, and moreover, a wall would feel confining and exclusionary.

Interviewee B6 thought the wall idea was "awful" because it would stoke fear in people while disempowering them:

> I don't want to go to a Pride celebration where there's no march, because you guys are saying it's too dangerous to march in the street and now we're going to be in this giant fenced area to protect us? Doesn't that just feel so disempowering? You're just telling people that they should be scared.

As the interviewee explained, many community members did not feel safer but rather more constrained with the cancellation of a Pride parade through Hamilton streets. Building a wall would have replicated carceral logics of promising safety through segregation and confinement, in this case the confinement of Two-Spirit, queer, and transgender people (Davis, 1974; Phillips-Osei, 2018; Shabazz, 2014). In reaction to the rapid loss of queer spaces and organizations in the city, the solution was not to take over public space, cordon it off, and claim it, as such a move would reproduce rather than oppose colonialism and gentrification. A public space drawn off by harsh barriers for excluding people impedes queer existence.

"Let's make a huge fucking banner and we can bring it there!" was the most popular idea floating around community meetings leading up to Hamilton Pride 2019 (Interview B6). Along with using noisemakers and drums, community members would hold up a huge banner to block the protesters' signs and presence in the queer space. Unlike a wall, which felt restrictive, the banner would create a "'black hole' for the haters to disappear into," explained writers with North Shore (2019):

> What if the haters' strategy of showing up and flying their twelve-foot scriptures and calling us all sinners while screaming in our faces for the entire day fell flat? What if instead of getting to stand face-to-face with

Pride and spew their nonsense, they were forced to stare at a black wall all day?

Unlike previous years, when the community response was spontaneous, haphazard, and reactive, organizers in 2019 wanted to engage in a planned direct action that would intimidate the protesters (Interview B7). An affinity group[7] worked on the logistics of the new tactic and constructed a black banner that was 30 feet wide and 9 feet tall, held together by seven pieces of lumber. They practiced moving and holding the banner together and checked in on people's comfort levels with potential violence and arrests (North Shore, 2019).

The affinity group, later named the Pride Defenders, had positioned scouts around the park to alert people when the protesters arrived. Once the protesters were spotted, members of the affinity group pulled on pink masks, unfurled the black banner, and joined with dozens of community members who were confronting the protesters. "The thing that will live in my body the most from that whole time," said a member of the Pride Defenders, "was the moment of holding that banner with a group of people and marching across the lawn of Gage Park [ . . . ] All of a sudden everybody looked up and just saw this group of pagan black-clad folks just proudly marching through the grass carrying this enormous banner. And most of them had no idea what the fuck it was" (Interview B7). The Pride Defenders raised the black banner, blocking out the far-right protesters, and "the crowd erupted in applause that these assholes had temporarily been erased" (North Shore, 2019). Community members joined the action:

> I've heard a lot of people reflect on what a beautiful thing it was that there was a fairly small group of people who planned this action. But it wouldn't have been successful if it wasn't for the fact that by time things were really popping off, there were like 50 or 60 Pride attendees over there. (Interview B7)

The far-right protesters quickly became agitated by the black banner and tried to move around it. Initially, the Pride Defenders repositioned the banner to stop the protesters from getting further into the park toward the festival area, but they were careful not to physically confront the protesters: "We wanted to see how this tactic played out. Each of us had agreed that we weren't going looking for a fight but were ready if they started one" (North Shore, 2019).

Momentum tipped as the protesters tried to push through the black banner (Interview B7). With no police in sight (Interview B6), the Pride Defenders closed the banner around one person, trapping him for a minute. They also grabbed a few of the protesters' cameras and signs, which seemed to incite the protesters further, and fights broke out (Interview B6).

> A couple of the people there who were more prepared for combat started to get really shovey, and people on our side started to get shovey back. Things very quickly turned into an open brawl that swell and dissipated many times over the course of 20 minutes [ . . . ] It was a fairly chaotic scene. (Interview B7)

The Pride Defenders, and community members who joined them, noticed that a few of the far-right protesters were wearing body armor and helmets and belonged to "more nefarious white supremacist street-militia-type organizations like the Proud Boys and the Soldiers of Odin" and seemed "ready to engage in combat" (Interview B7). The white supremacists had come as backup to the usual protesters, to apparently defend them against the queers. Interviewee B6 heard from a friend that Chris Vanderweide, a known white supremacist from Kitchener, Ontario, said he was there "to fuck up some queers."

> I got my nose broken in that skirmish. That helmet guy [Vanderweide] swung his helmet and broke two of our noses within a couple seconds. I fell to the ground and blacked out for a second. [There] was just water-falling blood out of my face. (Interview B7)

A radical street preacher named John Mark Moretti kicked another person in the head (North Shore, 2019). One of the people holding the banner, an Indigenous, Two-Spirit, cis femme anarchist, was punched in the face, and she ducked under the banner, where she realized her mouth was bleeding and her tooth was chipped. While someone was helping her, she saw her friend sitting on the ground with blood on his face; his pink mask was removed because he could not breathe (Interview B6). A white, queer transwoman and anarchist had stayed at home and watched as her friends returned from Gage Park with broken noses, bloody faces, and black eyes. She said she had seen her friends get hurt at other protests, but this one felt worse because it happened at Pride and the protesters attacked her friends in front of a crowd with seeming impunity (Interview B4).

## "People Punch People; What Are We Going to Do?"

Private security was hired for the day by Pride Hamilton, but they were not able to handle the situation, reported the Office of the Independent Police Review Director (2019).[8] As a volunteer with Pride Hamilton watched the fights, which were already loud and violent, she could see only "a couple of police officers" in the area (Interview B3). When four officers approached the crowd, volunteers with Pride Hamilton tried to talk to them, to explain the situation, and to help them de-escalate the fights. One volunteer said the police would barely talk to them. She watched nervously as the police officers did nothing (Interview B3).

According to the report (Office of the Independent Police Review Director, 2019), a community member said they asked the police, "If I can walk over there, why can't you? You have a gun and a uniform. If I can walk closer to the event to witness what is happening, why can't you?" (p. 15). Another community member questioned the police's inaction, to which the police officer responded, "people punch people; what are we going to do?" The community member said the police should stop them, and the officer replied, "there [are] only four of us; we can't do anything" (p. 29). In this case, police neglect enabled far-right violence. Several people, including a journalist, phoned 911. It took at least 45 minutes for more police to arrive,[9] which is a long response time "when there's violence going on," said a volunteer (Interview B3).

When more police officers arrived, they began dividing people in the crowd to attempt to stop the fights (Office of the Independent Police Review Director, 2019). The damage—to communities' sense of safety and their scant remaining trust in the Hamilton police—had been done, however. "It was another circumstance where the police looked horrible," said a white, queer, nonbinary community member; the police "looked really bad. They looked feckless, completely feckless. And they looked like sympathizers to white supremacists, which they have proven themselves to be, time and time again" (Interview B8). Hamilton police had routinely ignored the threat and actions of far-right organizing and had instead focused on left-wing activists, including Indigenous land defenders, environmentalists, G8 (Group of Eight) protesters, and anarchists (Jones, 2019). Two-Spirit, queer, and transgender community members were the first people arrested and charged in relation to the events at Gage Park (Howells, 2019), fulfilling Interviewee B2's fear that police would target, as opposed to protect, marginalized communities.

Even before the arrests, the police's supposed neutrality—merely separating the far-right protesters from the Pride Defenders and holding a line between them—was seen as defense of and support for the protesters, who had intended to disrupt Pride and harm Two-Spirit, queer, and transgender people. As with Dunnville Pride (where police negotiated for homo/transphobic street preachers to address the festivalgoers) and with the city hall protests, police were accused of enabling the far-right groups under the guise of protecting their free speech and right to protest. A Pride Defender sarcastically recited the police's justifications for their inaction: "[The police are] just holding a line, they're just there to keep the peace, it's their right to protest, we can't kick them out of the park, because this is their free speech and blah, blah, blah, and we're just here to make sure it doesn't escalate, right?" (Interview B6). The line cut through queer space, so by holding that line, police were facilitating the far-right protesters' encroachment on queer space. The effort to bring order to public spaces facilitates hetero/cisnormal gentrification and efforts to "clean up" public spaces for the comfort, safety, visual consumption (Kennelly, 2015), and profits of developers, business and domestic property owners, and consumers. Police organizations, therefore, are seen as sanitizing public space to ensure that the city is welcoming and tolerant of those who choose to abide by the rules of hetero/cisnormal order.

Four days after the events at the park, Hamilton police chief Eric Girt spoke on the *Bill Kelly* radio show and drew an equivalence between the far-right protesters and the Pride Defenders, calling them "people, who either extreme left or extreme right, wanting to engage in fundamentally criminal acts" (Bergman, 2020, p. 63). Such rhetoric resembles former American president Donald Trump's reference to "very fine people on both sides" in his framing of the 2017 white supremacist march in Charlottesville, Virginia. In his independent review of the Hamilton police at Pride Hamilton 2019, Scott Bergman (2020) found that "many view the Chief's comments as morally equating the conduct of hateful anti-LGBTQ Agitators with that of Pride Defenders" (p. 63). Chief Girt was seen as attempting to demonize the Pride Defenders, equating them with far-right protesters and painting them as destructive and looking for a fight.

This attempted smear did not alter the opinions of the Pride Defenders. Dozens of Two-Spirit, queer, and transgender people had witnessed and then joined the Pride Defenders while the police callously watched. Many of the community members I spoke to said that they were most moved by the community solidarity that emerged during the confrontation. Solidarity took the form of Pride Defenders and festivalgoers physically fighting the protesters: "Over a hundred Pride participants jumped in to stave off the haters. Queers who refused to allow their presence to go unchallenged were attacked but fought back. Homosexuals are no cowards, and queers aren't fragile snowflakes" (The Tower, 2019). Community members said they engaged in physical violence principally as a means of self-defense and the defense of one another, and those in attendance seemed to agree that the violence was necessary. The community solidarity also took other forms, including providing first aid to those who were injured, all while making sure that the black banner remained raised. As Pride Defenders were being attacked, many worried that they would drop the banner, effectively giving in to the far-right protesters. To their surprise and relief, community members took over holding the banner.

Through solidarity and mutual support, Two-Spirit, queer, and transgender communities strategically and successfully pushed the far-right protesters out of their queer public space. "The Black Hole stayed intact and standing until the haters left the park," observed writers with the North Shore (2019): "What matters here is that instead of sitting back and praying for the police to save us, a huge group of people rallied together and drew a line—that Pride was not a safe space for homophobic preachers." The far-right protesters began to leave the park as one of them announced through a megaphone, "OK well, since all of you faggots are being so violent, we're going to have to leave. We knew you were like this" (Interview B6). A few of the protesters complained to police about their injuries and stolen signs and cameras. The police did not usher them out of the park; communities there got them to leave.

> The preachers actually left. To me that's the most important part of the story—for the first time in probably three or four years of these people showing up regularly to Pride events in southern Ontario, they left before they had planned to leave. Whether or not people got hurt or people felt violated because there was violence at Pride, it was, in my opinion, an enormous win that they left. The general understanding from everybody that I spoke to was that if [the far-right protesters] would show up at a Pride again, they would do it in a very different way and feel much less confident in being able to just do what they want and take up as much space as they want, knowing that they would be met with some level of resistance. (Interview B7)

In the proceeding hours, days, and weeks, Two-Spirit, queer, and transgender community members were both energized and shaken by the confrontation. Many felt proud of the "awe-inspiring community bravery" (North Shore, 2019) and of the people who put their bodies on the line (Interview B8). But the intensity of the day, the violation of the community space, and the jarring violence all took a toll. "[I was] really shook and upset when one of my oldest friends got home from the hospital. It was a horrible feeling," shared a white, queer transwoman and anarchist (Interview B4). "I remember just walking away from the whole thing," said an Indigenous, Two-Spirit, cis femme anarchist, "and being like, fuck, this is actually so frustrating to me, to be standing there and feeling so helpless" (Interview B6). Several people, including the Anishnaabe Ojokwe activist and lawyer who opened the day, felt that Pride Hamilton, the private security, and the Hamilton police failed to provide proper protection to them and their family:

> I do feel, and I have been very open with the Pride committee, that they failed to provide me with the adequate safety measures that needed to be in place on that day that would help protect me and my family who were coming. We had to flee. They failed and the police failed for not asserting their right and their obligations to provide service to a function that was happening in a public space. That's a responsibility. (Interview B2)

Thus, although many were galvanized by the events of the day, some declaring it a victory, there were Indigenous, racialized, and vulnerable Two-Spirit, queer, and transgender people who felt they could not stay in the space, much less push back against the far-right protesters, because the police were an imminent threat.

## "Don't You Remember That We Weren't Invited to Pride?"

Even though the police did have the power to intervene, regardless of Pride Hamilton's decision, several police officers at Gage Park, and later Chief Girt of Hamilton police, attributed police inaction to the fact that they were not invited to participate in the Pride Hamilton events. This reasoning mirrors how police have blamed victims of sexual assault, particularly sex workers, for the violence they experience (Lyons et al., 2017). A queer white woman, who was trying to get the police to stop the far-right protesters, overheard a police officer say, "Well, if we would have had a booth here, this wouldn't have happened." She added, "I remember hearing him say that and going like, are you shitting me? People have been dragged down to the hospital, and this is what you're saying?" (Interview B3). There were also reports that another officer said, "Don't you remember that we weren't invited to Pride? We're just going to stand here, not my problem" (Scrappy Jew, 2019).

On the *Bill Kelly* radio show already mentioned, Chief Girt said that the police would have responded appropriately if they had been welcomed to the Pride Hamilton event: "We would have had people in the crowd pretty much the whole time, on the property. It's pretty simple" (CBC News, 2019). Chief Girt pointed to the denial of the department's request for a recruitment booth and to the lack of an invitation and said that a sufficient number of officers were at the perimeter of the park out of respect for Pride Hamilton's request. "It's kind of a no-win situation," he continued, "where you're asked not to be there, and then when you're not there, how come you weren't there?" (Bergman, 2020).

In his independent report, Bergman (2020) concluded that the police did not purposely deny protection to Two-Spirit, queer, and transgender communities, but the police were inadequately prepared for the events and consequently failed to provide adequate protection. Bergman added that community members "consistently conveyed" to him that they believed the police intentionally withheld protection because they were denied a recruitment booth and were not invited to the event (pp. 89–90). Two-Spirit, queer, and transgender community members were torn as to whether the police's inaction was negligent or malicious:

It was definitely a popular impression that there was some malicious intent rather than a breakdown in communications. (Interview B1)

I think it's intentional. I think it's purposeful. I think it's a way to try and punish people. (Interview B5)

It became very clear, especially to those of us who already do not trust the police, that they let that happen, because they were mad that they didn't get invited. That was a very obvious thing; they're extremely petty like that, but it took I'd say the wider community maybe six months to fully accept that that had happened. (Interview B6)

The police chief's backtracking and Bergman's report could not undo the damage done. The police officers and their chief had said the implied part— the part that racialized and marginalized community members experienced and knew well—out loud: police protection was conditional. For Two-Spirit, queer, and transgender communities, the conditions were that the police should not only be welcomed into queer spaces but also be able to use the queer space to recruit more people for their institution. Yet even meeting the conditions of the police would not have guaranteed police protection for Indigenous, Black, and racialized Two-Spirit, queer, and transgender people.

The day after the festival at Gage Park, Pride Hamilton released a statement acknowledging the "long-standing issues between the LGBTQ+ community and Hamilton Police Services that remain unresolved" and still maintaining that "this was an opportunity for police to demonstrate that they were there to protect and act in solidarity with the community" (Pride Hamilton Board, 2019). Pride spaces and festivals become gentrifying forces when police usher good, white, family-friendly gay citizens through public streets and parks, carving out homonormative publics. Although Pride Hamilton bucked against the police's insistence that they be welcomed to Pride, it maintained that the police were expected to enter the space to provide protection and, moreover, that providing protection in their queer space was a means toward bettering relations with LGBTQ+ communities.

This expectation of protection comes from privileged white experiences with the police, and it does not acknowledge that any form of police intervention—even in the form of protection—is a threat to Indigenous, Black, and racialized community members. In the aftermath of the Gage Park incident and the police chief's comments, a white, queer, nonbinary anarchist observed a shift among some white, queer, and transgender people in Hamilton who

> subconsciously internalized an idea that they deserve police protection, where other communities do not. In some cases, it felt like a betrayal to people who had fallen for this idea that the police are there to protect them and felt like they had been betrayed in that moment. (Interview B1)

Those good gay citizens who bought in to gentrification and its attendant promise of police protection for their freedom and safety were never fully protected from state intervention (Duggan, 2002). Yet as Interviewee B1 bemoaned, these white people's perspectives shifted only after the violence at Gage Park, when they personally experienced the consequences of police neglect, and they did not heed what racialized community members had said long before June 15, 2019.

## Conclusion

The direct-action tactic—of using a black banner to defend queer space against far-right protesters in the absence of police—was both imperfect and galvanizing. The action was limiting, as many marginalized and racialized Two-Spirit, queer, and transgender people could not risk provoking the far-right protesters, much less the police. Those who were able to participate succeeded in keeping the banner raised and pushing the far-right protesters out of their queer space, inspiring communities across Canada that were confronting hate groups and the police in their own queer spaces. Some interviewees remarked this:

> One of the cool things that happened after Pride Hamilton was that Pride organizers in three different cities, including Toronto, London, and St. Catharines, all reached out to us and asked if they could borrow the black banner. It ended up getting shuttled from city to city. (Interview B7)

> I think it was Calgary Pride where somebody erected a giant wall of speakers, and they cited inspiration from the tactics in Hamilton. (Interview B1)

The Gage Park action also primed Hamilton activists for future waves of protest, including when the police arrested several alleged Pride Defenders in the weeks following the festival. Anti-police sentiment grew in Hamilton over the next two years, moved by calls from Black Lives Matter activists throughout Canada to defund and abolish the police after the murders of George Floyd and Breonna Taylor in the United States, and Andrew Loku, Abdirahman Abdi, Eishia Hudson, and Chantel Moore in Canada. A coalition of activists in Hamilton, including Defund HPS, called for the reallocation of funds from police toward community-centered services for housing and mental health and for the removal of police resource officers from schools.

As people fought to curtail, defund, and abolish the police, a fear remained that the reach of the police would continue to extend. Some community members held that the police should provide protection against discrimination and hate crimes and that Two-Spirit, queer, and transgender communities needed to work with the police to establish trust so that the police would be welcomed into queer spaces. Other community members feared that the police would try to use the chaos and violence at Gage Park as a justification for increasing police presence and interventions in queer spaces and future Pride events. As support swells for police defunding and abolition, Two-Spirit, queer, and transgender communities must question why police insist on being in their queer spaces.

*Notes*

1. I conducted the interviews as part of my larger research project, "The Changing Relationship between LGBTQ People and Police Organizations in Canada," funded by the Social Sciences and Humanities Research Council. The plan for this study was approved for its adherence to ethical guidelines by the Athabasca University Research Ethics Board.

2. I contacted the Hamilton Police Service for interviews, but no one responded to my request.

3. I did not include the names or organizational affiliations of any of the interviewees in this chapter due to ongoing police cases involving a few of them. That said, there are some interviewees who could be identified based on information in this chapter. In such cases, the interviewees consented to those details being shared. The interviewees' self-identified race, sexuality, gender, and pronoun(s) are used to contextualize their perspectives, experiences, and statements.

4. Hamilton, Ontario, is situated on the traditional territories of the Erie, Neutral, Huron-Wendat, Haudenosaunee, and Mississaugas and lies between Lake Ontario and the Niagara Escarpment. It is the third-largest city in Ontario, known for manufacturing and the associated working-class and trade union politics. As of 2016, 18.6% of the population was racialized, according to Statistics Canada (CBC News, 2017). In recent years, Hamilton has seen an influx of people moving out of Toronto in pursuit of more affordable housing, often facilitating gentrification in the process.

5. The yellow vest movement emerged in Canada in 2018, copying the yellow vest attire but not the politics of the yellow vest protests in France. The Canadian version was a far-right coalition espousing racist, anti-Indigenous, anti-Semitic, Islamophobic, and homo/transphobic views, while supporting oil pipelines and opposing immigration and the carbon tax.

6. The North Shore is a platform for sharing news, analysis, and events concerning the anarchist communities of the north shores of Lakes Erie and Ontario, Georgian Bay, and along the Ottawa River.

7. An affinity group is a subgroup within a social movement, which is nonhierarchical and works together to develop activist plans, tactics, and safety protocols for a specific action or campaign.

8. Private security companies, part of para-police organizations, have been found to be poorly trained and held to lower standards than state-funded police organizations (Thumala et al., 2011).

9. Police response times vary depending on the population and geography of the jurisdiction and the size and practices of the police organization. Response time is a contested metric of police effectiveness. Maslov (2016) argues that the public's perception of police response time matters more than the actual response time. In the case of Gage Park, many festival attendees reported that the response time was too slow and thus enabled violence (Bergman, 2020).

PART 2

# Intersections with Marginality

# 4. TRANSGENDER AND NONBINARY PEOPLE'S PRESENTATION MANAGEMENT DURING ENCOUNTERS WITH POLICE

Max Osborn

Valerie, a Black and Hispanic transgender woman in her early fifties, decided to go for a walk one day in her Bronx neighborhood.[1] "I saw a bunch of trans women that I knew," she recalled. "They were talking, they were hanging out." Noticing that the lace of her boot had come untied, Valerie stopped and sat down for a moment at the edge of the curb to fix it. The other women recognized her and came over to say hello, and the group chatted casually for a few minutes. Then the police arrived.

The officers told the women to "break up" their conversation and leave the area. Although the other women quickly complied and kept walking, Valerie finished retying her bootlace. "After I finished fixing my boot," she remembered, "I'm walking back to where I was going. And [the police] stopped me. And they gave me a ticket, said I was loitering, 'cause they told me to move. I moved." When she objected, pointing out that she had in fact left, the officers told her she "didn't move fast enough."

Luckily, Valerie was able to contest the ticket in court, where the case was eventually thrown out. Yet the experience of being surveilled, harassed, and profiled by police was a familiar one, and one she expects to repeat. Reflecting on the incident, she expressed nonchalance and a degree of resignation, speculating that because it had been the end of the month, the officers must have had a ticketing quota to meet. "It's just how it goes," she shrugged. Quota or not, however, Valerie felt confident that the police had targeted her because of her race and transgender identity. As a Black transgender woman who had begun her transition decades earlier, at the age of 20, she was used to police treating her as suspicious regardless of where she was or what she was doing. "Basically, their famous line is, you fit the profile," she told me. "So, me and 10,000 other people could fit the profile. But why'd you stop me?"

## Literature Review

Valerie's experience is hardly an unusual one. Transgender and nonbinary people experience an elevated risk of being targeted and harassed by police, a long-standing piece of the context of systemic violence against—and criminalization of—sexual- and gender-minority people (see Mogul et al., 2011, for a review). Throughout most of U.S. history, laws have existed prohibiting homosexual conduct and gender-nonconforming behavior—and therefore, the responsibilities of police officers explicitly included surveilling and policing queer and transgender bodies, identities, and spaces. In some jurisdictions, "sumptuary laws" explicitly prohibited cross-dressing, and in others, gender presentation was regulated by the application of statutes on "disguise," "masquerading," or "impersonation" (Capers, 2008; Ryan, 2019). (Valerie distinctly remembered being subjected as a young woman to what was known as the "three piece" rule; if stopped by police, one could be arrested if found not to be wearing at least three pieces of clothing "appropriate" to one's sex assigned at birth [Craig, 2007; Faderman, 1991].) Police scrutinized citizens not just for gender-nonconforming dress and appearance but also for nonconforming behavior (Ritchie, 2017). These statutes existed in many jurisdictions until the 1980s. Although they are no longer in effect, their impact lingers, with police continuing to single out people who appear transgressive or unusual as being inherently suspicious and potentially criminal (Buist & Lenning, 2016; Mogul et al., 2011).

These patterns of police behavior can be understood within a framework of order maintenance and social control. Scholars of these topics assert that the fundamental role of police is not necessarily to end crime but rather to end disorder (Neocleous, 2000). Thus, an intrinsic part of police work involves identifying people who are "out of order" or "out of place" (Kennelly,

2011; Moran & Skeggs, 2004; Neocleous, 2000). Transgender, nonbinary, and gender-nonconforming people often fall into the category of those perceived to be disorderly or disruptive. Gender and sexuality scholar Brandon Andrew Robinson (2020a) explains that

> enacting and embodying expressions of gender in a way not in line with one's gender assigned at birth threatens heterosexuality—especially in sexual situations—and the gender binary. People objectify and scrutinize gender-expansive people and gender-expansive bodies because expansive expressions of gender challenge dominant social structures. (p. 10)

Those whose embodiments or presentations transgress binary understandings of gender upend social scripts about appropriately gendered behavior (Craig, 2007), and they may be met with harassment or violence in public spaces as a result (Westbrook & Schilt, 2014).

Although laws prohibiting gender nonconformity may be a thing of the past, transgender people continue to be arrested and incarcerated at disproportionately high rates, and many report being unjustly stopped and questioned by police (see Stotzer, 2014, for a review). National surveys show that transgender people frequently experience mistreatment by officers, including misgendering and deadnaming, verbal harassment, and in some cases physical or sexual assault (Amnesty International, 2005; James et al., 2016). Police regularly use transphobic language, like *he/she*, *it*, and *freak*, against transgender people and often subject them to invasive, humiliating body searches in public places (Amnesty International, 2005).

Transgender women, and particularly transgender women of color like Valerie, report especially high levels of harassment and victimization at the hands of police (Amnesty International, 2005). The National Transgender Discrimination Survey (Grant et al., 2011), which included over 6,000 responses, demonstrated that Black and Latina transgender women were more likely to be arrested or detained solely for their gender presentations than were other transgender people: 41% and 21%, respectively, compared to 7% for the overall sample of transgender respondents. Police often assume transgender women of color are sex workers, regardless of whether there is evidence to support it; over 33% of Black transgender women, 30% of multiracial transgender women, and 25% of Latina transgender women reported experiencing such profiling, compared to only 11% of white transgender women (James et al., 2016). These instances of profiling are ubiquitous enough to have given rise to a phrase, *walking while trans*, to describe the experience of being stopped by police while going about one's daily routine such as grocery shopping, waiting for the bus, or taking out the trash (Carpenter & Marshall, 2017; Daum, 2015; Make the Road New York, 2012).

These disparities reflect the crucial role police play not just in enforcing the law but also in deciding when and where to do so—and importantly, whom to target (see Mogul et al., 2011). Typically, officers are given a significant amount of discretion in how to do their jobs. Laws that were ostensibly written to be neutral can therefore be applied in discriminatory ways. For example, police may choose to look the other way when some people commit low-level "quality of life" offenses such as "disorderly conduct," "public lewdness," or "failure to comply," while harshly enforcing the same statutes against others. Laws associated with these offenses are often ambiguously worded or subject to interpretation, allowing officers the freedom to decide whom to treat leniently and whom to single out for enforcement. Previous research shows that "quality of life" infractions are frequently used as justification for stopping or arresting transgender women (Amnesty International, 2005). The ticket Valerie received for loitering is just one such example of this disparate treatment.

These everyday small-scale interactions of being surveilled, targeted, and treated as out of place or out of line can have a serious cumulative impact on people's mental and emotional states over time. Moreover, the formal threats posed by police and other institutions often interact and overlap with more informal social pressures toward conformity and self-regulation (Foucault, 1977). Just as police can directly control civilian populations by threatening physical harm or legal consequences, civilians are also encouraged to modify their behaviors to better comply with social norms (Foucault, 2003). Transgender and nonbinary people learn to anticipate negative consequences for expressing gender nonconformity in public spaces and, therefore, often end up changing their behaviors and appearances to avoid standing out or drawing attention from either the general public or the police (Dwyer, 2015). This often means hiding or downplaying one's transgender identity and conforming to the cisnormative social expectation "that those assigned male at birth always grow up to be men and those assigned female at birth always grow up to be women," which privileges cisgender identities and presentations over transgender, nonbinary, or gender-nonconforming ones (Bauer et al., 2009, p. 356).

## Methodology

The current study examined the experiences of transgender and nonbinary people during encounters with police. Transgender and nonbinary participants completed qualitative interviews as part of a larger study on safety and risk, encounters with police, help-seeking processes, and service access by the LGBTQ+ community. Advertisements were posted in online spaces catering to LGBTQ+ people in the New York metropolitan area. Eligibility was limited to people aged 18 or over who identified as LGBTQ+, had lived in New York City for at least a year, and had at least one interaction with police they were willing to discuss. Interviews took place via videoconferencing or phone calls, and most lasted an hour to an hour and a half. Interview topics included presentation and visibility, risk and safety, interactions with police, help-seeking decisions, and access to formal and informal sources of care and support. All interviews were audio recorded and transcribed verbatim, then analyzed using a modified grounded theory approach to identify recurring or important themes in the transcripts (Charmaz, 2006). The study was approved by an institutional review board, and each participant was compensated $50 for completing an interview.

Of 42 LGBTQ+ people interviewed, 31 identified themselves as falling within the category of transgender and/or nonbinary, with about two-thirds of those 31 participants indicating a nonbinary identity. Transgender and nonbinary participants' ages ranged from 21 to 56 years old, with a mean of 25.9 years. All participants were invited to describe their gender identities, racial backgrounds, and sexual orientations in their own words. (Thus, whenever a particular participant is quoted or described here, their own language about gender, race, and sexuality is used.) To describe their genders, participants used 24 unique terms or combinations of terms (e.g., transgender masc/fluid, queer, transgender woman, nonbinary hard femme). Grouped more broadly, 9 participants (29%) identified as transgender men or transmasculine, 7 participants (22.6%) identified as transgender women or transfeminine, 11 participants (35.5%) identified as nonbinary without reference to masculinity or femininity, and 4 (12.9%) identified as other gender categories. Participants used 19 unique terms or combinations of terms to describe their racial/ethnic backgrounds. In terms of racial categories, 13 participants (41.9%) were white, 7 participants (22.6%) were mixed race, 5 participants (16.1%) were Black, 4 participants (12.9%) were Asian, and 2 participants (6.5%) were Latinx or

Hispanic. Participants used 16 unique terms or combinations of terms to describe their sexual orientations, with the most common being pansexual (7, or 22.6%) and queer (6, or 19.4%). Participants' occupations encompassed a range of jobs, including student, high school teacher, theater technician, and social worker. Notably, 9 transgender and/or nonbinary people (29%) were unemployed at the time they were interviewed.

## Findings

### Experiences of Profiling and Harassment

The transgender and nonbinary people interviewed described a variety of experiences of profiling and harassment by police, often in ways that highlighted or appeared to be predicated on their transgender identities or lack of gender conformity. Those who believed their transgender identities were visible to observers, or who presented their genders in ways that were nonconforming or ambiguous, thought this put them at elevated risk of attracting negative attention from police. This belief was expressed by many transgender women and transfeminine participants, as well as by nonbinary people who attempted to adopt gender-neutral presentations or who mixed and matched masculine and feminine signifiers. By contrast, transgender and nonbinary participants who were often perceived to be cisgender and/or gender-conforming thought they drew less scrutiny and were less at risk of experiencing harm from police for their gender identities.

Police harassment functioned as a constant in some interviewees' lives. Paula, an African American trans woman in her mid-fifties who had begun her transition in the early 1980s, estimated that she had been arrested about 80 times over the course of her life. "I was always discriminated because I was a Black transsexual drug addict," she explained. "Whenever they'd see me, they would take me to jail. Even if I wasn't doing anything, they were saying that I was standing around trying to prostitute myself, and they would take me to jail." Tuesdays and Thursdays, she recalled, were quota days when police tended to pick up anyone they had arrested on previous occasions and could recognize on sight in order to boost their activity statistics. Transgender women, who were often highly visible and had few resources with which to push back against police discrimination, made easy targets.

Karen, an African American transgender woman in her late thirties, had also had more than her fair share of altercations with police over the years, particularly when she was younger:

I used to get into so many physical altercations with them. Like when they used to lock me up for prostitution, there were nights where I wasn't even prostituting, because the Village itself, back in the '90s, that's where we used to hang out. To see other trans people. To just hang out and have fun and socialize. So it would be nights where I was just wearing my jeans and my sneakers and regular clothes. And I'm laughing with the other trans and stuff. And they would just come up to us and just lock us up and say, oh, we were prostituting. And we weren't prostituting that night [ ... ] Yeah, so I feel like they manipulated the situation. And they made me have a bad record, from—because they figure okay, this stupid bitch got locked up 30 times already, we could lock her up another time, and it'll just fly that she's a prostitute. So they did that. And that precinct, they did that to so many girls, and they were wrong for that. They were really, really wrong for that.

Like Paula, Karen thought that police were quick to profile transgender women as sex workers whenever they appeared in public, regardless of the circumstances. Although it was clear to her that officers targeted transgender women based on little to no evidence, there was little she could do to contest this treatment.

In some cases, a transgender person's gender might suddenly become the focal point of a police encounter due to a discrepancy between their gender presentation and identification documents. "My ID says one thing and [ ... ] the way I present says another," explained Diana, a Black and Puerto Rican woman in her late thirties. Once they realized she was transgender, she said, police tended to treat her more disrespectfully. Similarly, when Nate, a white man in his early twenties, was arrested at a protest, officers used the mismatch between his presentation and ID as an excuse to publicly humiliate him during the booking process:

It was a lot of transphobia. 'Cause I looked like a guy, and they thought I was a guy until they saw my ID. And then they're like, are you a guy or a girl? I'm like, I'm a guy. I'm a guy. And I kept telling them, but they would call me either she or it [ ... ] The one moment that just really sticks out was [ ... ] they took our photos, and then they would separate us by gender. And so they took my photo, and the people at the jail started taking me to be with the guys. And then the—my arresting officer was like no, no, no, no, it's—it's a she, it's a she. And made this whole thing in front of everyone. And the people were confused, 'cause I looked like a guy. So they're like, what do you mean? They were arguing about where I should go. And just calling me it and saying that like, it's a she. Like, it's female, put it—put it with the girls.

Jay, an Indigenous and Hispanic queer person in their mid-twenties, experienced a different problem related to their ID. When Jay was pulled over while driving, the officer treated them with increased scrutiny and suspicion until they showed identification. The officer appeared relieved to find that the gender marker on Jay's ID listed them as male and made a point of addressing them as "mister" throughout the rest of the interaction. Jay, whose gender presentation was somewhat ambiguous, speculated that the officer "felt uncomfortable" with the idea of dealing with "a person who [he] wasn't able to identify right away" and was glad to find an excuse to sort them into a binary gender category and resolve that confusion.

Being subjected to regular harassment from police had both emotional and logistical consequences. Cookie, a Puerto Rican and Black woman in her early fifties, described an incident where she and another transgender friend had been spat on and harassed by a stranger and had then called the police. Instead of helping the two women, the police refused to arrest the man and began mocking and misgendering the women in front of a crowd of people that had gathered. After the incident, Cookie's friend, who was in recovery for drug use, became so upset that she nearly relapsed. "It's just like you reach the top, and somebody pushes you down and says you're not worth [ . . . ] it's really, really a hurtful feeling," Cookie recalled. "It's so disgusting, we felt like shit." The mistreatment she experienced was compounded by the fact that she called the police in the hope of receiving protection and assistance. "I believe it's worse than a group of guys in the street calling you out," she continued. "Cause you see these people as professionals. To help us. Protect us. And make sure we're okay. They were doing other than that." Many interviewees who had experienced mistreatment by the police thought that they had few viable options for seeking institutional help in the future, and they were therefore less likely to report other instances of victimization or interpersonal harm.

## Self-Regulation and Pressure to Conform

Because of the heightened scrutiny they had experienced during encounters with police, many of the transgender and nonbinary participants intentionally adapted their presentations to better conform to gender norms, hoping to minimize the negative attention they attracted from officers. Importantly, this often involved their anticipating the way police were likely to perceive and categorize them, and then adjusting their presentations accordingly, to match whichever binary gender they believed police expected them to be. This process of presentation management illustrates the pervasive pressure that transgender and nonbinary people feel to self-regulate; such pressure constitutes a form of informal social control over populations often seen as disorderly or disruptive to the status quo (Dwyer, 2015).

To feel safer around police, participants would often attempt to present themselves as straight and cisgender. Transgender participants who generally attempted to be "stealth" in their daily lives, meaning they avoided disclosing their transgender identities and hoped to be perceived as cisgender, tended to experience less harassment and mistreatment. "If you look like a woman, and you carry yourself like a woman," explained Paula, an African American transgender woman, "then no one knows. Then you don't have a problem." For those who did not necessarily attempt to hide their transgender identities across all contexts, interacting with police might necessitate a sudden shift in demeanor or appearance. "It's an automatic thing that happens, that I change my presentation," said Steven, a white nonbinary genderqueer person in their late twenties. "Like my emotional presentation, you know? And vocal presentation and things like that [ . . . ] The body language, it changes automatically [ . . . ] I feel like it has to. In a certain way, I feel like a compulsion to that." Steven noted that their other queer friends also tended to engage in this automatic process of presentation management whenever police showed up. "It's a weird thing with authority almost," they continued, "that kind of makes you feel compelled to resort, or revert, to a—whatever you think the more socially acceptable presentation would be [ . . . ] I feel like that's what comes out when I interact with the police." Steven said their ability to present as a cisgender white man caused police to take them more seriously and to treat them with greater respect, which made them safer than if they were more open about their gender identity during these encounters.

Other white participants who could also enact presentations of normative cisgender masculinity made similar observations. "Even though I'm incredibly marginalized," explained Tyler, a white transmasculine nonbinary person in their mid-twenties, "I'm disabled, I'm trans, I'm queer, I have lived experience of homelessness, low income, all of this other stuff. That stuff isn't visible to police." Although Tyler guessed that police most often perceived him as a cisgender man, encounters with officers remained anxiety-provoking because he worried that he would be treated as suspicious or harmed if his gender identity became known. "They would fuck me up," he asserted. "They would really screw me over." Tyler's experience demonstrates that the temporary privilege or status gained by passing as cisgender is "often tenuous, context specific, and revocable" (Pfeffer, 2014, p. 11). Moreover, it shows that multiple facets of identity can impact police encounters simultaneously. In his case, although Tyler noted that his whiteness and perceived masculinity afforded him a certain degree of privilege around police, those aspects of his identity might not be enough to outweigh his transgender identity were the police recognize it. Because of this potential threat, Tyler worked to enact a straight, cis presentation when around police. "I very much try to adopt any male behaviors," he said. "I just lower my voice, try to just not be seen as queer in any way. And this might be intentional, it might be unintentional. I know that it's a safety thing for me."

Participants who would enact presentations of cisgender manhood often hoped to gain authority, respect, or negotiating power when interacting with police, while those performing cisgender womanhood wanted to be viewed as innocent, sympathetic, or nonthreatening. Transgender and nonbinary participants who thought they were likely to be perceived as cisgender women adopted a corresponding set of presentations, enacting a normative, binary feminine manner around police to avoid being seen as suspicious or out of place. Lin, a Vietnamese nonbinary person whom others often assumed to be a woman, noticed that police treated them very differently from their masculine-presenting friends, many of whom were Black or darker-skinned people of color. When these friends were with them, Lin adopted a feminine presentation during interactions with police, which involved emphasizing not only their assumed womanhood but also their "tiny" size, youthful appearance, and cooperative demeanor:

> [Officers'] impressions of me are already like, helpless woman [ . . . ] I'll use that to my advantage, of being extra demure to them, so then they don't see me as a threat. But on top of that, their flags aren't raised about the people that are around me [ . . . ] I'm not a threat, right? So that must mean my friend's not a threat.

In these instances, transgender and nonbinary participants who were successful in passing as cisgender, or who experienced privilege from other aspects of their identities, hoped that by manipulating their presentations they could secure safety not only for themselves but also for people around them whose intersections of identity might make them more vulnerable to police violence.

## Visibility, Race, and Safety

The strategy of adopting a cisnormative presentation to avoid negative attention was simply not available to some of the transgender and nonbinary interviewees. Some found it difficult or impossible to successfully downplay their visible transness and to pass as cisgender. For example, several transgender women indicated that although they experienced less police harassment during periods of their transition when they were less likely to be "clocked" or "spooked" (i.e., identified by observers as transgender), they still felt highly conspicuous in most social situations, and often they felt that the safest option was to avoid public spaces entirely. "I can't go anywhere. Literally anywhere," declared Ruth, a white transgender woman in her late twenties, who added that she did not feel able to change her appearance to avoid attracting attention. "I can't walk down the street without being on display in some way." Previous studies on transgender women's experiences demonstrate that transfeminine bodies are not only visible, but hypervisible, across many contexts and are more vulnerable to harassment and violence as a result (Bettcher, 2007; Lubitow et al., 2017; Serano, 2007).

Others said they could not conform to officers' gendered expectations because they were unsure of how their genders were being perceived and categorized—and thus they did not know what the officers' expectations were in the first place. Anomaly, a Filipino transgender man who was short and youthful-looking, said that he was "pretty much not built to conform to the societal expectation of what a man is." Therefore, he sometimes found it difficult to anticipate how others might gender him and what subsequent assumptions they might make about him. On one occasion, another man assaulted Anomaly, and the two ended up in a fistfight, which resulted in police intervening. When interacting with the police, Anomaly had no way of knowing whether they would assume he was a young woman who had been attacked by a man and was therefore deserving of sympathy, or a young butch or masculine woman whose gender nonconformity would be seen as transgressive, or a young man of color who would be unlikely to get the benefit of the doubt in a physical altercation. Unable to guess how the officers would see him, Anomaly felt anxious and unsure about how to proceed. "I just really find it difficult," he explained, "because I don't know how I'm gonna be perceived, gender-wise."

Moreover, some transgender and nonbinary participants thought they would always be conspicuous to police because of their racial identities, regardless of how they altered their gender presentations. People of color, particularly Black people, related being followed, stopped, or questioned by police on a regular basis. Some believed police singled them out for additional harassment because of their visible gender nonconformity on top of their race; this is consistent with literature by transgender writers of color showing that gender ambiguity is perceived as more conspicuous and more transgressive when embodied by people of color, whereas white people often have more freedom to express gender nonconformity without being harmed for it (Gossett & Huxtable, 2017; Ritchie, 2013; Snorton, 2017).

Some interviewees attributed their mistreatment by police primarily to racism rather than gender presentation. As Kavitha, an Indian American nonbinary/genderqueer person, explained:

> When I'm by the police or near the police, the identity that's primarily the thing that is going to put me at risk is me being a brown person [ . . . ] I already feel unsafe. Do I fear that if they find out that I'm a queer person [ . . . ] that I'll be treated even worse in custody and stuff like that? Sure. But they're already [ . . . ] willing to do anything to me.

For Kavitha, a feminine-presenting person whose nonbinary identity often went unnoticed by strangers, race was a much more salient factor than gender in their interactions with police. Similarly, Dale, an Afro-Indigenous nonbinary person, asserted that no matter how they enacted their gender, there was no possible way to eliminate the risk that police posed to them because of their race. As they put it, "There's literally nothing that I can possibly do to look like a safe person who's not going to get hurt."

## Conclusion

The findings from these interviews demonstrate that transgender and nonbinary people continue to experience a range of harms from police, including profiling, misgendering, and harassment. Moreover, interviewees described being subjected to greater police scrutiny and negative attention when their transgender identities became the focus of an interaction or when their gender presentations were perceived as ambiguous, confusing, or uncategorizable. Because of the increased risk they attributed to being visibly transgender or gender-nonconforming, many transgender and nonbinary people attempted to mitigate this risk by preemptively altering their appearances and behaviors to better fit binary cisnormative expectations about gender presentation. These processes of presentation management and self-regulation constitute a mechanism of social control by which "disorderly" or disruptive populations are compelled to conform to social norms to avoid negative consequences (Dwyer, 2012; Foucault, 1977). During encounters with police, transgender and nonbinary participants altered their presentations in response to the simultaneous threats of formal state power and the more implicit social pressure to conform to norms.

Because this was a qualitative study relying on a relatively small and diverse sample, one must be cautious about generalizing its findings. As with other qualitative research informed by queer and feminist methodologies, the data described here are intended to provide insight into the experiences and perspectives of members of a specific population, rather than to make broad claims. Moreover, the study's setting in New York City, a major urban area with a large police force and a large queer and transgender community, may make it difficult to extrapolate its findings to suburban or rural settings, where queer and transgender visibility may function differently and elicit differing responses from both police and community members. Lastly, as the data for this project were collected in 2020, during a period of widespread protest against police violence, the social context may have influenced participants' attitudes about police and safety.

The study's findings highlight possible avenues for policy changes and future research. Some participants expressed a desire for increased accountability for police officers who harm or target civilians based on gender and sexuality, although others focused more on the lack of available resources and social services tailored to queer and transgender populations. When providers and institutional actors lack sufficient knowledge about LGBTQ+ identity and service needs, people seeking services may feel additional pressure to conform to norms, take on the burden of educating providers, or avoid accessing services altogether. Allocating more funding to expanding culturally competent service provision (e.g., victim services, housing assistance, mental health treatment), as well as training existing providers on best practices for engaging with LGBTQ+ people, could help convince queer and transgender people that institutional assistance is truly available and accessible. Another possibility for minimizing harm experienced by LGBTQ+ people at the hand of police would be to reduce the number of encounters between these groups by altering the scope of policing and crisis response.

For example, many participants mentioned that they would prefer having access to other ways of responding to emergency situations that did not involve police, such as relying on trained conflict mediators or mental health workers to resolve interpersonal conflicts.

Beyond the current study, future research could examine attitudes and behaviors of police to pinpoint areas of bias and determine how these may translate into the mistreatment of civilians, particularly those who present as visibly queer and/or transgender. Moreover, these interviews illustrate the overlapping and compounding risks experienced by transgender and nonbinary people who cannot manage their presentations so as to make themselves less conspicuous to police, either because they cannot make their transgender identities any less visible or because their racial identities mean they will always be conspicuous to police regardless of their gender presentations. Further research should therefore inquire into the specific risks for police violence experienced by transgender and nonbinary people of color.

*Note*

1. This work was supported by funding from the CUNY Graduate Center, the Association of Doctoral Programs in Criminology and Criminal Justice, and the American Society of Criminology's Division on Women and Crime.

# 5. INEQUITIES AMONG LGBTQ+ YOUNG PEOPLE
## Organizational Roles in Police Departments

Sean A. McCandless

Young people who identify as LGBTQ+ experience many inequities across policy, administrative, and societal contexts (Dolamore & Naylor, 2018). For instance, LGBTQ+ young people are more likely to be victims of violence in the family home, become homeless if kicked out of the family home, and have disproportionately high contact with police and greater presence in the criminal processing system (Johnson et al., 2018; Kimble, 2015; Norman-Major, 2018; Quintana et al., 2010). From a systemic perspective, these inequitable experiences of LGBTQ+ young people do not "simply happen." Rather, such experiences and their outcomes are the results of numerous societal, familial, policy, and administrative factors, especially ones found in public service agencies like police departments.

This chapter uses Bolman and Deal's (2017) four-frames model of organizations to chart and parse factors within police departments that impact equity for LGBTQ+ young people, especially those experiencing homelessness. The four-frames model of organizations asserts that organizations can be understood in terms of their structure, human resources, politics, and symbolism. The chapter contextualizes this discussion with an overview of several key experiences of LGBTQ+ young people who are homeless, reviews major dynamics in each of the four frames, and concludes with patterns across the frames and suggestions for improving equity. Furthermore, LGBTQ+ young people can experience bias and discrimination due to negative social constructions of numerous aspects of their identities—such as age, sexuality, gender expression, race, ethnicity, and more (Irazábal & Huerta, 2016). As such, to provide as full of a picture as possible of the inequities faced by LGBTQ+ young people, literature concerning race and intersectionality is reviewed throughout the discussion below.

## Experiences of LGBTQ+ Young People

LGBTQ+ young people have a disproportionate likelihood of contact with police due to experiencing homelessness, engaging in recreational drug use, performing sex work to survive, and experiencing prejudice and discrimination from societal actors (e.g., in public, nonprofit, and private sector entities; family; community members) (Dwyer, 2015; Gaynor & Blessett, 2022; McCandless, 2018b). Underpinning these experiences is the social construction held by many powerful societal actors that LGBTQ+ young people are deviants. This social construction is laden with numerous negative potentials when contacts with police occur (Dwyer, 2011b; Dwyer, 2014a). Police can be ill equipped to help LGBTQ+ young people, due to gaps in knowing how to interact with them and how to get them the help they need. Additionally, across public service agencies, biases like heteronormativity, cisnormativity, homophobia, transphobia, and racism could influence the outcomes from both individual street-level encounters and higher-level official and unofficial department policies and practices (Dwyer, 2011a; Dwyer, 2014a; Dwyer, 2014b; Dwyer, 2015; McCandless, 2018b; Naylor, 2020).

LGBTQ+ young people thus tend to disproportionately experience inequities in four major dimensions of social equity, namely, access to public services, processes of creating public services, quality of public services, and outcomes from interactions with public service agencies (Drake & Matuszak, 2019; Hooker, 2020; National Academies of Sciences, Engineering, and Medicine, 2022). In terms of access, LGBTQ+ young people are less likely to trust public service institutions to keep them safe, whether when accessing shelters, obtaining medical treatment, or reporting and seeking meaningful amelioration of abuses perpetrated by others in society, including administrative actors (Fish, 2020; McCandless, 2018b; Shelton et al., 2017). In terms of processes, LGBTQ+ young people are more likely to have negative interactions with public service professionals, especially police, whether through being ignored or being more likely to experience verbal, mental, and physical aggression from public service professionals (Côté & Blais, 2021; Robinson, 2021). In terms of quality, LGBTQ+ young people are less likely to benefit from public services because the quality of service they receive is not equal to that experienced by other members of the population for multiple reasons, such as not getting helpful assistance from public service professionals, not being informed of life-improving or lifesaving services (e.g., food, shelter, medical treatment, education and job opportunities), and not getting or having insufficient help in obtaining those services (Dolamore & Naylor, 2017; Norman-Major, 2018). Finally, their outcomes are also inequitable in that bias and prejudice and an increased likelihood of administrative contact mean that LGBTQ+ young people are more likely to be arrested and suffer longitudinal consequences related to being incarcerated or living in transitional housing, including negative impacts on their educational attainment, job prospects, and mental and physical health (National Academies of Sciences, Engineering, and Medicine, 2022; Robinson, 2020b; Snapp et al., 2015). These inequities become starker when compounded by other challenges young people face at home, at school, and in interactions with numerous societal actors (Hail-Jares et al., 2023).

Moreover, the experiences of LGBTQ+ young people are deeply intersectional (Ream & Forge, 2014; Reck, 2009). LGBTQ+ young people can experience bias and discrimination against any one identity of theirs or against combinations of historically marginalized identities, including age, sexuality, gender identity, and race (Blessett, 2020 Johnson et al., 2018; Norman-Major, 2018; Stulberg, 2018). Intersectionality grows more complex when factoring in homelessness.

## Structure

The operations of public service agencies like police departments can be understood in part through examining their structures. Bolman and Deal (2017) refer to structures as the ways that organizations are put together. Depending on agency mission, location, legal expectations, resources, and community context, agencies can and do differ from one another in terms of their structures. Key dimensions of structure include the formation of hierarchies, the diversification and integration of jobs, communication flows, and ways in which agencies create, use, differentiate, and integrate teams. Structures extensively affect social equity outcomes for all LGBTQ+ young people but particularly those experiencing homelessness.

First, few police departments, or public service agencies in general, are structured in ways to facilitate dedicated outreach with historically marginalized populations (Johnson & Svara, 2015; McCandless, 2018b; Nolan, 2006; Quintana et al., 2010). This is partly a result of the history of policing, in that governments (as well as business and community interests) have often called upon police departments to deal with vagrancy. Police are frequently tasked with disbanding camps of persons experiencing homelessness, removing them from businesses, and keeping them out of public sight. Depending on their department, as well as their exercise of street-level discretion, police officers may not help or be able to help a person experiencing homelessness to find shelter, whether transitory or permanent (Brunet, 2015; Goodison et al., 2020; Irving, 2021). Further, given how police have often not reached out to historically marginalized populations in general, intersectionality theory becomes relevant, because when numerous historically marginalized identities are evident, LGBTQ+ young people experiencing homelessness could suffer inequities due to prejudice and discrimination against their sexuality, gender identity, race, ethnicity, color, experiences of homelessness, and more (Fenley, 2020; Gaynor & Blessett, 2022).

Second, policing practice, especially in the United States, emerged from practices meant to keep populations in what elites socially constructed as the "proper place" for these groups. In part, modern policing stems from slave patrols capturing runaway slaves and, treating them as property, returning them to their "owners." Moreover, policing has long been a mechanism for controlling populations socially constructed as deviant. Given such social constructions, the notion of engaging in outreach with marginalized populations was antithetical to policing and, indeed, to public service institutions in general (Gaynor, 2018b; Gaynor & Blessett, 2022; Headley, 2020; Ingram et al., 2019).

Third, societal acceptance of LGBTQ+ people has expanded over time. These expansions have resulted in numerous legal, political, and managerial changes to public service agencies in many areas of the world. In the United States, homosexuality is no longer classified as a mental disorder by major medical associations; both statutory and case law have expanded recognition and protection of LGBTQ+ rights; and there is greater societal acceptance of LGBTQ+ people in general and throughout popular media (Cleghorn et al., 2018; Gaynor & Blessett, 2014; McCandless & Elias, 2021; Naylor, 2020).

These broad historical contexts influence structures within all public service agencies, including police agencies, that, in turn, affect outcomes for LGBTQ+ young people, especially those experiencing homelessness. Historically, along with courts and prisons, police departments have been the public agencies most directly involved in marginalizing LGBTQ+ populations, again through socially constructing these populations as deviant, especially when intersectionalities regarding race and ethnicity are factored in (Gaynor, 2018a; Gaynor & Blessett, 2022; Giwa et al., 2021; Goodison et al., 2020). Additionally, police departments have often not had positive relations with LGBTQ+ communities. The Stonewall riot, for instance, occurred in large part as a response to police brutality against the LGBTQ+ community in New York City over decades (Bullough, 2002; Carter, 2010; Giwa et al., 2022).

In tandem with greater societal acceptance, legal mandates, and even departmental culture changes, some police departments have begun acknowledging their role in marginalizing numerous populations, including LGBTQ+ populations. One increasingly common structural method adopted to address these inequities is creating LGBTQ+ liaison programs, such as those in Dallas, Texas (Dallas Police Department, 2021), and Seattle, Washington (Seattle Police Foundation, 2021). Such programs have multiple, broad goals, but they typically share some type of outreach strategy directed to a specific community in order to, at least in principle, promote greater equity for this community (Giwa et al., 2022; Maccio & Ferguson, 2016; Mogul et al., 2011). From a structural perspective, however, at least two major issues often compromise such a program, in that only a handful of officers or even only one officer may belong to it and its office may be structurally isolated from the main body of the department, thus limiting its abilities to influence wider practice (Dwyer, 2014a; McCandless, 2018b).

Structural imperatives in carrying out police work can also lead to inequities. Police officers may answer numerous calls during a single shift, which implies competition among values of efficiency, effectiveness, economy, and equity (Brunet, 2015). For instance, in terms of efficiency and economy, police are expected to answer as many calls as possible in as little time as possible. When such expedience leads to police profiling, psychological harm can result, and trust in police erodes (Epp et al., 2017). Concerns for effectiveness tend to prioritize officers dealing with an immediate situation and moving on, thereby relegating "social issues" like homelessness to other public or nonprofit workers, if at all. For someone engaging in sex work to survive, using drugs, or experiencing homelessness, policing structures can result in an officer dealing with the immediate situation without addressing inequities the person may be experiencing (Woods et al., 2013) and with the officer believing it is not their job to ameliorate these conditions (see Gaynor & Blessett, 2022; McCandless, 2018b). In terms of equity, or the mandate to treat everyone fairly, police may simply stop, search, remove, arrest, or in some circumstances kill people committing a crime or suspected of committing a crime because other public services—such as courts, jails, prisons, or social services—are there to handle the next steps (Carpenter & Marshall, 2017; Gaynor, 2018b; Gaynor & Blessett, 2022; Headley, 2020; McCandless, 2018a).

Thus, with these structural imperatives working in concert, any person from a group or groups socially constructed as "deviant," including those experiencing homelessness, has an increased likelihood of contact with police. This is true for LGBTQ+ young people in particular, and depending on the reason for police contact and on an officer's discretion, they could experience vastly different outcomes. Thus, the structural frame points to specific issues of organizational dynamics that make it difficult for officers who witness issues on the street that evidence inequities to make such concerns known apart from filing reports that defer the issue up the chain of command. Outside agencies (especially courts), news outlets, and organized societal groups may act to compel agencies to respond to prioritize equity.

## Human Resources

Whereas structure helps chart ways in which the organizational and hierarchical expectations of police work can lead to inequities for LGBTQ+ young people, considerations of human resources reveal how inequities are also consequences of who works in public service agencies. Thus, Bolman and Deal (2017) center the human resources frame on who is recruited, hired, supported, promoted, and fired in an organization as well as on the dynamics involved in those processes, especially representativeness. For any issue suggesting inequity in public service, the human resources frame prompts examination centered on the degree to which agencies are demographically representative of the populations they serve and, thus, the effects that representativeness (or the lack thereof) has on agency practice.

Representative bureaucracy is a multipart concept. For one, agencies are often not demographically reflective of the populations they serve. For another, agencies that are more representative can promote greater awareness of inequities faced by historically marginalized populations and work more effectively to promote equity (Headley, 2020). Representative bureaucracy includes both a passive dimension, or simply the presence of a demographic group, and an active dimension, or a person from a particular group being in a position of influence and engaging in substantive decision-making that promotes awareness of inequities and develops policies to redress them (Keiser, 2010; Sowa & Selden, 2003).

Many police departments are not demographically representative. In the United States, for instance, police departments disproportionately employ white cisgendered heterosexual men (see Colvin, 2012; Myers et al., 2004). From the lens of representative bureaucracy, such agencies may be ill equipped to acknowledge and address issues of LGBTQ+ inequity (Mallory et al., 2015). Some departments, though, are more demographically representative of the populations they serve, including LGBTQ+ representation. From the human resources frame, promoting representativeness is a necessary but not sufficient condition for promoting equity, such that a lack of LGBTQ+ representation among officers likely negatively influences outcomes for LGBTQ+ populations. Therefore, recruiting, hiring, and supporting LGBTQ+ officers is critical (Copple & Dunn, 2017).

Furthermore, departments are becoming subtly more representative of LGBTQ+ identities (Colvin, 2012; Giwa et al., 2022). As but one sign, police departments commonly sponsor representation in Pride parades, perhaps even featuring LGBTQ+ officers, although there have been attempts to minimize such presence (Fitzsimmons, 2018; Giwa et al., 2021). In some locations, like New York City, Pride parade committees have banned police from participating, disheartening gay officers (Associated Press, 2021). Regardless, representativeness has limits to its ameliorative effects on equity (Headley & Wright, 2020; Wilkins & Williams, 2008; Wright & Headley, 2020). LGBTQ+ officers may still feel marginalized within departments and not respected (Colvin, 2012; Giwa et al., 2022); they may experience homophobic talk, feel like outsiders, encounter tokenism, and more (Colvin, 2009; Giwa et al., 2022). And some officers have initiated lawsuits claiming discrimination in the workplace and unsafe workplace environments (see Lam, 2019).

In sum, passive representation does not guarantee active representation, which likely is required to promote LGBTQ+ equity (Copple & Dunn, 2017). A public servant may identify as belonging to a particular population yet still enforce what, to an outsider, looks like prejudicial behavior. In this way, the positive effects of passive representation can be muted if policing cultures exalt the intersections of cisgendered heterosexual white men and adopt policies that marginalize populations not identifying with this intersectionality. In short, many police agencies do not have a critical mass of LGBTQ+ officers and allies to change practices, and even with greater representativeness, policies for human resources that promote inclusive environments may be nonexistent or not enforced.

## Politics

The discussion of representativeness evokes considerations of politics, or the determinations of who gets what, when, why, and how. Bolman and Deal (2017) note that the political frame examines how power dynamics within agencies affect what an agency does and how it performs. The presence of competing power dynamics yields differentials in who can and cannot exercise power and, thus, who is privileged versus who is marginalized. Further, who exercises power is in part a function of what position they hold, such as someone holding an official position or having unofficial influence (thus harkening back to both the structural and human resources frames). These power dynamics mean that any organization will have competing factions to some degree, that is, different groupings of people with distinct interests, needs, agendas, and resources. Which groups enjoy favor and who creates policy are in large part a function of considerations related to power, history, critical mass of supporters, resources, and support from other groups. Thus, within organizations, different groups can and often do compete for attention, resources, and power. Alliances can form within agencies to promote interests or, at the very least, marginalize others' interests (Bolman & Deal, 2017).

Both within individual police departments and within policing in general, politics are evident. Perhaps most pressing for this chapter are the politics surrounding whether issues related to LGBTQ+ equity and homelessness among young people are indeed problems. If something is to be a problem, it must first be defined so, leading to debates on whether and how the problem can be addressed by public service organizations, including police. Police agencies can have factions opposed to notions of LGBTQ+ equity (or indeed social equity in general) as well as factions in favor of promoting social equity.

Indeed, some factions within departments may be united in believing that social equity in general is antithetical to policing. If a union perceives that a particular initiative is detrimental to its interests, which some unions do regarding equity initiatives, the union may resist its implementation. One manifestation of this centers on the desirability and efficacy of equity training. For instance, politics are evident in debates about whether trainings (1) take away resources better used elsewhere; (2) are efficacious; (3) are desirable; and (4) make so-called real policing more difficult (Copple & Dunn, 2017; McCandless, 2018a; McCandless, 2018b). Additionally, within police academies, issues related to equity may be sparsely covered (McCandless, 2018a; Harmon, 2009; Soss & Weaver, 2017). Still, in the United States, it is becoming more common for police departments to mandate LGBTQ+ training, although some departments do so only as a result of lawsuits (Toesland, 2021).

Related to the structural frame, political factors (especially competition over resources) may mean that personnel assigned to an office mandated to promote equity are structurally sequestered from the core body of a police department. As noted earlier, consequences of this political and structural relegation are that such offices are likely to be underfunded and understaffed, and their abilities to affect policies and practices widely may be limited for want of political support from other groups in the department (Brunet, 2015; Daum, 2015; Dwyer, 2014a; McCandless, 2018b).

Additionally, external politics can shape agencies' internal politics. For instance, the work of police can be affected by signals given to police leaders by key community players, such as elected leaders, other agencies' leaders, or business and community leaders. These leaders could pressure or even require police to act in a particular way concerning an issue of equity (McCandless, 2018b; Mountz, 2016; Weaver et al., 2019).

## Symbolism

Finally, agencies do not consist solely of structures, human resources, and politics. Agencies' work has symbolic functions. For Bolman and Deal (2017), symbolism generally refers to the meaning of organizations' work, which, in turn, is reflected in ceremonies, events, symbols, values, beliefs, stories, myths, heroes, and villains. Although the lessons of the symbolic frame are implicitly woven throughout the other frames, the symbolic frame accentuates how, from the broadest perspective, public policies are often aligned against LGBTQ+ populations, especially young people experiencing homelessness (Johnson et al., 2018; Kimble, 2015; Mogul et al., 2011; Sellers, 2018).

As already mentioned, from an intersectional perspective, policing has symbolically revolved around constraining "youth," homelessness, and those who are socially constructed as "deviants" (Gaynor, 2018a; Gaynor & Blessett, 2022; McCandless, 2018b). Taken further, state agencies (especially those that are part of the criminal processing system) have also perpetrated violence directed at Black people, Indigenous people, and people of color. Thus, the symbolism of policing—particularly its values and beliefs—posits a "thin blue line" between anarchy and order, drawn to preserve societal values and suppress deviancy (Harmon, 2009; Johnson et al., 2018; Wilkins & Williams, 2008).

Conceived broadly from the perspective of symbolism, public agencies like police have engaged in both hierarchical and exclusionary violence. Hierarchical violence refers to "keeping groups in their place," whereas exclusionary violence refers to eliminating groups, whether through killing them, denying the legitimacy of their identities, or even denying that such groups exist (Gomez, 2013). Thus, to some police, promoting social equity is antithetical to the symbolism of policing itself and something associated with community policing. Despite the popularity of community policing, some officers have opined that it is not "real" policing, and both formal and informal cultures within departments reinforce this symbolism (Gaynor, 2018a; McCandless, 2018a; Soss & Weaver, 2017).

## Conclusion

Taken as a whole, the experiences with police of any historically marginalized population, particularly LGBTQ+ youth and those experiencing homelessness, do not "just happen." Rather, from the organizational perspectives of structure, human resources, politics, and symbolism, outcomes of police interactions are numerous and overlapping.

The four frames offer insights both separately and collectively. The structural frame highlights how inequities result in part from policing's historical association with controlling "deviancy," including LGBTQ+ populations, through police officers' on-the-ground work, the way departments are structured, and the messaging about equity affirmed through hierarchy. The frame of human resources charts how police agencies are often unrepresentative of the communities they serve because they favor officers who embody, normalize, and exalt identities that are cisgender, heterosexual, white, and male. LGBTQ+ persons may not be represented in agencies or be barely so, may not be in positions to foster active representation, or may themselves follow departments' formal and informal cultures on the treatment of LGBTQ+ populations. In this way, policing can become a means to create benefits for the privileged and marginalize those populations socially constructed as deviant. The political frame captures how police agencies can and do have competing internal groups, so support for LGBTQ+ initiatives, indeed any social equity initiative, may hinge on which groups are privileged and which are marginalized, and on the messaging police leaders receive. Finally, the symbolic frame charts how the nature of police work has, historically, embodied beliefs and values viewing LGBTQ+ individuals as deviant, therefore making work toward equity, to some, not "real" policing. Thus, all the frames work both singly and together.

Obviously, the organizational dynamics implicated in creating inequities are complex, and not every dimension of what happens in a police encounter is captured. Still, by better understanding the causes and effects of inequities, especially in terms of structure, human resources, politics, and symbolism, it is possible to design agencies that act inclusively and substantively to remedy inequities (Gooden, 2014). Part of this process entails recognizing that social equity itself is socially constructed in that what is considered "fair" is also a function of who defines what is fair (McCandless & Blessett, 2022). Power dynamics and societal position help determine who is in place to define the meaning of fairness as well as what does and does not become public policy and administrative practice. In this way, the determination of what to do about LGBTQ+ equity, indeed whether it is even a concern at all, is also socially constructed.

Both the literature on organizational dynamics and the four frames model suggest strategies to improve equity for LGBTQ+ young people in their contacts with police (Bolman & Deal, 2017; Copple & Dunn, 2017). From a structural perspective, the most important strategy for fostering equity centers on ensuring that messaging on and action toward promoting LGBTQ+ equity occur throughout a police agency, not just through liaison officers. Police leaders and managers at all levels, especially among patrol officers who are the most likely to encounter LGBTQ+ young people, need to enforce the importance of equity in every daily encounter and to better understand the concerns these young people face and to have the capacity to offer meaningful assistance. Relatedly, the structural frame suggests that LGBTQ+ liaison offices should not only become more common but should also not be organizationally isolated from daily workings in departments, especially with patrol officers, and have only casual contact with colleagues. Rather, structural contact—whether through meetings, memos, team work, or informal communications—is a necessary (but not sufficient) condition to promote equity (Giwa et al., 2022). From a human resources perspective, it is desirable to hire more LGBTQ+ officers. Although greater representation is not by itself enough to promote equity within police departments, it can, slowly, change administrative cultures (Colvin, 2009; Colvin, 2012; Giwa et al., 2022; Headley & Wright, 2020; Wilkins & Williams, 2008). Even if hiring more LGBTQ+ officers is not possible, hiring processes can be improved, especially to center the promotion of equity under required qualifications and to prioritize hiring those with equity mindsets. And even if such hiring improvements do not occur, police organizations can still establish human resources policy that mandates and measures equitable behaviors, rewards desired behaviors when they do occur, and sanctions undesirable behaviors. Such policy will only work, though, if administrators at all levels take it seriously and actively follow it (Charbonneau & Riccucci, 2008; Charbonneau et al., 2009; McCandless, 2018a, 2018b).

From a political perspective, factions clearly exist within police departments, including those who support equity policies and those against them (McCandless & Vogler, 2020). Police leadership at all levels needs to enforce LGBTQ+ equity messaging both formally and informally to counter "cabals" of officers who are against LGBTQ+ equity (Giwa et al., 2022). Further, LGBTQ+ liaison offices should not only become more common but should also have substantive resources available to them, especially recourse to hiring and supporting dedicated personnel and to providing sufficient funding for events and trainings. Finally, from a symbolic perspective, promoting different messaging and activities, both within agencies and through agencies' public relations, is critical. Given that the symbolism of policing is historically anti-LGBTQ+, promoting symbolic actions that counter and replace such past symbolism, whether through outreach, events, or public documentation of efforts (both successes and failures), can advance equity for LGBTQ+ young people.

Obviously, any organized hierarchy, including in the public sector, can encounter friction in instituting any type of change. As charted by Bolman and Deal (2017) as well as by organizational scholars like Heifetz et al. (2009) and Northouse (2022), instituting change can be difficult when members of an organization are resistant to change, especially to changing paradigms that give meaning to an organization's work, to modifying an organization's repertoire of behaviors and strategies, and to redefining the problems an organization faces. Such suggested changes, however ideal, may be resisted by many police officers. Taking guidance from organizational theorists, resistance to change could manifest itself in multiple ways: agency members could assert (a) that proposed changes are preferable but not practical; (b) that funding is unavailable for such changes; (c) that equity problems are overstated or misunderstood by the public; or (d) that proposed changes are undesirable, unfeasible, and would make policing more difficult. Overcoming such resistance is possible, but instituting reforms will likely require not only changes to agencies' organizational dynamics but also greater pressure from and accountability to elected leaders, courts, and business and community members (see Dolamore & Naylor, 2018; Norman-Major, 2018). Regardless, the list of potential strategies to foster greater equity for LGBTQ+ young people is extensive (Johnson et al., 2018), and the goal—of promoting better access, processes, quality, and outcomes for public services—is well worth the effort.

# 6. LGBTQ+ POLICING IN THE SOUTH
## A Look at Protections and Police Reforms

Mitchell D. Sellers

Southern U.S. states stand out on many fronts, but much is left to be desired when it comes to the criminal legal system. The American Civil Liberties Union (2022) notes that the United States represents only 5% of the world's population yet has 20% of the world's incarcerated population. Incarceration statistics are even more staggering when focusing on southern states. The Sentencing Project (2022) reports that 8 of the 10 states with the highest rates of imprisonment in 2019 were southern states (Louisiana, Oklahoma, Mississippi, Arkansas, Kentucky, Georgia, Alabama, and Florida). West Virginia topped the list for highest juvenile custody rate in 2019. Policing strategies and policies affect social injustices and can encourage recidivism and impact a person's entire future: jobs, housing access, engagement with government, and overall quality of life. These facts, combined with the overwhelming evidence that lesbian, gay, bisexual, transgender, and queer (LGBTQ+) communities are incarcerated at higher rates, warrant further review of the policing of LGBTQ+ communities in the South.

Although less stigmatized today, LGBTQ+ people continue to be confronted by bias from citizens and police alike (Stryker, 2008). Southern states are among the most socially conservative in the United States. The Pew

Research Center (2022) surveyed citizens' support for homosexuality in all states. Only 51% of respondents in southern states said homosexuality should be accepted (ranging from 40% to 64% in support), and 41% of southern respondents said that homosexuality should be actively discouraged (ranging from 28% to 54%). This finding differs considerably from the rest of the nation, where 64% said homosexuality should be accepted (ranging from 45% to 82%), with 29% of respondents saying homosexuality should be actively discouraged (ranging from 12% to 47%). The Republican Party has strong control of state legislatures and governorships in the South and is heavily aligned with socially conservative evangelicals in the Christian Right (Jelen, 2017). Conservative politicians stoke culture wars to galvanize support from social conservatives, and LGBTQ+ rights frequently come under attack, especially transgender rights in recent years.

Conservative states pushed through a slew of anti-transgender laws in 2021, instituting discrimination in health care access, education, and access to public accommodations, with many proposed laws aimed specifically at transgender minors. Gallup (2021) found a heavy partisan divide among support for transgender people, with Democrats significantly more likely to support transgender rights, which helps to explain the presence of so many new bills in Republican-controlled states. These new laws create barriers for LGBTQ+ people when interacting with government and in day-to-day life functions, and at times they encourage police investigation of LGBTQ+ people. Despite state opposition, many major progressive cities in the South adopted their own reforms to improve relations with LGBTQ+ populations, thus creating a situation where law enforcement policies vary from city to city, even within the same state.

The current study explores the landscape of laws and policing policies affecting LGBTQ+ communities in the southern United States. It asks the following questions: (a) what cities and states have reformed policing practices in the South to improve LGBTQ+ interactions with law enforcement; (b) what do southern states require to change gender markers on personal identification; and (c) what protections and services are offered by southern cities to LGBTQ+ people? It uses data from the Human Rights Campaign's State of Equality Index and Municipal Equality Index, along with the ID Document Center of the National Center for Transgender Equality. These sources allow for an analysis of legal frameworks at the state level, along with an in-depth analysis of the policing practices of the most pro-LGBTQ+ southern cities.

## Policing and LGBTQ+ Communities

Research consistently finds that LGBTQ+ people are disadvantaged at all stages of the criminal processing system (e.g., Mallory et al., 2015; Russell, 2019; Sentencing Project, 2022). This results in higher incarceration rates and distrust of law enforcement, which is even more pronounced when people are part of multiple marginalized groups, such as people of color or undocumented residents (Mallory et al., 2015). Research also shows reluctance on the part of LGBTQ+ people to turn to law enforcement for help (Owen et al., 2018), partly because at times the perpetrators are law enforcers themselves. Russell (2019) asserts that the rhetoric surrounding policing and LGBTQ+ communities evolved dramatically from targeted oppression decades ago to modern-day police chiefs heralded as advocates. She argues, however, that the reforms are superficial in that support relies on an assimilationist depiction of LGBTQ+ citizens. When discourse focuses on a hypothetical good queer citizen, a range of different experiences and life situations gets ignored. Duggan (2002) argues that superimposing existing social hegemonies on LGBTQ+ people creates a homonormativity that permits only a narrow form of identity expression to be viewed as "acceptable."

Laws continue to criminalize LGBTQ+ people today. A prime example of this is laws that criminalize HIV. Deliberately exposing people to HIV is illegal in all states, but many states leave room to criminalize people living with HIV (Goldberg et al., 2019). Enhanced sentencing and requirements to register as a sex offender are common for individuals convicted under HIV laws. Age-of-consent laws also criminalize sexual practices. Although most states reformed their laws so that the age of consent is the same for heterosexual and homosexual relations, several states limit loopholes for young adults who are close in age to heterosexual couples only (Human Rights Campaign, 2020).

Recent reform efforts promoted by Black Lives Matter and organizations in favor of defunding police would aid LGBTQ+ communities as well. Trickle-up social justice gains in recent years include limiting direct interaction with law enforcement, removing laws targeting homeless populations, decriminalizing sex work, and facilitating access to health care, which provides viable alternatives to black-market hormones for transgender individuals. Although not police reform, these changes make social workers, rather than police officers, the point of first contact with government for many members of LGBTQ+ communities. This change can save lives because social workers and police are trained very differently on how to confront special populations (Giwa, 2018).

Harassment and profiling of LGBTQ+ people are widespread across the nation. In the meta-analysis of Mallory et al. (2015), study after study found discrimination, harassment, and/or misconduct on the part of law enforcement, with officers commonly being the assailant (2%–24%, depending on the study). The police recording of Brandon Teena the week before he was murdered by his rapists presents a prime example of law enforcement focused on policing gender rather than sexual and aggravated assault. With qualified immunity, stand-your-ground laws, and gay/transgender panic as valid legal defenses across most of the country, being outed as transgender can turn quite deadly. Overlaying this with already-built-in racial, socioeconomic, and gendered biases further punishes gender minorities in all aspects of the criminal legal system, including initial contact, filing reports, arrest rates, and sentences.

## LGBTQ+ Policing Reforms in the South

Despite many calls for police reform since George Floyd's murder, few comprehensive police reform bills passed into state law in the South in 2020 and 2021. According to the National Conference of State Legislatures (2022), Georgia established a reform study committee in 2020 for law enforcement, and Louisiana created the Police Training, Screening, and De-escalation Task Force. Additionally, Alabama, Arkansas, Kentucky, and Virginia revised their statutes on punishing or documenting police misconduct. Most of the bills proposed and enacted focused on broader police reforms backed by contemporary activists, but few of the proposed bills dealt directly with LGBTQ+ people.

The South has long criminalized many parts of LGBTQ+ life. *Lawrence v. Texas* overturned the remaining sodomy laws in the United States in 2003, but other laws that govern norms for sexuality and gender expression persist. Cross-dressing bans remain on the books in many cities (Goldberg et al., 2019). Even the State of New York—one of the most liberal states in the nation—had what advocates referred to as a "walking while trans" law from 1976 until 2021 (Diaz, 2021). The law criminalized loitering for the purpose of sex work, but it was broadly applied. In practice, it was used to target transgender women of color, which led to the stopping and arresting of transgender people for things such as clothing, carrying condoms, alleged solicitation of sex, and similar charges associated with stop-and-frisk laws.

Anti-loitering laws and those targeting sex workers endure in the South (Palmer & Kutateladze, 2021). These broad and vaguely written laws enable police to claim probable cause in order to detain and question LGBTQ+ people. From 2005 to 2019, hate crime laws rose in popularity for prosecuting racial discrimination, which was later expanded in some states to include gender identity, HIV status, and sexual orientation (Palmer & Kutateladze, 2021). These laws extend the sentences for convictions of crimes against persons, but it is difficult to prove in court that attacks were motivated by hate; additionally, Palmer and Kutateladze (2021) find considerable underreporting of hate crimes against LGBTQ+ persons.

## Policing LGBTQ+ Bodies

The identifying documents that we carry daily permit the policing of gender-diverse bodies. "Passing" or "going stealth" allows gender-diverse people to avoid being targets, but many are put in dangerous situations when law enforcement or others inspect their unaltered identification. A routine traffic stop can turn deadly for transgender people or may lead to unwarranted searches, often resulting in violence or disproportionately high rates of incarceration. Incorrect docu'ments can prompt being strip searched by officers of the wrong gender and placement in correction centers inconsistent with a person's gender identity and expression—leaving transgender women at particular risk of assault and rape. The National Center for Transgender Equality (n.d.) notes that 15 states allow *M*, *F*, or *X* on birth certificates and that 21 states allow these options for denoting sex on driver's licenses. No southern state allows for a third gender marker on birth certificates, but Arkansas and Virginia allow gender marker changes on licenses without requiring provider certification. Dwyer (2008) asserts that as queering of public spaces continues to occur, we are seeing a shift in policing practices. This will change the way law enforcement interacts with LGBTQ+ communities and may create challenges for police administration, for example, in how individuals are processed when arrested (Dwyer, 2020).

## Research Methods

This study analyzes state and local data. For the state analysis, data from the Human Rights Campaign's (2020) State of Equality Index provide information on law enforcement policies and LGBTQ+ people, and the National

Center for Transgender Equality's (n.d.) ID Documents Center supplements discussion on gender marker changes. I also analyze data from the Human Rights Campaign's (2021) Municipal Equality Index. This index creates a scorecard for municipalities based on LGBTQ+ protections provided, inclusion in government employment, municipal services offered to the LGBTQ+ people, and law enforcement reforms involving LGBTQ+ people. It samples the largest cities in every state, along with a selection of small, medium, and large cities, to provide an accurate depiction of the country.

This study uses the Municipal Equality Index to explore police reforms on the local level. Analysis includes all local southern governments that have at least one pro-LGBTQ+ policy. Cities that had protections only because of the state or county were excluded from analysis. This is assumed to be a comprehensive list of all southern cities with LGBTQ+ reforms. There were 127 cities in the data set for analysis. Of the 127, 66 had an LGBTQ+ liaison for law enforcement, 63 had a LGBTQ+ liaison in the executive's office, and 99 reported their 2019 hate crime statistics. A manual search was made of all police and/or city websites in December 2021 to determine if the policing manual was made public online and whether the website referred to any police policy that affected LGBTQ+ communities.

## Results

### State Criminal Law and Policies

Focusing on state-level policy presents a bleak outlook for southern states. Table 6.1 shows laws affecting the entire LGBTQ+ population in each state. Florida is the only state to prohibit law enforcement officers from profiling people based on their actual or perceived sexual orientation. Louisiana is the only state to require that law enforcement officers receive sensitivity training but only regarding sexual orientation. Another pattern that emerges in southern states is the criminalization of HIV for low or negligible risk of transmission: 12 states criminalize low-risk activities. Of the remaining two, West Virginia can use existing communicable disease law to criminalize HIV. Additionally, Arkansas, Louisiana, and Tennessee may require those who violate these HIV laws to register as sex offenders.

The remaining policies are focused on minors, which might lead to the arrest or recidivism of young LGBTQ+ people. Florida, Georgia, Kentucky, Louisiana, North Carolina, Tennessee, and Texas prohibit discrimination against LGBTQ+ young people in juvenile justice systems. A handful of states

*Table 6.1: Criminal Justice and LGBTQ+ People in the South*

| Law or Policy | States Where Enacted |
|---|---|
| Prohibits profiling based on LGBTQ+ status | Florida (sexual orientation only) |
| Bans gay/transgender panic defense | None |
| HIV criminalization for low-risk behaviors | Alabama, Arkansas, Florida, Georgia, Kentucky, Louisiana, Mississippi, North Carolina, Oklahoma, South Carolina, Tennessee, Virginia |
| *Regarding LGBTQ+ Youth* | |
| Juvenile justice LGBTQ–inclusive | Florida, Georgia, Kentucky, Louisiana, North Carolina, Tennessee, Texas |
| LGBTQ+ minor access to homeless shelters | None |
| Inconsistent age-of-consent laws | North Carolina, Texas |

Source: Human Rights Campaign, 2020

nationwide created similar policies to prevent harassment and discrimination for homeless LGBTQ+ young people, but none are in the South. Another policy that can potentially harm LGBTQ+ young people is the criminalization of their sexual contact. Age-of-consent laws vary across the states, with most states setting the same age of consent for heterosexual and homosexual activity. Romeo and Juliet laws allow for exceptions for young teens in many states, but in the case of North Carolina and Texas, these exemptions apply only to heterosexual couples (Human Rights Campaign, 2020). Consequently, LGBTQ+ minors can be prosecuted for sexual activity when their heterosexual peers are exempted.

### Hate Crimes and Gender Marker Changes

Some statewide pro-LGBTQ+ policies exist in the South. Figure 6.1 shows hate crime laws inclusive of LGBTQ+ people overlayed with municipalities with policies that protect LGBTQ+ people. Seven states (Alabama, Arkansas, Mississippi, North Carolina, Oklahoma, South Carolina, and West Virginia) do not have hate crime laws that protect sexual orientation or gender identity. Georgia, Tennessee, and Virginia include sexual orientation and gender identity as protected classes in hate crime laws. However, Tennessee does not require law enforcement agencies to report crime statistics to the federal government. Texas and Florida require reporting of crime statistics but protect sexual orientation only. Finally, Louisiana and Kentucky protect sexual orientation alone but do not require reporting of statistics.

State laws are vital for establishing blanket protections within a state, but cities have also worked to reform their policing strategies. Figure 6.1 presents all municipalities that have at least one LGBTQ–inclusive policy on the books. The light-gray areas denote cities that reformed law enforcement practices involving LGBTQ+ interactions—in the form of hiring LGBTQ+ liaisons within law enforcement, the executive's office, and/or by reporting 2019 hate crime statistics. These steps show a willingness for transparency and inclusion of LGBTQ+ communities. The dark-gray areas denote cities that have any other pro-LGBTQ+ policy in place. From this perspective, southern cities are doing much better than they are typically credited to be. Most of the heavily populated cities have reforms that directly shape government relations with LGBTQ+ communities—either through mitigating relations or reporting hate crimes.

Simple administrative changes can remove potential bias in routine police stops. Interacting with law enforcement often involves showing identification documents with a gender marker that can disclose the gender-diverse status of transgender people. Unfortunately, as Figure 6.2 illustrates, changing one's documents in the South is not an easy task. Elias and Colvin (2020) show considerable variation in policies that allow for nonbinary options, with certain jurisdictions imposing burdensome costs, time delays, or medical requirements required before changing documentation. Although the study of Elias and Colvin did not include southern states, similar barriers exist in the region. Oklahoma, Tennessee, and West Virginia prohibit gender changes on birth certificates, with Oklahoma and Tennessee requiring that individuals have proof of surgery, a court order, or an amended birth certificate before changing the gender on a driver's license. Florida and Virginia are the only states that do not require surgery or a court order to amend birth certificates. Changing gender on a Florida driver's license requires provider certification but does not require surgery. Virginia is the only state in the South to have clearly outlined protocols for both birth certificates and driver's licenses. The remaining states allow for gender amendments on birth certificates, but

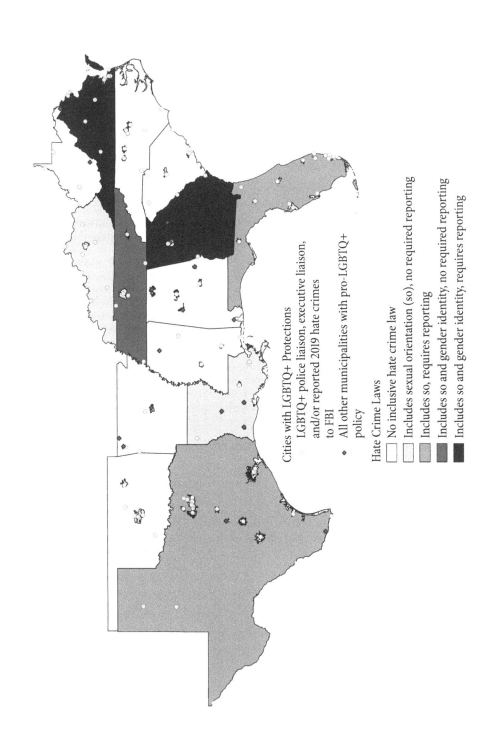

Cities with LGBTQ+ Protections

LGBTQ+ police liaison, executive liaison,
and/or reported 2019 hate crimes
to FBI

◆ All other municipalities with pro-LGBTQ+
policy

Hate Crime Laws

☐ No inclusive hate crime law

☐ Includes sexual orientation (so), no required reporting

☐ Includes so, requires reporting

☐ Includes so and gender identity, no required reporting

■ Includes so and gender identity, requires reporting

the process either requires surgery or other medical intervention. Furthermore, seven of the states (Georgia, Kentucky, Louisiana, Oklahoma, South Carolina, Tennessee, and Texas) require people to have proof of surgery, a court order, or an amended birth certificate to change their gender on their driver's license.

*City Reforms*

Local governments demonstrate how federalism can lead to LGBTQ+ progress even in the most conservative states. Table 6.2 depicts city policies according to whether they instituted the aforementioned police reforms (LGBTQ+ liaisons and/or reporting of hate crime statistics) or any other pro-LGBTQ+ policy (right column). Most cities had LGBTQ+ liaisons for law enforcement (52% for all; 61% for police-reformed). An overwhelming majority also reported hate crime statistics for 2019 (78% for all; 92% for police-reformed). The police manual was available in approximately half of the cities. Among all cities with LGBTQ–inclusive policies, 36% of police manuals reference

*Table 6.2: Municipalities with LGBTQ–Inclusive Policies*

| Police Reforms | All | Police Reformed |
|---|---|---|
| Police LGBTQ+ liaison | 52% | 61% |
| Reported 2019 hate crimes | 78% | 92% |
| Police handbook made public | 51% | 56% |
| Police policy on LGBTQ+ issues | 36% | 42% |
| Executive LGBTQ+ liaison | 50% | 58% |
| *Changes Possibly Preempting Police Intervention* | | |
| Conversion therapy ban | 11% | 13% |
| LGBTQ+ services for minors | 28% | 32% |
| Homeless LGBTQ+ services | 17% | 20% |
| LGBTQ+ elderly services | 13% | 15% |
| Transgender services | 12% | 14% |
| HIV services | 37% | 39% |
| *N* | 127 | 108 |

Source: Human Rights Campaign, 2021

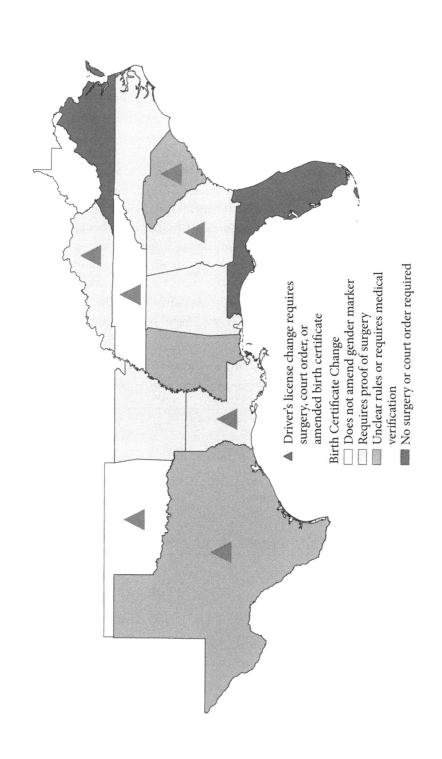

Driver's license change requires surgery, court order, or amended birth certificate

Birth Certificate Change
- Does not amend gender marker
- Requires proof of surgery
- Unclear rules or requires medical verification
- No surgery or court order required

LGBTQ+ people. This is even higher (42%) among cities that reformed policing to be inclusive of LGBTQ+ people. LGBTQ+ liaisons in the executive's office were also common, with 50% of all cities having this position and 58% with reformed policing having it. Many cities went beyond trying to improve relations by offering services that could preempt interactions with law enforcement, such as special outreach programs for LGBTQ+ minors, homeless populations, and people living with HIV. These proactive measures lead to interactions with social workers or health care workers rather than law enforcement, and they could prevent incarceration as a result of homelessness or bias from police officers.

## Discussion and Conclusion

Federalism complicates discussion of policing in the South because of the extreme ideological differences between state legislatures and local officials in progressive cities. Southern states offer little guidance to law enforcement to aid LGBTQ+ people. However, major cities stepped in to fill the void by adopting proactive measures to improve relations, such as creating LGBTQ+ liaisons, adopting nondiscrimination policies, and training officers on special needs of the population. This helps to reduce bias in policing and enables LGBTQ+ people to access services without fear of arrest or harassment. Among the cities with LGBTQ+ reforms, about half promote transparency by posting policing manuals, and approximately 40% posted efforts online to improve LGBTQ+ relations with police. Most state policies, however, spell trouble for LGBTQ+ citizens in the South. Only Louisiana requires sensitivity training for law enforcement, and this is exclusively for sexual orientation. Likewise, Florida is the only state to prohibit police officers from profiling people based on real or perceived sexual orientation.

States have made some progress in sexual orientation policy but continue to lag regarding gender identity and expression. No southern state offers police training on gender identity, nor does any prohibit the profiling of gender-diverse people. Moreover, all southern states allow legal defenses based on bias, such as gay or transgender panic. This is particularly dangerous when combined with the presence of stand-your-ground or self-defense laws enshrined in all southern states, except for Virginia (National Conference of State Legislatures, 2020). Everything combined enables perpetrators of LGBTQ+ hate crimes to claim a range of perceived threats grounded in bigotry involving race, gender, or sexual orientation.

The barriers to correcting gender markers in many states require knowledge of the legal system, along with being born and/or living in the right state. Gender-diverse people born in states that do not amend birth certificates, as well as people who do not want medical intervention, cannot change their documents in much of the South. This dooms many to have identification incongruent with their gender identity and places them at risk. Such was the case for Brandon Teena, who attempted to report rape only to be dismissed and repeatedly questioned by police about his gender and behavior. He was murdered a week later by the rapists whom law enforcement failed to protect him from. No southern states prohibit profiling based on gender identity or expression, which is particularly troubling. Failure to provide guidance on how to interact with LGBTQ+ individuals can perpetuate the high rates of incarceration and discrimination seen by LGBTQ+ people in criminal legal systems.

Fortunately, cities are taking strides to redress failures at the state level. Many municipalities in the South have policies that support LGBTQ+ communities. The most direct reforms involve creating liaisons in police departments or in the executive's office, along with filing hate crime statistics. These reforms are all important signs of accountability and an awareness of LGBTQ+ citizens. Liaisons serve a symbolic task supporting all constituents, but they also facilitate a change in department culture and aid in training everyone in the field. This can translate to better interactions between LGBTQ+ communities and law enforcement. Similarly, transparency in documenting and reporting hate crimes provides a form of justice, albeit limited. Another strength in southern cities is that of providing services in the community that can reduce interactions with law enforcement. A common critique of reform advocates is that police are called for a range of purposes that would be better handled by social workers. That is particularly true for individuals facing multiple forms of marginalization. Cities that provide services to LGBTQ+ minors, homeless populations, and older people offer alternatives for those in need of social services without their having to interact with law enforcement.

This study presents a snapshot of the current state of LGBTQ+ recognition by law enforcement in the South. Policing manuals were accessible in a little over half the municipalities, but few manuals explicitly instruct personnel on how to interact with LGBTQ+ people, so caution should be taken when speculating on how successfully these new protocols are improving interactions with police. The study's strength is that its analysis pooled all municipalities in the South with pro-LGBTQ+ policies.

The South is sure to be a battleground for LGBTQ+ activists for years to come as social conservatives turn to culture wars to mobilize supporters. State legislatures and progressive local governments in the South are taking radically different approaches. Major cities are stepping in to fill in gaps in the guidance that state governments fail to provide, for example, in the form of conversion therapy bans, protections in public accommodations, and some third of government jobs offering transgender-inclusive health care. Cities also offer protections from discrimination and other services that attract LGBTQ+ people to move there. This shows progress, but there is a widening gap in conditions for people across the country. Until the federal government adopts reforms, the South will continue to have a patchwork of policies governing how law enforcement interacts with the LGBTQ+ community.

# 7. POLICING QUEER KINK
## Misconceptions, Preconceptions, and Confusion

Emma L. Turley

The police have long had a contentious relationship with queer kinksters, often arising as a result of homophobia and common misconceptions about consensual bondage, discipline, dominance and submission, and sadism and masochism (BDSM) (Haviv, 2016). The legal ambiguity of activities classed under the umbrella of BDSM, along with preconceptions that all kink is abusive, influences the way that queer practitioners of consensual BDSM are treated by police. Police have been criticized for treating all BDSM or kinky encounters as abusive, and the semi-criminalized status of these activities, as well as increased police focus on intimate partner violence, obscures issues of autonomy and consent (Weait, 2007; Wright, 2018). This chapter traces the pathologization of BDSM to its current status as a recognized psychological disorder, which in some ways parallels the historical pathologization of lesbian, gay, bisexual, transgender, queer, and plus (LGBTQ+) sexualities and gender identities.

This chapter focuses exclusively on queer kinksters because research has demonstrated that BDSM interests and preferences differ significantly between heterosexual and LGBTQ+ people, with a higher prevalence of queer people, particularly gay and bisexual men, involved in kink practices (Hérbet & Weaver, 2014; Holvoet et al., 2017), and work focusing on only queer BDSM communities in their relations with police is rare. The chapter examines the ways that queer consensual kink is regulated and policed. Beginning with an overview of consensual BDSM, the chapter discusses how historical and contemporary sociomedical perspectives influence criminalization of consensual BDSM activities. The chapter then highlights the implications of BDSM's ambiguous legal status for its practitioners and explains how intersections of police homophobia, transphobia, and kinkphobia, and a conflation of BDSM with intimate partner violence (IPV), can result in unnecessary criminalization and discrimination for practitioners of consensual BDSM. The chapter concludes with a call for additional training for police in the differences between consensual BDSM and IPV and in a sex-positive approach to queer kinksters.

## Overview of BDSM

Bondage, discipline, dominance and submission, and sadism and masochism are a collection of consensual embodied activities involving an erotically charged shift of power and the use of intense physical and/or emotional stimulation (Barker et al., 2007; Turley & Butt, 2015). Consensual BDSM is referred to by many terms both within and outside the BDSM community, including kink, sadomasochism or SM, WIITWD (what it is that we do), and play (Moser & Kleinplatz, 2007). Although the activities that can be considered BDSM are not homogenous, a key feature of them is that an eroticism is overlaid on activities not usually associated with Western positivist notions of sexual activity (Turley, 2022). Such activities can include, but are not limited to, inflicting or receiving physical pain, humiliation, restraint using ropes or harnesses, and the use of fetishist clothing and other items (Moser & Kleinplatz, 2007). BDSM can take many forms and is constrained only by one's imagination or fantasy limits (Turley et al., 2018). Although BDSM, SM, and kink can encompass a similar range of practices and activities, the commonly used term BDSM is used throughout this chapter for the sake of clarity.

Practitioners of consensual BDSM adopt either a dominant or submissive role. Those whose role preference falls toward the dominant end of the spectrum can refer to themselves using such terms as top, master/mistress, sadist, and domme/dom. Individuals who prefer submissive roles use terms such as bottom, slave, sub, and pet. There are also those who like to adopt either role, depending on the circumstances of the BDSM; these practitioners are known by the terms switch and flexible (Moser & Kleinplatz, 2007).

Consensual BDSM is practiced by people from across the gender and sexuality spectrums, so practitioners of BDSM are not a homogenous group in their gender identities, sexualities, or BDSM interests. People who use a particular label to signify their role preference do not necessarily participate in the same BDSM activities as other persons using the same label, and meanings behind the labels are not interpreted in the same ways by every practitioner of BDSM (Moser & Kleinplatz, 2007).

Although consensual BDSM is perceived to be a rare sexual interest, research on its prevalence in Western populations indicates that it is not especially uncommon. Estimations range between 10% and 22% for adults who express some interest in BDSM-related activities (Kinsey et al., 1953; Masters et al., 1995; Moser & Kleinplatz, 2006), and a systematic review of the literature found that BDSM-related fantasies were common, occurring in 40%–70% of the populations included in the review (Brown et al., 2020). Demographically, practitioners of BDSM tend to be white, well educated (with a baccalaureate), and middle or upper class, and they do not have higher rates of mental health issues or relationship problems than the general population (Brown et al., 2020; Langdridge & Barker, 2007). There is little research on BDSM participation cross-culturally; the majority of studies include Western participants, so the research represents a culturally homogenous group.

Research has demonstrated that BDSM interests and preferences are fundamentally different for heterosexual and LGBQ+ people, with more prevalence of BDSM interests among nonheterosexual people (Alison et al., 2001; Hérbet & Weaver, 2014). Gay men tend to have their first BDSM experience at a later age than heterosexual men, and their activity preference is distinct. Gay men exhibit a preference for hypermasculine, sadistically oriented activities, focused around masculinization of sexual behavior using leather and uniforms in their BDSM activities. Heterosexual men's preferences focus on submissive behavior such as verbal humiliation, sensory deprivation, and pain (Nordling et al., 2006). Research looking exclusively at women's experiences is limited; however, bisexual and gay women's interest in BDSM is higher on average than that of heterosexual women, although their types of preferred activity are broadly similar, involving bondage and domination (Tomassilli et al., 2009). Research exploring the sexual desires, fantasies, and sexual interests of subgroups of the LGBTQ+ community is sparse; subgroups that are neglected are bisexual, transgender, asexual, and nonbinary or genderfluid people, and research on BDSM exhibits the same pattern of sparsity (Nimbi et al., 2020).

## Pathologization, Medicalization, and Murky Legal Status

BDSM is a particularly stigmatized subculture due to misperceptions about matters of consent and abuse and about the activities that occur in BDSM experiences (Turley, 2022). Issues around pathologization, medicalization, and the legal confusions relating to consensual BDSM contribute to this stigmatization, particularly when queer BDSM is examined in the context of heteronormative sexual practices (Goffman, 1963; Turley, 2022). This section of the chapter explores these issues by tracing BDSM's historical medicalization and its development into a categorized psychiatric disorder.

Victorian sexologist Richard Krafft-Ebing categorized types of nonnormative sexualities and sexual behaviors. An interest in sadism and masochism he classified as abnormal and therefore in need of medical intervention (Turley & Butt, 2015). Krafft-Ebing's work produced a taxonomy of "sexual perversions," which continues to influence Western biomedical and clinical thinking about sexuality (Spinelli, 2006). Foucault (1978) theorized that the Western sexual ideal is "procreational heterosexuality"; therefore sexual activity that did not meet this criterion was positioned as "perverted." BDSM's perceived link with pathology is reflected in the *Diagnostic and Statistical Manual of Mental Disorders*, or the *DSM*, of the American Psychiatric Association, which is the taxonomic and diagnostic authority consulted by psychologists and psychiatrists. Editions of the *DSM* have categorized consensual BDSM as a psychiatric disorder, with the most recent edition, the fifth, classifying it as a "paraphilic disorder" (American Psychiatric Association, 2013). Although the *DSM* criteria specify that a diagnosis of a paraphilic disorder depends on the presence of clinical distress and/or a victim, and notes that many people with non-normative sexual interests do not have a psychiatric disorder, any inclusion of BDSM interests in the *DSM* is likely to attract significant stigma for practitioners of consensual BDSM, particularly when definitional nuance is lost. As a result of these continuing psycho-medical perspectives, it is unsurprising that public opinion is likely to agree that an interest in consensual BDSM points to mental illness, often leading to the conclusion that its practitioners are mad, bad, or dangerous. This association of BDSM with psychiatric disorder and pathology is often reinforced by the media (Weiss, 2006), and therefore it is reasonable to assume that police officers' thinking about BDSM is influenced by, and reflective of, these common misperceptions.

The concept of abnormality was used historically to medicalize transgressive and non-normative sexual activity. However, research evidence is lacking that links consensual BDSM with pathology and mental illness (Ahlers et al., 2011; Richters et al., 2008, 2014; Wismeijer & van Assen, 2013), and in fact, it has been reported that practitioners of BDSM had lower scores on clinical depression scales (Connelly, 2006). Research aimed at understanding the people and practices involved in consensual BDSM have produced findings that challenge common prejudices and misunderstandings around pathology, danger, abuse, and consent (Hammers, 2019; Langdridge & Barker, 2007; Newmahr, 2011; Turley, 2022; Weiss, 2011). Moreover, recent research has found that engaging in consensual BDSM can have multiple positive outcomes for practitioners, including improved well-being, enhanced spiritual connection or transcendence, relaxation in the form of leisure, and an enriched sense of playfulness (for example, see Ambler et al., 2017; Carlström, 2021; Faccio et al., 2020; Fennell, 2018; Turley, 2016, 2022; Williams et al., 2014).

Although the premise of BDSM often revolves around loss of power, abusive activities, and danger, practitioners of consensual BDSM approach risk and safety with serious care and consideration. Consent is present as a central feature. Organized BDSM communities tend to adhere to a code of conduct and refer to the mottos "safe, sane, and consensual" and "risk aware consensual kink" to describe attitudes toward safety when participating in BDSM (Langdridge & Barker, 2007). Codes of conduct such as these explicitly acknowledge that those participating are aware of the potential risks involved in BDSM (Williams et al., 2014). Safety measures are implemented by a variety of means, including open and explicit negotiation of the BDSM scene, roles, and activities that will take place; a discussion of the hard and soft limits of the people involved; and the use of a safe word. A safe word is a word, phrase, or gesture, agreed on beforehand, that signals to participants that the scene should be paused or stopped. A traffic-light system is sometimes used to classify someone's preferences for BDSM activities: activities a person enjoys are coded green, activities that person would like to try are coded amber, and activities that are off limits are coded red (Turley et al., 2018). As with any subcultural community, there are instances when problems occur, but breaches of a code of conduct are often handled within the community rather than within a legal framework (Turley & Butt, 2015).

Contrary to fact, non-consent in BDSM is presented as the norm by the media, particularly in television, film, and true-crime podcasts, which draw heavily on stereotypes of BDSM practitioners as abusive. Despite the increase in BDSM-related media content over the last decade, higher levels of exposure do not lead to increased understanding or acceptance of the practice (Sand, 2019). The media tends to split BDSM activities into "acceptable" and "unacceptable" categories, and increased representation in TV shows, novels, popular music, and advertising often fails to challenge the stigma associated with BDSM or portrays only normative and "accepted" activities, such as spanking and light bondage, while othering more extreme forms of BDSM (Simula, 2019; Weiss, 2011). Again, it is likely that police officers draw upon this misinformation when dealing with queer BDSM practitioners in their work.

The legal status of BDSM is unclear, and laws on consensual violence are often just as murky. In many Western legal systems, participating in BDSM may not in itself be criminalized. However, certain aspects of BDSM or particular activities may break laws and provoke a criminal response (Weait, 2007). As mentioned earlier in the chapter, safety and consent are considered central to practicing BDSM, yet the recent increased interest in BDSM arising from popular culture, such as the film *Fifty Shades of Grey*, has led to a rise in new BDSM practitioners who may be unfamiliar with the subcultural norms and therefore may play unsafely (Langdridge & Barker, 2007; Sagarin et al., 2019).

Even when BDSM activities are explicitly consensual, practitioners can find themselves subject to prosecution. A key legal case comes from Operation Spanner, a three-year investigation into same-sex BDSM in the late 1980s in the United Kingdom. The investigation culminated in the prosecution of 16 men who were charged with a range of crimes, including bodily harm and unlawful wounding, despite the facts that the case had no complainants and that the defendants testified that all activities were consensual. The subsequent *R v. Brown* (1994) AC212 judgment ruled that it was not legally possible to consent to sadomasochistic harm and is still the basis for contemporary U.K. case law (Beresford, 2016). The implications of this ruling set a legal precedent that particular consensual acts can be criminalized without a victim complaint. Australian legal cases have focused on consensual BDSM that went wrong, rather than on cases with no victim complaint. However, it is noteworthy that U.K. cases often have a "persuasive" effect on Australian courts (Bartle, 2018). In the *R v. Stein* manslaughter case in Victoria, the court stated that consent was irrelevant to the case because the victim had suffered significant physical injury from suffocation (Bartle, 2018). The legal status of consensual BDSM in the United States is ambiguous. Although there is no penal law targeting BDSM specifically, other laws prohibiting assault or battery are applied, and courts refuse to acknowledge a defense of consent (Ludwig, 2017). Many U.S. jurisdictions base this refusal on the *R v. Brown* judgment (Ludwig, 2017), and to date there has been no court decision that accepted consent as a defense in a BDSM-related case (National Coalition for Sexual Freedom, 2022).

The extensive research of Moser and Kleinplatz (2005, 2006) suggests that the scientific justification for including BDSM in the *DSM* is flawed. The inclusion lacks empirical support and is value-laden, which may lead to misunderstandings, misuse by authorities, and miscarriages of justice. There is a dearth of information and training available to assist police in differentiating consensual from nonconsensual harm in BDSM. When coupled with kinkphobia and a heteronormative bias, misinterpretation of BDSM activity may lead to spurious legal charges and unnecessary prosecution of LGBTQ+ practitioners of consensual BDSM.

The pathologization of sexual and gender minorities parallels the pathologization of practitioners of consensual BDSM. Homosexuality was included in the *DSM* until 1973 and was considered a psychiatric disorder resulting from a deviation from "typical" and "normative" heterosexual development. The presence of "atypical" same-sex attraction was viewed as a symptom of defective development (Drescher, 2015). Diagnosis for gender minorities followed this same pattern and was included in editions of the *DSM* under various guises, including transvestism, transsexualism, and gender identity disorder. In the current version of the *DSM*, gender identity disorder was replaced with gender dysphoria, shifting the diagnostic focus from an identity issue to a distress issue. The shift marks an improvement on past categorizations, but it remains problematic. A legitimized notion of sexual and gender minorities as psychologically damaged has intersected with the historically criminalized nature of LGBTQ+ identities to result in the perpetuation of transphobia and homophobia, including in criminal processing systems. The following section of the chapter explores police prejudice against non-cis-heteronormative identities.

## Homophobia and Transphobia in the Police

The relationship between queer communities and the police has been, and remains, a turbulent one due to homophobia and the unfair treatment of LGBTQ+ people by police (Dario et al., 2020; Dwyer, 2014b). Research has demonstrated that LGBTQ+ people hold more negative perceptions about the police than their heterosexual counterparts (Miles-Johnson, 2013a; Owen et al., 2018). This is unsurprising given that members of LGBTQ+ communities are subject to false arrests, harassment, homophobia, sexual and physical violence, and other forms of police discrimination (Ritchie & Jones-Brown, 2017). This discriminatory treatment dissuades some LGBTQ+ people from reporting crimes or decreases the likelihood of their cooperating with the police (Mallory et al., 2015).

Historically, LGBTQ+ people were subject to higher-than-average criminalization for a variety of reasons. Criminal laws against sodomy were disproportionately enforced against same-sex participants (Dario et al., 2020), criminal charges were filed for infringements such as loitering or dressing in a "disguise" when dressed in drag, and gay bars and nightclubs were regularly raided by police (Cain, 1993). Woods (2017) reports that members of the LGBTQ+ community were generally regarded by police as deviant sexual offenders. Although laws prohibiting homosexuality have been abolished in most Western jurisdictions, the consequences of this historical criminalization of the LGBTQ+ community remain in the forms of over-policing LGBTQ+ people in social and leisure spaces and under-policing the victimization of LGBTQ+ people, as well as the stigmatization and discrimination experienced by queer communities more broadly (Dwyer, 2007).

Although it is unlikely that police today will demonstrate the overt, violent homophobia that was common in the past, history demonstrates that interactions between police and LGBTQ+ persons remain strained across several dimensions. These interactions are affected by a range of intersecting factors including sexuality, gender, gender identity, race, age, and economic status (Amnesty International, 2005; Giwa & Jackman, 2020; Moran & Sharpe, 2004). Dwyer (2011b, 2015) reports a particularly high prevalence of negative encounters with police among young gender-nonconforming people and young people who "read" as queer by police from visible bodily cues. Gender presentation influences interactions with police, and gay and bisexual men attempt to appear more masculine in the presence of police officers, while lesbian and bisexual women try to maximize their femininity to avoid maltreatment by police (Nadal et al., 2015). Transgender people, particularly transgender people of color, report higher instances of negative interactions with police, which indicates the intersectional nature of these encounters (Hodge & Sexton, 2020; Moran & Sharpe, 2004).

Despite police attempts to improve their relationship with queer communities through various programs and initiatives, the relationship remains fraught, primarily as a result of systemic and structural issues within the police and wider criminal processing systems. Police foster a culture of hegemonic masculinity to reinforce the power of heterosexual men over women and sexual and gender minorities (Connell & Messerschmidt, 2005). This culture values hypermasculine traits and thus rewards stereotypical gender roles (Dario et al, 2019; Rabe-Hemp, 2009). Officers who do not match masculine stereotypes are viewed as ineffective and a risk to the successful completion of operations (Bernstein et al., 2003; Giwa et al., 2022). Despite initiatives by police departments to recruit more women and gender and sexual minorities, the homophobia and heteronormativity persist (Giwa et al., 2022; Lyons et al, 2008), coloring police interactions with LGBTQ+ people and undermining the community's trust in the police.

## Kinkphobia

Compared with police interaction with LGBTQ+ persons, research that examines police interaction with those interested in kink is much more limited. Existing research does highlight that practitioners of consensual BDSM are reluctant to report to police any crimes, such as sexual assault, that take place in the context of BDSM (Haviv, 2016). The current police response to crimes such as sexual assault and rape is inadequate and is likely to result in secondary victimization, particularly for sexual and gender minorities, who frequently experience negative interactions when reporting to authorities (Greeson et al., 2014; Kennedy & Prock, 2018). Reporting sexual crimes is difficult for anyone, but this difficulty is compounded for those belonging to a stigmatized subculture (Haviv, 2016). BDSM practitioners' reasons for not reporting sexual crimes to the police include fears that their interest in BDSM and membership in the community will be publicly exposed or that they will experience victim blaming from police (Haviv, 2016; Murphy-Oikonen & Egan, 2022). Women reported apprehension on two fronts: fear of sexual objectification from male officers, who would likely view them as sex objects because of their sexual interests, and the difficulty of providing proof of a crime, especially when some acts of BDSM were consensual. These fears were underpinned by the expectation that police would fail to understand that BDSM is not supposed to be abusive and should always be consensual (Haviv, 2016). Practitioners highlighted that reporting and policing tend to occur within the BDSM community itself through warnings and blacklisting, and also that support was available within the community for victims of sexual assault (Dunkley & Brotto, 2020; Turley & Butt, 2015). It is reasonable to assume that existing homophobia and heteronormativity in the police are exacerbated by intersecting kinkphobia and misconceptions about consensual BDSM.

It is useful to draw on Rubin's (1984) charmed circle to characterize the intersectional threads that constitute Western societal perceptions of acceptable and unacceptable sex and sexualities and the multiple ways these perceptions lead to regulatory power. The more normative the sexual behavior, the more central the position in the circle. According to Rubin, sex that is conceptualized as "good, normal, and natural" is at the center of the circle and includes sex that is heterosexual, within marriage, monogamous, occurring in private, noncommercial, and reproductive. Ranked low on Rubin's hierarchy of sexual values are behaviors that are out of wedlock, nonreproductive, commercial, or involving the use of pornography. Along with promiscuity, nonheterosexual sexualities, and cross-generational sex, BDSM is positioned at the outer limits—outside the charmed circle. The social constructions of good/acceptable and bad/unacceptable for LGBTQ+ identity can also be characterized with Rubin's charmed circle. In the 40 years since Rubin's publication, views of homosexuality in most Western countries have moved closer to acceptability as attitudes toward sexual minorities improved. However, contemporary constructions of the "good gay" as monogamous and the "bad queer" as promiscuous are relevant and operate in the same regulatory spaces (Stychin & Herman, 2000).

Given criminal processing systems' heteronormative legal and cultural framework at present, queer practitioners of BDSM are at risk of being perceived as doubly deviant by authorities, including the police, as a result of both their sexuality and their unconventional sexual interests. Add to this the semi-criminalization, misunderstandings, and legal confusion around consensual BDSM, and the levels of stigmatization by authorities heighten (Turley, 2022). Goffman (1963) conceptualized stigma as unwanted difference that is discrediting to the individual, and the differences are amplified for queer BDSM in the context of heteronormative sexual practices. Issues of sex negativity are pertinent to his argument; they describe attitudes, beliefs, and behaviors that construct sexuality as dangerous and generally immoral (Sears, 2016). The impact of sex negativity can affect the provision of, and access to, services such as social services and police (Williams et al., 2015), and it is unsurprising that kinkphobia is strongly embedded in sex-negative attitudes (Downing, 2013; Khan, 2016). This collection of perceived deviant intersections creates multiple layers of stigma that BDSM practitioners are required to manage during encounters with police and other criminal processing agencies to protect themselves and their communities from unfair treatment, possible exposure, and discrimination. It is not difficult to understand how practitioners of consensual BDSM can become victims of discrimination from a range of authorities, including during child custody cases (Wright, 2006), during domestic violence cases, while seeking employment (Ridinger, 2006), and during criminal proceedings (Monica, 2011). As a result of the stigmatization caused by the combination of pathologization, criminalization, and misconception, LGBTQ+ practitioners of consensual BDSM must employ complex stigma and impression management strategies to protect themselves against discrimination and victimization by regulatory authorities saturated with heteronormativity.

## The Conflation of Intimate Partner Violence and Consensual BDSM

Police have been criticized for treating BDSM or kinky encounters as abusive, and the semi-criminalized status of these activities, along with increased police focus on IPV, obscures issues of autonomy and consent. Police have often conflated IPV with BDSM and have used laws designed to offer protection from nonconsensual violence to legally prohibit and sanction consensual BDSM (Kieran & Sheff, 2016). The World Health Organization (2017) defines IPV as inclusive of physical, psychological, and sexual harm and mentions aggression, sexual coercion, and controlling behavior. To the unfamiliar, it may appear as though BDSM practices overlap with IPV. However, there are important differences between the two.

The most profound difference is the presence or absence of consent. IPV is not consensual; however, in BDSM, consent consists of an ongoing, interactive, and dynamic process, which foregrounds protection measures. This includes an open discussion of desires and hard and soft limits (Holt, 2016), as well as a discussion of preferences and desires before the encounter begins (Kieran & Sheff, 2016). In addition, there should be a mutual definition of terms (Turley et al., 2018), along with shared notions of responsibility and transparency among practitioners (Holt, 2016). The recognition that consent is ongoing and can therefore be withdrawn is a central feature of BDSM, and safe words and/or safe gestures used to signal a wish to stop the activity are respected by partners (Jozifkova, 2013). In consensual BDSM, control is willingly relinquished and given over by submissive partners to dominant partners, whereas in IPV, power and control are taken from someone through violence, coercion, or manipulation (Kieran & Sheff, 2016). The intentions are markedly different and delineate BDSM apart from IPV; the purpose of BDSM is to pleasure and excite, and even to bond, whereas the intention of IPV is control and abuse (Dunkley & Brotto, 2020; Kieran & Sheff, 2016). The outcomes of each are also different. Outcomes of BDSM can be sexual and nonsexual and can include sexual and erotic satisfaction, personal growth, and spirituality (Turley, 2022). Outcomes of IPV are marked by disempowerment, victimization, anger, and helplessness (Kieran & Sheff, 2016). There is usually no lasting psychological harm or permanent physical damage as a result of engaging in consensual BDM, which is not the case with IPV. Patterns of violence and reconciliation, common in IPV situations, are not present in consensual BDSM relationships (Jozifkova, 2013). Aftercare is a usual feature of consensual BDSM and occurs at the end of a session and consists of affectionately attending to each partner after intense feelings of a physical or psychological nature that frequently occur during BDSM.

Intimate partner violence is a global issue of concern, and police responses have been criticized for failing to take IPV and family violence seriously and for adopting a heteronormative approach where women are viewed solely in relation to men (Douglas, 2019; Goodmark, 2009; Hanmer et al., 1989). As a result, there has (rightly) been increased police focus on IPV and a shift toward more proactive policing with a strong emphasis on policies, procedures, and risk perceptions (Meyer & Reeves, 2021). A shift in social and legal responses to IPV in Australia has led to legislative commitment and ongoing policy reform in a range of organizations including the police (Meyer & Reeves, 2021). Given that police already conflate BDSM and IPV, education and training about consensual BDSM is important.

Training on consent in the context of BDSM would allow police to better differentiate BDSM from actions committed in IPV, and markers for distinguishing BDSM from abuse—such as voluntariness and communication—should be highlighted (Dunkley & Brotto, 2020). Moser (2006) has detailed physical indicators that assist professionals in recognizing the differences between consensual BDSM and abuse. These include facial bruising and defensive wounds, which are not usually present after BDSM. wounds that occur during BDSM are usually present on fleshy parts of the body and are concentrated in one area or in a pattern typical of BDSM, whereas wounds from physical abuse have no set pattern and are randomly distributed. Kieran and Sheff (2016) have prepared a list of questions that act as communication guidelines for professionals, which focus on consent as the primary distinguishing factor from IPV. This collection of resources could be employed to assist police in recognizing consensual BDSM and interacting better with BDSM practitioners, which would help to avoid the conflation with IPV and unnecessary criminal justice interventions.

## Conclusion

This chapter covered the range of intersectional factors that influence the police's negative perceptions of practitioners of consensual BDSM. The lasting influence of BDSM's pathologization as mental illness and the semi-criminalization of its practice laid the foundations for kinkphobia and misconceptions about BDSM. An overlay of homophobia, which in many ways has paralleled the pathologization and criminalization of BDSM, illustrates how additional intersecting factors compound misconceptions and kinkphobia. Police have been criticized for treating all BDSM or kinky encounters as abusive, and the semi-criminalized status of these activities, along with increased police focus on IPV, obscures issues of autonomy and consent. Additional police training to recognize the difference between BDSM and IPV, to foreground sexual citizenship, and to take a sex positive approach to queer kinksters would be useful in avoiding over-policing and spurious criminal justice interventions for queer practitioners of consensual BDSM.

PART 3

# Intersections in Uniform

# 8. TRANSITIONING IN UNIFORM
## Identity and Conflict within Policing

Heather Panter

The expansion of lesbian, gay, bisexual, transgender, queer, and plus (LGBTQ+) identities, as outlined by Herek (2010), has been seen as a modern shift from an antiquated male heteronormative conceptualization of sex and gender to inclusive concepts of LGBTQ+ identities. Previous studies have highlighted complex LGBTQ+ experiences within police culture (see Dwyer, 2011a, 2011b; Dwyer et al., 2020; Giwa et al., 2022; Miles-Johnson, 2015, 2016a, 2016b, 2019), with some academics examining occupational experiences of LGBTQ+ people within policing (see Bernstein & Kostelac, 2002; Colvin, 2009, 2012; Giwa et al., 2022; Jones & Williams, 2015; Miller et al., 2003; Panter, 2017, 2018; Rumens & Broomfield, 2012).

Yet, with said expansion of LGBTQ+ communities and our understanding of sex and gender, inclusive concepts can cause complexity in understanding group variability and the complexities that lie within (Parent et al., 2013). For example, although the *T* (for transgender) has an obvious place in the conceptualization of gender, there are possibilities for intangible separations with respect to LGB+ (i.e., non-heteronormative sexuality) (Parent et al., 2013). When considering intersectionality and the LGBTQ+ policing community, gender identities and sexuality are often indistinguishably linked because gender identity is often seen as an interlocking component of sexuality (see

Panter, 2018). This nexus of gender identity and sexuality, with respect to intersectionality theory, arguably operates in overlapping and connected ways (see Crenshaw, 1991). As such, this chapter aims to contribute to policing studies by examining transgender work experiences and identity formation. Further, this chapter examines how police culture may impact acceptance and/or unacceptance of transgender officers while transitioning.

## Transgender Work Experiences and Identity Formation in Occupational Settings

West and Zimmerman (1987) argued that people are always "doing gender," as gender is a social process that is constantly regulated performatively, rather than something that is innate to "men" and "women." In respect to gender performance, "the visibility of gender, as defined by social markers, creates unique challenging circumstances for individuals who are transitioning or planning to transition from one gender to another, as well as those who are gender nonconforming" (Sawyer et al., 2016, p. 21). Schilt and Connell (2007) contended that "everyone is accountable to gendered expectations, gender inequality is socially produced and maintained in interactions" (p. 600). As such, gender role expectations and gendered disparities are deeply embedded in workplace structures (Schilt & Connell, 2007).

Previous research has highlighted the occupational challenges that transgender people face while transitioning (see Brown et al., 2012; Budge et al., 2010; Schilt & Connell, 2007; Schilt & Wiswall, 2008), workplace policies that hinder transition (Colvin, 2007), and workplace discrimination and harassment (Davidson, 2016; Dispenza et al., 2017; Lombardi et al., 2002; McNeil et al., 2012; Panter, 2018; Waite, 2021). Yet Schilt (2006) found that female-to-male transgender people reported advantages after they had transitioned to a male identity. Schilt's participants described their perception that they had more authority, competency, recognition, and economic gains due to their new gender status (Budge et al., 2010). Notably, there is scant research examining transgender police officers' experiences when negotiating gender during transition (see Panter, 2017, 2018) as the acknowledgment of transgender identities within policing is minimal despite recruitment attempts (see Miles-Johnson, 2019).

Devor (2004) provided an informative analysis of transitioning and identity process for transgender individuals across various employment sectors. Devor's model was based upon gay identity formation and role exit theories, which state that people desire to "be witnessed for exactly who they are and to see themselves mirrored in others' eyes as they see themselves" (Budge et al., 2010, p. 2). Similarly, Gangé et al. (1997) found that transgender identity formation occurs through early transgender experiences, coming out to oneself, coming out to others, and resolution of identity. Part of this resolution of identity can be attributed to gender socialization theory, which highlights that gender is learned socially while establishing guidelines for appropriate and inappropriate gender behavior (see Schilt, 2006). Schilt and Connell (2007) noted that transgender workers who transition in workplaces have to renegotiate their gender differences through these gender performance expectations. Moreover, these socialized gendered expectations vary depending on different organizational cultures and occupational context (Connell, 1995; Schilt & Connell, 2007).

Budge et al. (2010) proposed a work transitioning model as a theoretical framework when examining the transition process of transgender identities within workplaces. Budge et al. stated that occupational studies on transgender experiences should be examined through three phases: pre-transition experiences, transition experiences, and post-transition experiences. Taken together, the literature that examines occupational experiences when transitioning advocates for taking a holistic account of how new gender status impacts occupational socialization across each step of transition and identity development.

## Theoretical Concepts of Gender and Identity within Police Work Cultures

Policing, even with occupational inclusion improvements, is still predominantly male and reflects desired masculine values (e.g., ideals of emotional control, concealing weakness, demonstration of toughness) (Silvestri, 2017). Policing tends toward a "cult of masculinity" (see Silvestri, 2017) with a continued existence of an "impervious white, heterosexist, male culture" (Loftus, 2008, p. 756). Fundamentally, police culture has been synonymous with hypermasculinity and dichotomous gender roles (i.e., hegemonic masculinity) due to the nature and components of the job itself (see Colvin, 2012; Loftus, 2008; Westmarland, 2001). Connell and Messerschmidt (2005) proposed that hegemonic masculinity describes how men structurally dominate within cultures while reproducing inequality. As such, the social construction and manifestation of hegemonic masculinity within policing can be seen in work assignments based on desirable performance traits that limit female officers to "women's issues" (e.g., domestic violence, child abuse investigations, sex crimes) and male officers to "male issues" (e.g., firearms, tactical units, narcotics) (Barlow & Barlow, 2000; Giwa et al., 2022; Westmarland, 2001).

Within policing, identities are not only reinforced and regulated, but they also contribute to attachment conflicts. For example, du Plessis et al. (2021) stated that occupational identity is a central feature in identity construction, and occupational identities allow for a sense of belonging from an identification with fellow officers. Bayerl et al. (2018) argued that this sense of belonging shapes collective meanings for the regulation of group members' behavior. Rabe-Hemp (2009) discussed this when she examined how cisgender women officers identify culturally as police officers while "doing gender" (West & Zimmerman, 1987). Rabe-Hemp further highlighted that policewomen both resisted and adopted heteronormative stereotypes held about femininity in policing, but they also regulated and reinforced existing gender differences during the process.

In addition to occupational gendered role expectations, policing not only recognizes (non)conformity but also socially regulates and reinforces ideological expectations of binary identities. This social dominance, and to a certain extent occupational desirability, of masculinity within policing further encourages a male dominance and reassertion. With this encouragement of a dominant masculine ethos in policing, the perceived antithesis of masculinity, that is, femininity, is perceived as undesirable and often is treated as such (see Panter, 2018). Therefore, theoretically, female-identifying police officers are expected to either accept their socialized perceived inferiority relative to masculine job performance expectations (and subsequently do more work to be considered legitimate in policing roles) or adopt the more "desirable" masculine traits within policing (see Panter, 2018).

Regardless, these nonmasculine performative actions within police culture require conformity to existing masculine ideologies that are structurally regulated by how binary gender is perceived. Policing, due to its behavioral practices of strict binary gender and to heteronormative assumptions about men and women, creates difficult occupational barriers for LGBTQ+ identities (Colvin, 2009, 2012; Giwa et al., 2022; Panter, 2018). Arguably this occurs because LGBTQ+ identities are the repository of whatever is symbolically expelled from hegemonic masculinity within patriarchal ideologies of police culture (Panter, 2018). Threats to the masculine police ethos cause further conformity to stereotypical models of binary gender regulation to compensate for any socialized questions about sexuality and/or gender presentation (see Miller et al., 2003). This regulation, as a result of desired conformity, can be validated through the subordination of women, heterosexism, genderism, authority, control, competitive individualism, and the capacity for bias as illustrated by the lack of social acceptance of transgender women, effeminate gay male identities, and femininity in general (see Colvin, 2012; Connell, 1995; Messerschmidt, 1996; Panter, 2018).

Nonbinary conformity and non-heteronormative identities could be perceived as a direct threat to socialized perceptions of occupational assumptions of "masculine" and "feminine" job performance expectations (see McCarthy, 2013; Panter, 2018). Panter (2018) found that the transgender policing community not only faced occupational bias as a result of gender presentation (genderism), but they also faced bias as a result of intersectional perceptions of how gender and sexuality are connected (heterosexism). Panter (2017) also found that some pre-transition individuals specifically enter policing as a way to ease internal conflicts from pre-transition distress and/or gender dysphoria, despite the known historical rejection of transgender identities within policing. Police culture can (in rare circumstances) bolster gender performance self-esteem in how officers regulate their gender performance (Panter, 2017). But gender androgyny or nonconforming gender is often not accepted within police cultures due to a failure to "fit in" with gendered job assignment expectations and police culture altogether (see Panter, 2017). Hence, LGBTQ+ police report having different occupational experiences, with "effeminate" gay men and transgender women reporting higher incidents of occupational bias and unacceptance compared with "masculine" lesbians and transgender men (Panter, 2018). This is why queer criminology should focus on examining the differences within each strand of the LGBTQ+ community, instead of making collective observations for all LGBTQ+ police.

## Methods

In *Transgender Cops: The Intersection of Gender and Sexuality Expectations in Police Cultures* (Panter, 2018), I examined the unique occupational issues that both British and American transgender police officers faced within policing. This book was a result of a four-year study I conducted. A former American cop turned academic, I had connections to both the policing world and the LGBTQ+ community that afforded access to communities normally difficult to reach for research (see Lum et al., 2012; Panter, 2018). Data were collected during police ride-alongs, attendance at police diversity training, participant observation of police at transgender Pride events, and multiple in-depth qualitative interviews. Subsequent data were collected from follow-up qualitative interviews with original participants over a span of two years. Therefore, this present study consists of two different sweeps of research activity over the course of six years: a reexamination of the original qualitative data published in Panter (2018) alongside follow-up qualitative interviews with the original participants.

This sample included both transgender police and cisgender police who work alongside transgender colleagues. Participants were never asked their identity during interviews, but they always disclosed their identification. Using a snowball approach, I followed up with contacts provided by original interviewees to recruit additional participants. Interviews ranged from 15 minutes to three hours; most were 40 minutes long. Interviews occurred over a span of six years, carried out at different time intervals organically in different sweeps of research activity. Therefore, like Coffey and Atkinson (1996), I did not perceive analysis as the last stage of research; instead, analysis had fluidity during my collection of interview data, because I was categorizing, thematically coding, thinking about, and connecting responses throughout the entire research process. I undertook a thematic type of analysis, "fracturing" (Strauss, 1987, p. 55) my data into specific codes so that "individual pieces can be classified or categorized" (Babbie, 2010 p. 402).

Despite my attempts to have minority racial and ethnic transgender participants, all participants who contributed to this research identified as white—a considerable limitation to this study. I tried to recruit minority racial and ethnic transgender participants through online forums, chat rooms, police public affairs offices, police agency websites, Black and minority police social groups, and with a snowballing method. Unfortunately, I was unable to gain any participants who identified as Black and transgender, Native American and transgender, Asian and transgender, and so forth. Ultimately, I was unable to explore the intersectional components of race, sexuality, and gender collectively. I suspect that the lack of Black, Native American, and Asian transgender police participants was due to a lower representation of these groups in policing in general. Or perhaps white transgender persons are more commonly drawn to policing. Further research would be needed before making this assumption. Regardless, my samples of cisgender and transgender participants, sorted demographically in Tables 8.1 and 8.2, contribute findings to policing studies and occupational studies on gender perceptions, gender expectations, and identity formation.

*Table 8.1: Demographics of Cisgender Sample*

| Self-Identification | American | British | Total |
| --- | --- | --- | --- |
| Heterosexual males | 8 | 3 | 11* |
| Heterosexual females | 2 | 1 | 3 |
| Lesbian | 3 | 4 | 7 |
| Gay | 2 | 2 | 4 |

* Three cisgender heterosexual males self-identified as "cross-dressers."

*Table 8.2: Demographics of Transgender Sample*

| Self-Identification | American | British | Total |
| --- | --- | --- | --- |
| Male-to-female | 4 | 5 | 9 |
| Female-to-male | 2 | 2 | 4 |
| Genderqueer/genderfluid | 1 | 2 | 3 |

## Findings

*(Transgender) Visibility, Transitioning, and Identity with Policing*

Most of the transgender participants, except for three, disclosed that they had transitioned during their police tenure. For some transgender individuals, there are gradual visual indicators of a transition status before, during, and after transition that can make disclosure an involuntary process. In a quotation taken from Panter (2018), Liv, an American transgender woman, put it this way:

> I think it is a lot easier to be the first LGB versus a T, because a T is a big difference for people. When you come out gay or lesbian, you don't really physically change anything; it doesn't impact on the people you work with per se, because they don't see you with your partner. But when you transition, they have to deal with it for a restroom issue, locker room issues, the pronoun issue, etc. They physically see you differently.

Most participants stated that some members of the transgender community have an easier time post-transition within policing. As Clair, a British transgender woman, stated:

You can spot a pre-op trans woman easily, but for some post-op trans women it is much more difficult, which is why pre-op women and cross-dressers have to put up with a lot. Trans men, on the other hand, pass easier than trans women. They can grow a beard and gain muscles quickly because of the testosterone.

Similarly, Tom, a British transgender man said, "Because I am now bald, most people do not question if I am a man or woman because of the test[osterone]. The only notable thing that people may question is my short height and my smaller hands."

Some officers, employed post-op or post-transition, stated they chose not to disclose their transgender status to protect themselves. Holly, an American transgender woman officer, explained that her first policing job resulted in an unwarranted termination pre-transition, because at the time she identified as a male cross-dresser and disclosed this to her agency. Holly took time off from policing after her termination:

> I took time off from policing, because initially I was assessing if I should stay in [policing] since they don't want me. They basically felt that it was incumbent on them to weed the people out who were gay, lesbian, or transgender. I took the year off and decided, you know what, that they didn't need to know, and if I could find a department where they didn't ask or didn't care, I would try there, so I did.

After her transition, Holly reentered policing with another agency without disclosing her transgender status out of fear that she would be fired again. In subsequent interviews, Holly explained why she has chosen to continue to "stay in the closet" with her current agency:

> They are just now getting used to gay people and lesbians . . . [C]an you imagine how it would be if I came out as trans when everyone knows me as a "straight woman"? It really isn't anyone's business also, and that is why I will not come out . . . I cringe thinking about what would happen if I was involved in an accident on duty and my medical history comes out, but HIPAA should protect me.

Notably, transgender identities can become visible once transgender status is disclosed pre-transition or post-transition while in policing. This disclosure process is unique because social stigma moves from possessing an invisible stigma to having a visible stigma and, for some, back to having an invisible stigma again (see Panter, 2018). In my subsequent interviews with transgender women, they stated that they felt they had to adhere more rigidly to heightened feminine presentations the further they transitioned. This is similar to Schilt and Connell's (2007) findings where they identified that new gender boundaries and conformity existed for transitioning employees in non-police employment. Holly described this pressure to conform:

> I must make sure that I am presenting myself, even post-op, as feminine at all times. I have to have long hair; I have to have makeup on, and so on. I mean no offense . . . but if I look like a butch lesbian or a masculine woman, it will be even harder for them to accept me as a woman.

Similarly, in another subsequent interview, Clair, stated:

> I have learned over the years it is harder to conform to feminine ideas of womanhood than it is to exist as a male based on my experience. It can be exciting, yet very exhausting; because women in general don't have a positive reputation in policing or in society . . . it isn't the same, you know, as men. You know a bloke is a bloke, but when you are a woman, you have to make sure that every little detail works. You want to make sure that your hair is more aligned with what you see on TV and such. Your clothing and style have to be on-point to make sure no one questions you if there are questions . . . [Y]ou don't want to draw attention to yourself when you are trying to blend into "normal."

Transgender women perceived that femininity was harder to perform within policing, where gender ideologies are rigidly upheld through visual performance. When I inquired about this gender conformity pressure, participants described what they do: grow their hair out in feminine styles; apply makeup; wear piercings; adhere to female uniform dress codes; change their posture in how they sit and walk; stick to "girl talk"; and mind their mannerisms and way of speaking. This is similar to findings for gender role socialization in Singh et al. (2010) and Brown et al. (2012) for non-police occupations.

By contrast, transgender men I interviewed rarely discussed how they visually "perform maleness"; instead they identified how maleness benefited them or gave them more privilege. As Dave, an American transgender man, stated:

> After my transition, I became one of the boys, you know? I now know what male privilege is because I now have it. Hell, I even gained rank. I don't think I gained rank because I am trans; I think I gained rank

because I am a man. I am much more respected because I am a male now compared to being a "butch" lesbian. Until you experience what it is to be both male and female in policing, you really don't know how male privilege works.

Participants' perceptions of how gender is performed or how it is visually perceived within policing are not a surprising finding due to the manifestation and institutionalization of male dominance within policing. Men are perceived as more valuable (see Griggs, 1998), and transgender men are more valued workers after transitioning than they were as women (see Schilt, 2006). Comparatively, transgender women lose their male privilege because women are a representative minority and have lower ranks in both American and British policing (see Westmarland, 2001). Furthermore, entrenched and accountable heteronormative expectations within policing lead to the social expectation that gender performativity should be visibly distinguished. Therefore, I contend that in hypermasculine environments like policing, "doing gender" (West & Zimmerman, 1987) and "gender performance" (Butler, 1990) are much more rigidly regulated on account of the heteronormative expectations in policing.

When I asked participants how they visually present their new identity and how they learned to do so, they often said they mirrored those around them. As Ellie, a British transgender woman, stated:

I watch what other women do with their hair and nails, and that is what I do. Mainly I copy their styles because I want to blend in, but also it reassures me what is acceptable within policing. Being a trans woman, you need to make sure that you don't stand out as a woman.

Dave spoke similarly of his experience:

I have had male colleagues tell me that they understand why someone would want to be a man, especially in policing . . . It is easier to present masculinity than femininity in general because you are surrounded by guys . . . I have learned a lot from my male colleagues and often mirror how they present themselves, like shaving for example. Often they help me be a man.

Notably Schilt and Connell (2007) described this process as "gender apprenticing" (p. 612), where same-gender colleagues take a transitioning colleague under their wing when transitioning, helping them with their visual male performance. In Schilt and Connell's study, a cisgender colleague aided a transgender man with knowledge on how to tie different types of neckties at work—an action that "typically is handed down from father to son" (p. 613). Yet Schilt and Connell stressed that although appreciated, gender apprenticing can coerce transgender colleagues into replicating established hegemonic performances of masculinity, putting more pressure on gender conformity. Further, Miles-Johnson (2016a, 2016b) argued that these heteronormative stereotypes regarding physical appearances can be "particularly problematic" (Miles-Johnson, 2019, p. 195) for transgender identities within policing because gendered notions of behavior and presentation are based on expectations of what constitutes "male" or "female" and often exclude transgender identities. As such, I argued in Panter (2018) that policing's strict binary gender behavioral codes, practices, and normative assumptions about gender make it more difficult for noncongruent transgender identities because gender differences are more visible or identifiable.

### LGB Minus the T: Visibility and Intra-conflict within the LGBTQ+ Policing Community

Understanding the intersectionality of gender within police culture is very complex, as I already mentioned. Besides encountering some of the same occupational bias that LGB police face, the transgender police I interviewed said that heterosexist language was the most reported administrative type of incident (see Panter, 2018). This is similar to Colvin's (2012) research on lesbian and gay American police, where 70% of participants disclosed that heterosexist words had been directed at them in workplace settings. American and British transgender police similarly revealed to me that they had been called slurs in the workplace: "bull-dyke; fag-hag, he-she, shim; queer faggot, he-she; faggot, tranny; and sissy faggot" (Panter, 2018, pp. 172–173). Often the derogatory terminology directed at transgender police is homophobic instead of transphobic. Still, I found that cisgender LGB police can be a major vector of bias toward the transgender community (see Panter, 2018). Notably, all cisgender American male participants (regardless of their sexuality) disclosed difficulty in interpreting the difference between "butch" lesbian identities and transgender masculine identities. As Fred, whose statements aligned with other American cis-male participants, stated in his first interview: "Is there such a thing as a trans man? I thought that was just a really butch lesbian." Here Fred, like all of the cisgender male participants, associated butch lesbians with transgender masculine identities due to his perception of appearances.

Tim, a gay cisgender American officer, shared views held by the other cisgender male participants:

> Trans men, while some may look good, are not real men. They don't have a penis; you know . . . that is why I would never date one. They don't have normal working male anatomy.

In a follow-up interview, Tim stated:

> I know people now say that me being a gay man means I should date a trans man, and if I don't, it means I am transphobic . . . but that is ridiculous; I am a gay man, not pansexual. I know what I am attracted to, and as a gay man I don't need people telling me who I should or shouldn't be attracted to. It is ridiculous . . . [S]ometimes the LGBT community shoots itself in the foot.

Some constables admitted that they had difficulty understanding the difference between gay men and transgender women. Simon, a cisgender British constable, said, "I don't think there is much difference between a gay man and a transsexual, because they are both biologically male and act feminine." Like Simon, Peter, a cisgender British constable, stated: "I think transgender women are just like gay men. They just take it up another level." In a follow-up interview, Peter stated:

> I think we are seeing more transgender people now than a few years ago because it has been more visible. It makes me question when are we going to stop . . . you have genderqueer and nonbinary now . . . [M]aybe some gay men are actually trans? I don't know . . . it is getting more confusing but I am trying my best to understand . . . [I]t seems with more acceptance the boundaries get more and more blurred and even more confusing.

Although gay sexuality could be considered conflicted with respect to the social ideology of dichotomous gender roles, cisgender participants indicated that transgender identities are more commonly perceived as not "female" or "male" enough, even in follow-up interviews. Participants, regardless of their sexuality, still disclosed that they perceived the possession of male or female genitalia as a defining characteristic of a person's gender regardless of their gender identity. This patriarchal dominance within policing culture, which associates binary genitalia with gender, was apparent even in perceptions held by cisgender LGBTQ+ police.

*Changes in Occupational Socialization within Policing*

Participants disclosed intersectional attitudes toward gender expectations when they transitioned on the job. Pre-transition, regardless of presented masculinity or femininity, participants revealed that they were included either in workplace "girl talk" (i.e., talk about appearance, romantic interests, and menstruation) with female colleagues or "guy talk" (i.e., conversation about sports, cars, and sexual objectification of women) with male colleagues. After transition, transgender officers and constables disclosed that their new cross-gender interactions notably changed. Transgender men were no longer included in girl talk, and transgender women reported similar exclusions from guy talk.

As Jessie, an American officer, stated: "Once I transitioned, I wasn't socially included in guy talk anymore. People assumed because I transitioned that my personality would change too." Much like American transgender participants, English and Welsh transgender constables stated that they were treated differently after transition. Clair stated, "I was in the army before, so I was used to the guy talk. Once I transitioned, that all changed. I felt socially rejected by men and women because I wouldn't be included in girl talk." Tom stated:

> I still like girlie things and I miss talking about those things sometimes. I mean, just because someone transitions, it does not mean that all your interest changes . . . There is an assumption that because I identify as a male, I am unable to identify with female stuff . . . I mean, I used to be female, but now I am treated socially much differently.

This finding is somewhat similar to Schilt and Connell's (2007) study of transgender workplace interactions in non-police environments. Schilt and Connell found that both transgender men and transgender women post-transition reported being included in gendered interactions. Schilt and Connell described post-transition gendered interactions as "a new sense of freedom" (p. 611), allowing transgender women to discuss feminine things denied to them pre-transition. For transgender men, Schilt and Connell noted that during pre-transition they were afforded more liberty to express masculine interests (Thorne, 1993). Yet Crocker and Lutsky (1986) speculated that transgender employees may falsely assume that because there are physical changes in the presentation of their gender identity, coworkers may think that they have changed their interests to stereotypical gender-congruent ones.

Acker (1990) and Gorman (2005) indicated that employers evaluate their employees' job performances and abilities in binary gendered ways (i.e., heteronormative). These gendered evaluations appeared to be highlighted when my research participants disclosed their transition from one gender to another and described how they performed gender during the process. Collins (2000) offered an explanation for these observations by suggesting that transgender identities are positioned as "outsiders within," allowing transgender persons to see past "natural" gender differences that exist within heteronormative standards. Arguably, this occurs because a post-transition transgender police officer experiences both intersectional social expectations of femininity and masculinity (see Panter, 2018).

For example, Dave presented himself as a masculine lesbian early in his policing career, and then he transitioned when "medical technologies in gender reassignment surgery had advanced." Dave was able to describe his observations and perceptions of masculinity reinforcement within policing during our original interview: "Being male or masculine is more acceptable in society, and if you are a man, I don't think being feminine is as acceptable. I think that an effeminate man may have a more difficult time in law enforcement." In a follow-up interview, Dave stated:

> Gay men are not accepted as much as butch lesbians in policing, you know? It makes sense that in a masculine profession that they are going to be more accepting of a masculine woman because they are conforming in a way to be good at the job. Like, you can trust that a butch woman will be strong and handle her business on their beat. That assertiveness that is needed in policing is not associated with femininity.

Liv stated that effeminate men and transgender women within policing are typically looked down on because there is a correlation between the presentation of masculinity and the proper performance of policing. As Liv stated, "Extremely, extremely feminine portrayals; you have a man on the job who has very feminine characteristics. Initially from the egotistical point of view, how is this person going to help or protect me?"

During my interviews with transgender police, participants frequently mentioned the "vulnerability" of feminine identities in occupational police settings, even during follow-up interviews. Femininity was generally viewed as less than desirable compared with masculinity in policing, and transgender feminine identities were perceived as having more vulnerability because they offend or complicate perceptions of both masculinity and femininity. Further, I found that transgender masculinity, much like components of lesbian masculinity, was not viewed as equal to cis-male masculinity (as described by Dave and others). The perceived performance of cis-masculinity, or a variation of it, was deemed as desirable both occupationally and for its social conformity by my American and British interviewees alike. This is similar to Schilt and Connell's (2007) notion of how binary gender is regulated and reproduced in non-police occupational settings, with gendered "hierarchies interwoven with heteronormativity and sexism" (p. 614). Further, this study also found that transgender men and transgender women were often frustrated with rigid gender binary socialization expectations within police occupational culture, but at the same time they reinforced heteronormative binary views held within policing.

## Critical Discussion

This chapter explored intersectional components with respect to gender and sexuality expectations and how each is perceived within police cultures in the United States and the United Kingdom. Analysis of data highlighted that cisgender perceptions of transgender women challenged socialized constructs of gender conformity because transgender women psychologically, socially, and medically distance themselves from aspects of their previous male body. Transgender men were viewed more positively than transgender women due to the culture within policing that praises masculinity and devalues femininity. Further, it was found that transgender women in policing are viewed as potentially more vulnerable to occupational bias from genderism than are cisgender lesbian and cisgender gay officers. In follow-up interviews, participants continued to suggest that certain transgender identities are perceived as less welcomed in police culture. They explained that cisgender heteronormative sex/gender/sexuality ideologies are seen to rest on the perception that there are two, and only two, opposite sexes who are attracted to each other, and these are determined by a person's physical body, primarily their genitals. This binary heteronormativity is reinforced by socialized gender perceptions and genderist ideologies within police culture. This presumption excludes transgender and nonbinary police, even in the views of the cisgender lesbian and gay police sample.

Three years after the publication of *Transgender Cops: The Intersection of Gender and Sexuality Expectations in Police Cultures* (2018), these findings still hold for the participants I interviewed. In other words, while there have been some occupational improvements in policing since 2018 with the inclusion and recruitment of more transgender officers, cultural components in policing remain where binary ideologies of gender (e.g., "desirable masculinity" and binary perceptions of "maleness" and "femaleness") are still enforced. Moreover, for transgender police officers, hypermasculine perceptions of femininity and masculinity are socially reproduced due to heightened and embedded gender hierarchies that result from heteronormativity.

All participants identified that these perceptions are the causes of occupational barriers that may affect future transgender integration and further acceptance in police culture. Identified occupational barriers often centered on the reinforcement of masculinity, often hypermasculinity, institutionally instilled in all facets of police culture, both American and British. Due to this regulation and reinforcement of hypermasculinity in police cultures, strict gendered divisions determine what is acceptable "female" presentation and "male" presentation, regardless of sexuality. Those whose identity conflicts with these binary ideologies (namely transgender and nonbinary identities) face occupational bias within policing similar to lesbian, gay, and bisexual officers. Further, participants disclosed that they perceived this bias as not just attributable to transphobic attitudes but as a result of intersectional components of both transphobic and homophobic attitudes rooted in heteronormativity.

This chapter explored the complexities of separating the interlocking concepts of gender and sexuality when examining LGBTQ+ police and occupational bias, and there was evidence of a perceived increase in "vulnerability" and likelihood of occupational bias for transgender feminine identities compared with cisgender performances of femininity. Therefore, future research could explore this finding in further detail while incorporating other intersectional identity components not present in my sample (e.g., race and transgender, Native American and transgender, and Asian and transgender).

# 9. EXISTENCE AS RESISTANCE
## The Case of Lesbian Police Officers

Lauren Moton

Policing has long been of interest to scholars of the social world. In particular, officer characteristics have been noted as important factors that impact their day-to-day work within the communities they are tasked with protecting and serving. Pioneering research has examined characteristics such as age, education, relationship status, and military experience (Friedrich, 1980; McElvain & Kposowa, 2008; Terrill & Reisig, 2003; Worden, 1990). However, these studies used samples that were overwhelmingly white, male, and heterosexual, which reflected the homogeneity among police forces at the time (Moton et al., 2020). As time has passed, police forces have become more reflective of the communities they serve, and it is important that we examine this development through theory and research.

Theories are used as frameworks to assist in contextualizing social phenomena. Specifically, queer theory—the study and theorization of gender and sexualities that exist outside a cis-heterosexual binary—is rapidly integrating within the field of criminal justice and often referred to as queer criminology. Queer criminology aims to critically analyze the ways in which criminal legal institutions reinforce heteronormative ideals and how this reinforcement impacts the lived experiences of queer people as victims, offenders, and practitioners. Further, queer criminology seeks to highlight how LGBTQ+ populations have been historically erased and simultaneously stigmatized, criminalized, and ostracized in criminological discourse (Buist & Lenning, 2016).

Policing is one sector of our criminal legal system that has traditionally reproduced notions of heteronormativity through its culture and norms. Because policing is largely white, cisgender, heterosexual, and male-dominated, the existence of lesbians within policing is in direct opposition to its status quo (Giwa et al., 2022). This is due to their gender identity as women and their sexuality as lesbians. Patriarchal hegemony has been perpetuated since the beginning of policing as we know it and is reflected through the exclusion of police officers who do not neatly fit the traditional idea of an officer. Research on LGBTQ+ police officers has found that officers possessing marginalized sexual identities experience differential treatment because of their sexuality (Colvin, 2009), have limited mentoring and promotion opportunities (Barratt et al., 2014), and sometimes report fear over whether their partner "had their back" in the field (Mennicke et al., 2018).

In this chapter, I explore the existence of lesbians in policing as an act of resistance to its masculine hegemonic social structure. Analyzing with the lenses of intersectionality and queer theory assists me in exploring how the existence of lesbian officers challenges various facets of policing through their representation of multiple marginalized identities. I argue that this existence represents a type of queer feminism that questions heteronormativity, challenges gender roles within traditionalist spaces, contests normative gender presentation, deconstructs hegemonic police culture, and affirms the importance of representative bureaucracy.

## What Is Known: Lesbian Officers

Though policing largely consists of male-identified personnel, there has been an increase in women joining the ranks over time. Women represent 12.6% of U.S. police officers, which is a significant minority within the occupation (Uniform Crime Report, 2018). It is not readily known, though, why women mostly steer clear of the police profession, because prior research indicates that women make tangible positive contributions to policing. Studies show that policewomen receive fewer complaints, engage in using force less often, and facilitate victims' crime reporting, particularly for gender-sensitive crimes like sexual assault or rape (Brandl & Stroshine, 2013; Dejong, 2005; Hoffman & Hickey, 2005; Paoline & Terrill, 2004). Apart from cisgender women joining the force, the policing profession today has more diversity than it ever has before, with an increase in racial, gender, and sexual minorities. Though policing has become more diverse and research on these diverse populations within policing has become more extensive, less is known about sexual minorities in policing, specifically lesbians.

Officers who identify as lesbians generally possess at least two social identities that are in direct opposition to the stereotypical officer. Lesbians are neither men nor heterosexual, the two primary demographics (i.e., straight men) of most police officers nationwide. What is empirically known about the lived experience of lesbian police officers dates back only about 30 years, with around 60 academic works including lesbian officer voices (Moton et al., 2020). Further, most of these studies do not have a sample of more than 40 lesbian officers, except for one study examining the experiences of lesbian, gay, and bisexual officers in the United Kingdom with a sample of 437 lesbian officers (Jones, 2015). Due to such a small number of studies with even smaller sample sizes, it is difficult to generalize about lesbian officers' lived experience (Colvin, 2009; Jones, 2015). What is known about the lived experience of this population, according to a review of the literature on lesbian police officers, relates to several categories: experiencing hegemonic masculinity and police culture, being viewed by their department as sexual deviants, managing and divulging their minoritized identities at a psychological cost, performing masculinity in a masculine hegemony, and building community and finding acceptance (Giwa et al., 2022; Moton et al., 2020).

Hegemonic masculinity is defined as the perpetuation and legitimation of the domination of men over women in society, while maintaining the subjugation of feminine and other nonmasculine, or gay, identities (Connell, 1995). It is a Westernized, capitalistic understanding of masculinity demonstrated through aggression, authority, technical competence, heterosexism, and the desire to dominate women. Hegemonic masculinity is associated with police culture because it sustains the patriarchal supremacy of white, cisgender, heterosexual men, who have traditionally been the majority in policing. Consequently, feelings of white, cis-heterosexual entitlement among the dominant demographic make existing in the profession difficult or uncomfortable as a minority (Moton et al., 2020).

Gradual acceptance of LGBTQ+ identities is a relatively new phenomenon. Police culture has historically fallen in line with homophobic views toward sexual minorities, positioning them as sexual deviants. In fact, prior studies found that 25% of anti-gay hate crime occurs at the hands of police officers themselves (Wolff & Cokely, 2007). This striking statistic has been theorized to result from policing's susceptibility to intolerance toward queer communities and officers' duty to uphold certain societal moral codes (Loftus, 2010; Miller & Lilley, 2014; Williams & Robinson, 2004). For example, sex between same-gendered people was illegal (thus immoral) up until 2003 in certain U.S. states (Chemerinsky, 2015). Herek (2009) puts forth a relevant theoretical framework—sexual stigma—that may account for why police culture excludes those who identify as sexual minorities. Sexual stigma asserts that homophobic predispositions are a result of an internalization of societal norms that reject sexual identities different from heterosexual orientations. This results in felt stigma (an awareness of stigma), enacted stigma (actions based on that awareness), and internalized stigma (acceptance of stigma as legitimate). Once people internalize stigma, they may be resistant to shifting their beliefs because they view the internalized stigma as legitimate.

In dealing with feelings of ostracization within their profession, lesbian officers often negotiate with the psychological toll of managing their identity and determining whether to disclose their sexual minority status to their fellow officers. Lesbian officers may choose to remain closeted to their colleagues as a form of protection from perceived homophobia. This forces the officers to manage their identity among the different groups they surround themselves with. Lesbian officers may keep their sexual minority status concealed at work and may keep their profession as an officer secret to people in LGBTQ+ communities. This causes stress for lesbian officers, who have to consistently remain conscious of what they have disclosed and to whom. Burke (1994, 1995) first put forth the idea of lesbian and gay officers having dual and conflicting identities, which often forces these officers to lead "double lives." Burke found that many lesbian and gay officers attempted to "pass" as heterosexual to deflect attention. Lesbian officers especially engaged in this practice because they already faced barriers at work for being women (Burke, 1994).

Women have historically been shunned from the police profession due to stereotypes about their physical capabilities in comparison with their male counterparts. When examining lesbian police officers' experience of discrimination on the job, Cherney (1999) found that they were more likely to experience discrimination based on their gender than on their sexual orientation (see also Giwa et al., 2022). This may be because the dimension of lesbian identity that is attracted to women is also a hetero-masculine trait, and this similarity might mitigate some of the discrimination against lesbian officers (Moton et al., 2020).

In response to these lived experiences within a profession that may not value all their differences, lesbian officers have developed ways to cope with microaggressions and discrimination. In Burke's (1994) interviews with lesbian officers, they discussed indirect ways to find kinship and solidarity with other lesbians on the job. They divulged that it was secretly known among the lesbian officers in one department to join the department's hockey team to find other women like them rather than to get involved in more obvious or formal associations like the Lesbian and Gay Police Association (LGPA).

For some lesbian officers, though, LGBTQ+ associations have served as valuable and productive means of facilitating community. For example, the Chicago Police Department (CPD) has historically not been well known for taking pride in its LGBTQ+ officers; however, in recent decades, it has overwhelmingly improved. It took the work of several lesbians to change the culture of the department through their creation of the LGPA in 1991. The women noted that they intentionally put the *L* at the front of the acronym because of past experiences with lesbian erasure (Keehnen, 2008).

One of the founders, Nancy Lipman—a 30-year veteran of the CPD—faced visceral homophobia throughout her career. Specifically, when she was still a rookie officer, she "heard a lieutenant at roll call say we should go back to Germany and bring back the ovens to use on 'faggots.'" Nancy later told the *Windy City Times*, "I wondered whether the officers sitting around me experienced even a fraction of the horror that statement evoked in me" (Keehnen, 2008, para. 1). This was a stark reminder that though she had made it through the police academy and finally attained her coveted position as a police officer, many of her colleagues subscribed to harmful ideologies about her sexual identity. Nevertheless, macroaggressions such as this did not discourage Nancy from getting heavily involved with LGBTQ+ advocacy throughout her career. Another founder, Susan Sasso—also a multi-decade veteran of the CPD—recalled a time when the psychological evaluation portion of the police exam asked questions about same-sex attraction framed as illness. These two instances revealed glaring homophobia ingrained within their department, which caused psychological stress for officers Lipman and Sasso.

Lipman and Sasso, along with three other women—Karen Calahan, Dorothy Knudsen, and Mary Boyle—filed the necessary paperwork to institute the organization, which the Fraternal Order of Police (FOP) did not take issue with. The real difficulty came when trying to get the FOP and CPD to treat them the same as any other organization. It took years of persistence on the part of the founders to gain recognition similar to that of other organizations under the FOP. For instance, the LGPA wanted to speak with new police recruits about LGBTQ+ sensitivity issues, but the CPD Training Academy repeatedly avoided processing the paperwork that would have allowed them to speak. Many years and several request letters later, they were finally granted a slot during recruit training, but it had to be their volunteered time that was not compensated (Keehnen, 2008). In speaking to the recruits, Susan Sasso made it a point to emphasize respect: "One of the things I told the recruits during training was that a person's sexual orientation has nothing to do with the job they do. What a person does in the privacy of their own home does not affect you, you must be professional and treat everyone with the respect you would want for yourself and your family" (Keehnen, 2008, para. 7). The humanization of queer people was important for the LGPA to convey to new police officers.

Education initiatives were not the only goals of the LGPA. This group engaged in several advocacy issues: Its members were instrumental in attaining domestic partnership and bereavement leave for city employees and their partners. Notably, they were responsible for adding sexual orientation to section 10-2 on discrimination issues in the FOP contract. Once the LGPA hit its stride, its members were active in recruiting queer officers from the community and were successful in implementing the first LGBT liaison officer into the historically gay and lesbian Ward 23 in Chicago. In this case, the LGBT liaison officer works for the police department, is trained on LGBTQ+ issues, and is available to members of the LGBTQ+ community when they have been a victim, offender, or witness to a crime (Dwyer et al., 2017). Having such culturally competent initiatives embedded in police agencies is imperative for the well-being and safety of the marginalized populations that police departments serve.

Additionally, the LGPA secured funding from the FOP for a float in Chicago's annual Pride parade. This was a hard-won battle with the FOP; the LGPA was repeatedly denied funding because it was not classified as an ethnic group. In years past, members of the LGPA had driven their personal vehicles draped with the LGPA banner in the Pride parade or marched on foot. It was even a struggle to be permitted to wear the CPD uniform during the parade. Many since-retired CPD officers thought that allowing LGPA officers to wear the CPD uniform when marching in the Pride parade was a "disgrace" to the uniform. After securing funding from the FOP for a float and the parade entry fee, LGPA officers were able to wear their uniforms in the parade with pride.

The LGPA's participation in the Pride parade was meaningful in several ways. The newfound representation was crucial for at-the-time rookie police officer Jamie Richardson, who attended the 1995 Pride parade in civilian street clothes, desperately hoping that none of the police officers serving as security would recognize her. It was not until she saw the LGPA float making its way down the avenue, with officers like Susan Sasso and Nancy Lipman proudly donning the CPD uniform, that Richardson decided right then and there that she was going to be an "out" police officer. She shared her reaction to the LGPA float with the *Windy City Times*: "I had to be one of them. That was when I decided that I was never again going to stand on the sidelines, and I would never again be going to go to work closeted" (Keehnen, 2008, para. 10).

In 2005, the LGPA merged with the Gay Officers Action League, which was founded in New York City in 1982. This merger aimed to expand the scope of the LGPA to include all public safety personnel, including firefighters, paramedics, security guards, 911 dispatchers, and state troopers. This expansion enabled officers to network with other LGBTQ+ public safety personnel within and across departments. And importantly, this expansion helped HIV+ officers in seeking medical assistance, as well as helping transgender officers in seeking gender-affirming care (Keehnen, 2008).

Over decades, the LGPA made enormous strides not only in improving conditions for LGBTQ+ officers but also in improving safety conditions for LGBTQ+ community members. However, its founding members can still recall the early days of holding secret meetings in members' basements, when many in the group were not comfortable being out at work, and of seeing the LGPA as a sanctuary from the homophobic sentiments held by their colleagues. Susan Sasso credited the LGPA for making progress: "Now we have out CPD commanders who would not have had such an easy time without LGPA breaking the ice" (Keehnen, 2008, para. 13). These early and persisting fears in the LGPA are directly in line with prior research into the lesbian police officer experience (Burke, 1994, 1995).

Although some scholarship asserts that lesbian officers may tend to remain closeted and seek out other lesbian officers through clandestine avenues (e.g., department extracurriculars) (Burke, 1994), other scholars, and the LGPA, found that with progressive policies and support from department superiors, homophobic tensions were eased with less-supportive officers in police departments (Belkin & McNichols, 2002). Allport (1958) put forth the "contact hypothesis," which posits that consistent contact with a group facilitates normalization and acceptance of the once "othered" group and lessens intergroup conflict. In thinking about lesbian officer experiences through this lens, one could contend that having more lesbians present in the traditionalist institution of the police, and with proper support available to them from groups like the LGPA, is a form of resistance to the masculine hegemony in policing (Moton et al., 2020).

## Lesbian Existence in Policing as Queer Feminism

Feminist theories examine how gender is constructed and how gender roles are assigned. Like many poststructuralist theories, feminist theory also has a political dimension that examines power imbalances and inequalities and how those imbalances are maintained in the social world (Klages, 2017). The feminist movement has a long history of advocating for gender equality through the lens of the particular political moment. Though feminism and feminist theory advocate for equities surrounding gender justice, this advocacy has been critiqued for being inadequate to theorize sexuality (Rubin, 1984). Lesbians largely identify as women, though gender identities outside the male/female sex binary are also possible, as lesbians have historically engaged feminist theory as a means to contextualize their lived experiences.

Queer theory was developed by Teresa de Lauretis in 1990 and originally aimed to complicate the inflexible complacencies of gay and lesbian studies, which she asserted neglected to bring race, ethnicity, geography, sociopolitics, and other social locations into its analysis. Queer theory offered a way to malleate rigid notions of deviance and preference. According to de Lauretis (1991), queer theories represent "forms of resistance to cultural homogenization, counteracting dominant discourses with other constructions of the subject in culture" (p. 219). In its development, queer theorists emphasized the fluidity of queer identity and how that identity shapes desire and choice and deconstructs heteronormativity (de Lauretis, 1991; Halperin, 1995; Watson, 2005). Though feminist and queer theory are different theoretical projects, it is important to demonstrate they can serve together to articulate how the complexities of gender and sexuality often crosscut each other (Jagose, 2009).

Intersectionality serves as a lens to synergize the multidimensional aspects of lesbian officer identity. Theorized by Kimberlé Crenshaw in 1989, intersectionality is an analytical framework that examines the interinfluence and overlapping structure of a person's social and political identities that, when combined, can create different modes of discrimination and privilege. Lesbian officers may have marginalized experiences as gender and sexual minorities, but they may also experience marginalization or privilege due to their race, ability, gender presentation, and other expressions (Moton et al., 2020). For example, a white, feminine-presenting, petite in stature, lesbian officer may experience some level of white privilege within her department but may also experience discrimination because of her feminine and petite presentation based on stereotypes of what is considered capable for the job.

The limited scholarship examining lesbian officers' experiences rarely includes an intersectional lens contextualizing their experiences. Experiences born out of marginalization are unique and require examination. Research that includes comprehensive analyses of gender, race, class, or other identities is virtually absent in the literature about police officers (Hassell & Brandl, 2009; Sklansky, 2005). Given the distinct intersectionality that lesbian officers bring to policing through their womanhood and queer status, it is necessary to investigate how their identities coalesce and how those identities influence their work.

There are several ways the existence of lesbians in the police profession can manifest as a type of queer feminism that can effect change in organizational structure. Lesbian officers often question heteronormativity. In Lewis's (2009) study of lesbians in the workplace, participants self-identified as "agents of change" and worked to actively spread awareness about nonheterosexual ways of being and helped colleagues reexamine heteronormative organizational practices. In addition, male colleagues engaged in dialogue about sexuality, which promoted an inclusive workplace culture that was described as "comfortable" and "accepting" from the perspective of lesbian workers. Lewis's findings are in line with Belkin and McNichol's (2002) findings, mentioned above, about a shift in workplace culture after supportive policies and backing from superiors eased tensions with cisgender heterosexual officers. Lesbian officers, with proper support, were able to enact change within their departments by questioning the heteronormative hierarchy reproduced in policing. Though lesbians are enacting change, there are still persistent negative stereotypes about women's abilities in the profession that impact their treatment.

There is a considerable and enduring belief that women are not capable of performing police work at the level that men perform (Giwa et al., 2022). This belief rests on the physical differences between men and women. In truth, though, most police work does not require great physical strength.

According to publicly available data, police in many cities across the United States spend less than 5% of their time dealing with violent crime; most of an officer's time is spent dealing with noncriminal calls, traffic violations, property crime, or other nonviolent crimes; being proactive; and responding to medical needs (Asher & Horowitz, 2020). These are important statistics to note because the stereotypes associated with police work are generally of strength-based actions such as fighting criminals or engaging in foot chases and shootouts, which are largely associated with men, and these stereotypes perpetuate gender roles in the workforce.

Gender roles are social roles that define the actions, behaviors, and attitudes that are considered socially desirable, expected, and appropriate for a person's sex assigned at birth or their perceived sex (Alters & Schiff, 2009). In the Western world, these roles are generally associated with femininity and masculinity. However, over time, society has moved away from an essentialist view that women and men drastically differ in terms of ability and success. Women, and lesbians more specifically, have challenged traditional gender roles associated with the police profession. Moreover, they have advanced to some of the highest ranks of police departments, all while existing within a largely cisgender, patriarchal, and heterosexual male-dominated space.

In addition, women defy stereotypes concerning not only what a police officer should look like but also how a police officer performs. Research has shown that women receive fewer grievances from the public, use force less often, and ease the crime reporting process, especially for gender-sensitive crimes like sexual assault or rape (Brandl & Stroshine, 2013; Dejong, 2005; Hoffman & Hickey, 2005; Paoline & Terrill, 2004). Women victims may feel more comfortable reporting a crime to another woman, especially if the perpetrator of the crime was a man. Further, attributes associated with femininity like expressiveness, communal orientation, and submissiveness (Conway et al., 1996; Fiske et al., 2002; Gerber, 2009) can serve as productive qualities in policing. As more police departments shift to community policing, traits like communal orientation and expressiveness better engage community members (Davies & Thomas, 2003; Heidensohn, 1992; Miller, 1999).

Lesbians present their gender in several ways. Gender presentation, or gender expression, is defined as a person's appearance, behavior, mannerisms, and interests related to gender in a specific sociocultural context, particularly having associations with masculinity or femininity. Common colloquial language used by the lesbian community has termed these associations *butch* when a lesbian woman is masculine-presenting and *femme* when a lesbian woman is feminine-presenting. There are many other terms, though, for lesbian gender presentations: stud, tomboy, lipstick lesbian, chapstick lesbian, stem (stud-femme), futch (feminine butch), and androgynous. These types of gender presentations are expressed through a personal desire to present differently from the traditionally constructed image associated with a particular gender. Judith Butler (1993) asserted that gender performativity may represent a strategy of resistance to traditional gender roles and expression. Butler put forth examples such as drag, cross-dressing, and portrayals of butch and femme identities that refute the socially constructed gender norms in society. This resistance by rejecting normative gender presentation may be employed by lesbians in policing. In a 2016 study, Swan found that more lesbians police officers than not (54%) reported presenting masculinity, and a large proportion of heterosexual women in policing reported this response as well. This may be attributed to the fact that a masculine presentation suits a male-dominated profession or that masculine-presenting women seek out occupations that celebrate masculinity. Nonetheless, non-normative gender presentation defies gender norms and expectations, which in turn challenges traditionalist cultures like that of policing.

The masculine hegemony that operates in the police profession is embedded so deeply that men not only make up 88% of its members but women also rise to leadership positions much less frequently than men. More and more women in the United States, however, are rising in the ranks to become sergeants, lieutenants, captains, sheriffs, and chiefs of police—but not without encountering significant structural barriers and discrimination. This opposition may be compounded by a woman's sexual orientation, depending on the type of discrimination.

For example, Ohio's first lesbian sheriff, Charmaine McGuffey, was elected in Hamilton County in April 2020, after overcoming many obstacles to achieve this position. She had a long career in the Hamilton County Sheriff's Office (from 1983 to 2017), where she rose in the ranks to major in command of jails and services. This position made her the highest-ranking woman in the history of the Hamilton County Sheriff's Office. Though McGuffey experienced success in the department, she reported being harassed after the forceful exposure of her sexual orientation to her superior and colleagues. McGuffey was closeted at work during her 34-year career until an incident where she and her friends were targeted by local police while fraternizing in front of a known gay bar outside her jurisdiction. She was violently arrested for public intoxication and disorderly conduct, but all charges were subsequently dropped. Although this incident did not give McGuffey a criminal record, she was forcefully outed to her colleagues at work.

Once her sexual minority status was known in the department, McGuffey reported that her direct superior, Sheriff Jeff Neil, filed an official complaint against her for using "her position to retaliate against employees, as well as engage in favoritism" (Avery, 2021). McGuffey reported that this complaint was used to discredit her. Neil went on to demote McGuffey to a lower-paying civilian position. She declined the new position and was subsequently fired. About a year and half later, in 2019, Charmaine McGuffey submitted her bid to run on a progressive platform against Jeff Neil for Hamilton County sheriff. In the primary election, McGuffey beat Neil with 70% of the votes, then went on to the general election and won, becoming Hamilton County's first openly lesbian sheriff (Avery, 2021). McGuffey experienced a harrowing journey to her current high-ranking position, and along the way she had to conceal her lesbian identity (which can cause stress and psychological issues; see Burke, 1994), was forcibly outed by another department, and was subsequently targeted by her superiors after her sexuality was disclosed. According to a 2019 National Institute of Justice report on women and policing, primary reasons why women often do not achieve higher positions on a police force are that they internalize sexist police culture, do not apply for higher-ranking positions, and fear discrimination (Starheim, 2019). The community of voters in Hamilton elected McGuffey to her position, and this may be an indication of a gradual societal shift toward a more progressive type of policing and a new face for police authority and personnel.

## Representative Bureaucracy in Policing: Pathways Forward

Representative bureaucracy provides a sensible framework for understanding the need for lesbian representation in the police profession, if the profession is to become more amenable to diverse identities. Representative bureaucracy, an idea from the field of public administration, conceptualizes the beneficial impact of minority representation in the public service sector (Hong, 2017; Meier, 1975; Sowa & Seldon, 2003; Wilkins & Williams, 2008). The central tenet of representative bureaucracy holds that public organizations are better equipped to serve their constituents when those constituents are demographically represented in the organizations.

Representative bureaucracy is characterized by three common principles: passive and active representation, client responsiveness, and symbolic effects. Passive representation refers to the degree to which public servants represent demographics similar to their constituents. Conversely, active representation reflects a public servant's ability to initiate and advance policies that serve the needs of their community (Hong, 2017). The second principle, client responsiveness, is defined as a bureaucrat's ability to garner community trust and support. Last are the symbolic effects enacted by public servants. These symbolic effects can have a positive impact on shifting public perception and legitimizing a public servant. Representative bureaucracy, even in its less powerful form of passive representation, has a positive effect on constituents' perception of public servants. The literature argues that when constituents see public servants who identify similarly to the community, those constituents are more likely to trust and support their work (Gade & Wilkins, 2013; Riccucci et al., 2014; Theobald & Haider-Markel, 2009). Passive representation can change citizens' perceptions and attitudes toward an organization and its employees, even with no evidence of an observable change having occurred in the organization's actions (Riccucci et al., 2014).

Colvin and Moton (2021) argue that though representative bureaucracy improves perceptions of a public organization and its employees, much of its application in research has looked at the representation of racial and gender minorities in public organizations. Applying the idea of representative bureaucracy to LGBTQ+ populations may be less clear, however, given that sexuality does not readily present itself as an observable characteristic. It falls to an LGBTQ+ bureaucrat to determine when or if they disclose their sexual orientation to the public (Chojnacki & Gelberg, 1994; Colvin, 2012). If LGBTQ+ public servants were to disclose their sexuality, there may be tangible benefits to the community that identifies similarly, such as in managing discriminatory policies and practices (Colvin & Moton, 2021).

Lesbian police officers who have disclosed their sexuality to their department may then have a positive impact on workplace climate and, importantly, on police-community relations. Historically, relations between the LGBTQ+ community and the police force have been strained. Research on this relationship reported that both women and men of this community felt unprotected by the law or discriminated against or harassed by police (Cherney, 1999; Williams & Robinson, 2004). Therefore, hiring and retaining police officers belonging to the LGBTQ+ community may reduce tensions between the two groups (Moton et al., 2020).

## Conclusion

Working as a lesbian officer in a profession that upholds white, cis, heterosexual patriarchy presents a set of challenges. Mild repercussions like microaggressions or implicit bias, as well as outright discrimination, prejudice, or violence, are all possibilities. Lesbian police officers represent a unique intersection of marginality within policing as a gender minority as women and a sexual minority as lesbians, which makes them a potential target of mistreatment. Despite these multiple marginalized identities, lesbian officers can disrupt the status quo of policing by existing in a space incongruent with their identity. Through queer theory and intersectionality, I have argued that lesbian police officers represent a type of queer feminism that questions heteronormativity, challenges gender roles within traditionalist spaces, contests normative gender presentation, deconstructs hegemonic culture, and affirms the importance of representative bureaucracy.

Prior research has illuminated lesbian workers' questioning of heteronormativity by their acting as agents of change through workplace practices of spreading awareness about nonheterosexual orientations to promote a more inclusive workplace. Such is the work of an organization like the LGPA (Lewis, 2009). In addition, lesbians in policing challenge gender roles by presenting the very traits that are used to stereotype them as ill qualified for the job. In fact, though, stereotypical traits associated with women, like expressiveness and communal orientation, have assisted women with facilitating community policing initiatives (Davies & Thomas, 2003; Heidensohn, 1992; Miller, 1999). Some lesbian officers contest normative gender presentation by engaging in gender expression in a more masculine way. Butler (1993) asserts that nonnormative gender presentation, through dress, behavior, and mannerisms, can be a form of resistance to concretized gender roles and norms. Not all lesbians present differently from what is stereotypically associated with womanhood (e.g., hyperfemininity), but some do, particularly in a masculinized profession such as policing. Lesbian officers can deconstruct hegemonic masculinist culture by pushing back on discrimination in the workplace and seeking out higher-ranked positions where they can effect change from the top down, like Sheriff Charmaine McGuffey did. Finally, the marginalization of lesbian officers as well as the strained relationship between the police and LGBTQ+ communities calls for more LGBTQ+ representation within police departments. I argue that representative bureaucracy provides a compelling reason for having more lesbian-identified women working in the field of policing.

# 10. GAY POLICE OFFICERS IN THE UNITED KINGDOM
## Current Scholarly Research

Nick Rumens

This chapter examines the state of research in the United Kingdom on gay male police officers. It highlights the scarcity of scholarship in this area, pointing out important knowledge deficits with a view to renewing emphasis on advancing the literature. Outlining the context of police policy and reform that has influenced how U.K. police organizations have engaged with lesbian, gay, bisexual, queer, transgender, and plus (LGBTQ+) officers, the chapter examines two areas of concern relevant to the study of gay male police officers: (1) gay male police officers' workplace experiences and (2) hypermasculine police cultures. The chapter discusses the implications of existing research for theory and knowledge that can develop scholarship in this area. In particular, the chapter provides options for police studies scholars, including critical perspectives on men and masculinities that address the gendering of sexuality and the concept of intersectionality. As a perspective, intersectionality is discussed as a fruitful approach to analyzing how differences are (re)constructed at the intersection of hierarchies of oppression. Additionally, queer theories are proposed as a way of problematizing heteronormative police organizations and work practices and of understanding how gay male police officers engage in negotiating experiences at work at the intersections of unstable and fluid identities.

The research on gay men employed as police officers in the United Kingdom tells an incomplete story. Although some, but crucially not all, gay male police officers have fared well under policy reforms and diversity initiatives that have improved equal opportunities for employment, training, and development, heteronormative work practices and cultures persist, with negative outcomes for gay men (Colvin, 2015; Jones, 2015; Jones & Williams, 2015; Rumens & Broomfield, 2012; Zempi, 2020). A similar story can be told about lesbian, bisexual, transgender and plus police officers (Colvin, 2012, 2015; Jones, 2015; Jones & Williams, 2015; Zempi, 2020). From the outset, it is important to note the dearth of literature that focuses singly on gay male police officers in the United Kingdom or in other regions of the world. Noting the same knowledge gap and shortage of research on lesbian and bisexual police officers in the United Kingdom, Jones and Williams (2015) observe that "the experiences of LGB police officers has been largely neglected for two decades" since Burke's (1993, 1994) formative research, which painted a bleak picture of widespread discrimination, sexual prejudice, and hostility toward LGB officers in England and Wales. Since 2015, scholarly interest in the experiences of LGB police officers in the United Kingdom has remained low (Jones, 2015; Zempi, 2020), with comparatively more research published on the relationship between U.K. police services and LGBTQ+ communities (Pickles, 2020).

LGBTQ+ police officers make up a vital segment of the national police workforce, but statistical data on the numbers and distribution of these officers are scarce. Rectifying this, the Home Office (the British equivalent to United States Department of Homeland Security), in partnership with the National Police Chiefs' Council and the College of Policing, recently developed a National Standard for Workforce Data to standardize the collection of data on protected characteristics, such as sexual orientation. As police officers are not obliged to include this information in their human resources records, glaring data gaps exist (45.7% of police officers have yet to provide it), although "experimental statistics" provide an early but imperfect indication that 4.6% of officers identify as gay/lesbian, 5.9% as bisexual, and 89.4% as heterosexual/straight (Home Office, 2021).

Studies in the United States and Australia on LGBTQ+ police officers reveal challenges similar to those facing gay male police officers in the United Kingdom: hypermasculine work cultures; sexual and gendered stereotyping of gay men as "feminine" and, thus, "unfit" to undertake police work; bias in hiring and promotion decisions; and discrimination from being openly gay in the workplace (Collins & Rocco, 2015, 2018; Dwyer & Ball, 2020; Mennicke et al., 2018; Miller et al., 2003). In Dwyer and Ball (2020), interviews with LGBTI (lesbian, gay, bisexual, transgender, intersex) liaison officers in Australia showed that some gay male police officers did not wish to be visibly aligned with the LGBTQ+ community as liaison officers. Despite acknowledging the potential benefits of liaison officers for LGBTQ+ people in need of police support, some gay male officers thought the personal risks were too great, as becoming visible in such a role would heighten the risk of discrimination. In the United States, Collins and Rocco (2015) found that gay male police officers learned tacit and informal "rules of engagement." These rules enabled them to foster a "survival consciousness" to cope with the ongoing hostility toward gay male police officers in hypermasculine police organizations. Although current empirical insights into the workplace experiences of U.K. gay male police officers seem to track closely with those in some other world regions, we cannot assume this to be the case, especially as cultural notions of sexuality and gender vary, as do other aspects of difference in the particularities of police work. This variation represents an important research area in its own right, with a potentially significant bearing on how we can begin to understand cultural differences in the workplace experiences of gay male police officers around the globe.

For the purpose of this chapter, the above strands of research channel toward a resounding conclusion: heteronormativity is a persistent and widespread workplace problem for gay male police officers. In what ways this is experienced by, for instance, gay male police officers at the intersection of race, disability, and age is unclear, both in the United Kingdom and elsewhere. In this chapter, I treat heteronormativity as a normative regime that is sustained by sexual and gender binaries—heterosexual/homosexual, male/female, masculine/feminine—that constrain how members of sexual minority groups (and many heterosexuals) are constituted as sexual and gendered subjects (Butler, 1993; Warner, 1993). Heteronormativity assigns normative status to heterosexuality, as "natural," "healthy," and "normal," against which LGBTQ+ sexualities and non-normative genders are understood as "abnormal." Heteronormativity is a pernicious social problem, manifested in and reproduced by institutions and organizations (Rumens, 2018). Like other work organizations, police services are heteronormative, as evidenced in research that documents barriers to equal opportunities (Colvin, 2015), disclosure and management strategies that hide sexual identity (Collins & Rocco, 2015; Miller et al., 2003), and overt and subtle forms of discrimination based on sexual orientation (Belkin & McNichol, 2002; Bernstein & Swartwout, 2012). Other studies have exposed heteronormative and hostile attitudes from heterosexual senior staff and peers (Lyons et al., 2008; Zempi, 2020), exclusion from specific areas of police work, and conditional or peripheral inclusion (Rennstam & Sullivan, 2018; Rumens & Broomfield, 2012). Research indicates that gay male police officers may experience workplace heteronormativity differently than lesbian police officers do, particularly when gay men are stereotyped as "feminine" and, thus, "unfit" to embody the masculine characteristics associated with traditional police work (Giwa et al., 2022; Praat & Tuffin, 1996; Jones & Williams, 2015; Rumens & Broomfield, 2012). Indeed, some research suggests that gay male police officers experience more barriers to equal opportunity than lesbian police officers (Colvin, 2015; Jones & Williams, 2015).

Although scholarship in the U.K. context provides some nuance to an ongoing narrative of heteronormativity experienced by gay male police officers, the topic remains empirically open. As such, the motive behind asking what scholarly research can tell us about gay male police officers in the United Kingdom comes from my concern with this knowledge void as well as a desire to renew emphasis on generating debate and scholarship in this area. Pursuing this, the chapter begins by establishing a policing policy and reform context against which existing research on U.K. gay male police officers can be located. Two areas of concern are discussed that are relevant to the study of gay male police officers: gay male police officers' experiences and perceptions of the workplace and the hypermasculinity of police cultures. The chapter concludes by outlining the implications of current scholarship for theory and future research.

## Policing Policy and Reforms in the United Kingdom

By way of context, I briefly consider the wider landscape of policy and reform in regard to policing and LGBTQ+ people as members of communities and as police officers. Notably, LGBTQ+ people in the United Kingdom, as in other countries (Dwyer, 2012; Russell, 2019; Stewart-Winter, 2015), have been over- and under-policed. The idea of homosexuality as deviant and morally corrupt has been responsible for its strict social regulation. Burke's (1993, 1994) pioneering research on LGB police officers in England and Wales exposed not only the legacy of over-policing but also the challenges confronting LGB police officers in heteronormative police work contexts. Tensions arising from claims of homophobic policing practices and police officers turning a blind eye to LGBTQ+ hate crimes (as an instance of under-policing) have damaged trust in the police for LGBTQ+ communities (Pickles, 2020). Rebuilding trust has become an abiding concern and challenge for U.K. police services as they strive toward inclusion and diversity in policing practices (Colvin, 2012).

One of the most influential turning points for reform was the 1999 publication of the Macpherson report, which set in motion a sweeping and politicized agenda of workforce modernization that extended far beyond its primary focus on institutional racism within the Metropolitan Police Service. Macpherson et al. (1999) corroborated accusations of institutional police racism and incompetence in the structures and practices of the Metropolitan Police Service, which led to the bungling of the murder investigation into Stephen Lawrence's race-related death. The report recommended measures to eradicate institutional racism in U.K. police services, and it precipitated widespread policing reforms that concentrated on, among other things, recruiting a diverse and inclusive police workforce that would have a positive impact on community policing. As Loftus (2008, 2010) submits, U.K. police organizations have relied heavily on diversity management initiatives to tackle inequality, prejudice, and discrimination experienced by officers belonging to minority groups. Some scholars have read this as a quantum leap, for, as Jones (2015) puts it, "less than 10 years after the emotive findings of Burke (1994), LGB people were being actively encouraged to join an occupation that was attempting to rebrand itself as diverse and 'gay-friendly'" (p. 67).

U.K. legal reforms may have helped to make police organizations more attractive as employers of choice. The Equality Act of 2010 brought together over 116 separate pieces of legislation to strengthen antidiscrimination law, including sexual orientation and gender reassignment protections. Furthermore, the establishment of the Gay Police Association and its successor, the National LGBT+ Police Network, has promoted equal employment opportunities for lesbian and gay police officers and improved relations between the police and LGBTQ+ communities (Colvin, 2015). In addition, organizational efforts to reinvent police services as LGBTQ+ inclusive have been afoot for several decades (Loftus, 2008, 2010). Some U.K. police services have maintained a recurring presence and participation in annual LGBTQ+ Pride events, viewing them as opportunities to foster relations of trust with LGBTQ+ communities, to demonstrate their commitment to LGBTQ+ diversity and equality, and to recruit new staff from these minority groups (Colvin, 2012).

Notable also is the growing number of police services that have participated in the Stonewall Top 100 Employers list, published annually by LGBT charity Stonewall. The list is compiled from the Workplace Equality Index, a voluntary exercise that enables employers to measure, verify, and improve their LGBT inclusion practice. Police services have featured prominently on the list over the last decade, appearing as employers of choice for LGBTQ+ people. However, in 2020, only four police organizations made the top 100, and London's Metropolitan Police Service was not one of them. Of the 43 geographic and specialty police services in England and Wales, Sussex Police attained the highest ranking, at position 68, with three other agencies ranking lower: British Transport Police, the Civil Nuclear Constabulary, and the Ministry of Defence Police.

One explanation for this decline is that some police services have cut ties with Stonewall due to cost (annual membership costs around £2,500), not getting enough value for the expense, and concerns over guidelines issued by Stonewall on how to deal with transgender and nonbinary people. Stonewall's transgender-inclusive initiatives, such as urging employers to use correct pronouns, adopting gender-neutral language, and providing gender-neutral training, have been roundly criticized by some politicians, journalists, and commentators (Somerville & Dixon, 2021). Attacked by what McLean (2021) describes as a "toxic" anti-transgender movement in the United Kingdom, Stonewall (among other organizations and public figures) is at the center of a firestorm raging between proponents and detractors of transgender rights. At the time of writing, legal action is being threatened by campaign groups claiming that to implement Stonewall's guidelines breaches police rules on political activity and associations, giving rise to conflicts of interest.

It is too early to tell whether the controversy surrounding transgender people's rights will impair the efforts made by police organizations to address the needs and interests of LGBTQ+ police officers. But the requirement for police services to deliver on the government's commitments in the LGBT Action Plan is pressing (Government Equalities Office, 2018). One aspect of the action plan, based on a national survey of over 108,000 LGBT people, promises to enhance LGBT safety: 40% of survey respondents had experienced a least one negative incident involving someone they did not live with, and 91% said they did not report the most serious incident they had experienced in the last 12 months. One strategy is to improve how police services respond to and record LGBTQ+ hate crimes. Although health and education took priority in 2018–2019 (Government Equalities Office, 2019), police services in England and Wales have been instructed to report on their effectiveness in identifying, recording, and responding to reports of hate crime.

To summarize, this necessarily brief sketch of the U.K. landscape of policing policy and reform helps to contextualize research on gay male police officers, which I turn to next. Although the external appearance of many police services as progressive and LGBTQ+ friendly contrast starkly with Burke's (1993, 1994) depictions of police organizations 30 years ago, later studies have shown that the realities of police work for LGBTQ+ police officers are still less than ideal (Colvin, 2012, 2015; Giwa et al., 2021; Jones & Williams, 2015; Rumens & Broomfield, 2012; Zempi, 2020).

## Gay Male Police Officers' Experiences and Perceptions

Given the poor track record demonstrated by U.K. police organizations in the past on issues of LGBTQ+ diversity and inclusion, it is not surprising that studies have shown that gay male police officers have not always viewed themselves as valued members of the police workforce (Burke, 1993, 1994). Nor have they always perceived the police organizations they work for as welcoming and inclusive of gay men. In Rumens and Broomfield's (2012) study, published almost two decades after Burke (1993), gay male police officers articulated the availability of career opportunities more positively than did those interviewed by Burke, as evidenced by openly gay men who had risen through the ranks from constable to senior roles (including inspector). Colvin's (2012) data set showed that 58% of gay and lesbian police officers in the United Kingdom felt that career advancement opportunities for them were the same as those of heterosexual officers. Significantly, though, a large percentage of gay and lesbian police officers felt they were not the same. While it is true there have been high-profile openly gay men in the U.K. police workforce, such as Brian Paddick, who attained the role of deputy assistant commissioner, it took until 2021 for the British Transport Police to become the first U.K. police service to have an openly gay man reach the rank of chief constable (at the time of writing, only on a temporary basis). Although these accomplishments have been heralded as "historic milestones" in police media, there is ample reason to ask, Why has it taken so long to scale these heights?

Research on the work experiences of gay male police officers provides some indication. Burke (1993, 1994) showed how gay male police officers anticipated and responded to heteronormative police work environments by adopting identity disclosure and management strategies of a self-protective sort. Some gay men "passed" as heterosexual by (re)constructing "heterosexual" identities and lives. Others adopted a "covering" strategy that did not draw attention to their sexual identities, by avoiding discussions about their personal life (e.g., male partners) or by signaling their anger with coworkers by making anti-gay jokes. Crucially, passing and covering could be deployed by some gay male police officers selectively so that a gay identity might be undisclosed in the workplace yet disclosed outside work, thereby avoiding the disclosure of a vocational identity (Burke, 1993, p. 92). This strategy of gay officers leading a double life or having a dual identity was a striking study finding that was symptomatic of heteronormative police cultures that obtained in the United Kingdom at the time.

Later, Rumens and Broomfield (2012) found no such evidence of a dual-identity strategy among gay male officers. Instead, findings showed identity disclosure and management processes based on integration and normalization. One normalizing strategy involved gay male police officers inhabiting dominant masculine norms that brought them closer to normative heterosexual masculinity (e.g., as competitive, assertive, in control of their emotions, rational), enabling some to claim that they were the "same" as heterosexual male police officers. The normalization of gay male sexualities can be an unconscious process of integration, but some gay male police officers were acutely aware of how normalization granted them conditional acceptance in police work contexts. In gendered areas of police work that demanded gender conformity, some gay male police officers distanced themselves from others who were perceived to be "too feminine." In these instances, Rumens and Broomfield found traces of homophobia in gay male police officers' disparaging assessments of other gay men they considered "feminine." Effeminate gay male police officers appeared to fare less well in their efforts to normalize, finding themselves othered and marginalized by senior officers and excluded from workplace rituals.

Colvin's (2012, 2015) U.K. survey-based research revealed that the "work lives of British lesbian and gay officers remain less than ideal" (2012, p. 74), which was made evident by reports of homophobic talk, being outed at work, differential treatment in transferring to a new post, work schedules, and promotions. For gay male police officers, the most commonly identified barrier to equal employment was joining or transferring to a police organization (2015, p. 341). One notable finding in Colvin (2015) was that gay men reported encountering more barriers and discrimination in police organizations than lesbian officers did, especially at higher levels and ranks. Colvin (2015, p. 345) postulates that one explanation for this is that supervisory and managerial discretion is less regulated at these levels. Another explanation is that gender stereotyping of gay men as "feminine" and "weak," and lesbians as "masculine" and "tough," may give lesbians an advantage in traditionally masculine police cultures.

Study findings from Jones and Williams (2015) seem to support this. Compared to lesbians, bisexual women, and bisexual men, gay male police officers were strongly associated with discrimination in all three employment areas studied (uniformed, length of tenure, rank). Jones and Williams draw on Praat and Tuffin's (1996) research in New Zealand to suggest that heteronormative gender stereotyping of gay men may be responsible for this pattern of discrimination, asserting that such stereotypes can be mobilized by recruiters to reject male candidates perceived or known to be gay. The problem of gender stereotyping is documented in Zempi (2020), a small-scale qualitative study, in which one gay male police officer reported homophobic attitudes from a coworker who feared he would be "unsafe" (i.e., "he feared I would rape him") if occupying the same patrol car (p. 38). That police officer refused to work with his gay colleague.

We have then, based on existing U.K. research, a relatively clear but incomplete picture of the perceptions and workplace experiences of gay male police officers. Although the researchers cited above state that U.K. police organizations have undergone reforms with profound effects on how they should engage with members of LGBTQ+ groups as rank-and-file officers, research still reveals negative disparities in employment experiences. The consensus is that although progress has been made, the current situation for gay male police officers, and other officers who hail from LGBTQ+ groups, remains problematic.


## Hypermasculine Work Cultures

One of the most serious problems identified in research that focuses on LGBTQ+ police officers is the ubiquity of hypermasculine work cultures that promote sexual prejudice and entrench heteronormativity (Burke, 1993, 1994; Collins & Rocco, 2015; Giwa et al., 2022). Historically, masculinity has shaped police organizations, policies, norms, and behaviors in particular ways, so much so that masculinity is synonymous with police work (Barrie & Broomhall, 2012). In police work environments, hypermasculine cultures are typically characterized by competitiveness, aggression, emotional distancing, and control, buttressing an idealized discursive template of what it is to be "male" and "masculine" (Miller et al., 2003). It is for this reason that police organizations render visible men and masculinities that otherwise might be hidden and unexamined in other work contexts.

Gay male masculinities are at risk of being exposed and penalized in hypermasculine police cultures, as dominant assumptions and norms about how "policemen" should behave often have the effect of privileging white heterosexual men (Loftus, 2008). Police officers who cannot or do not wish to approximate normative heterosexual masculinity have reported discrimination as a negative repercussion (Rumens & Broomfield, 2012). Indeed, in a U.S. context, Collins and Rocco (2015) argue that the anticipation of negative repercussions associated with coming out as gay carries more weight in hypermasculine police organizations for gay men. This is because gay male police officers are vulnerable to gender stereotyping as not being "real" police/men. As Myers et al. (2004) show, some find themselves having to work harder than their heterosexual male coworkers to prove themselves capable crime fighters.

Research also shows that hypermasculine police cultures and heterosexuality exist in a self-sustaining relationship that reproduces "compulsory heterosexuality" (Rich, 1980), in that heterosexuality is assumed, enforced, and treated as a political institution that entrenches patriarchy. Equally, normative heterosexuality sustains hypermasculine behaviors and practices that, in turn, maintain heteronormativity, the characteristics of which and its effects on gay male police officers are acutely apparent in some police organizations (Miller et al., 2003).

Although hypermasculine police cultures serve as barriers to inclusion for gay male police officers, an ideological shift has accompanied the move toward community policing that emphasizes the value of "feminine" skills such as relationship building, cooperation, communication, and compassion (Dick & Cassell, 2002). Arguably, "legitimate" spaces within police cultures have opened for women and members of minority groups to participate in police work based on the differences they are perceived to bring into the workplace (Loftus, 2010; McCarthy, 2013; Rumens & Broomfield, 2012). However, considerable resistance to the diversity initiatives deployed to support this new skill emphasis has been documented (Dick & Cassell, 2002; Loftus, 2008).

Hypermasculine police cultures may not be the bastions they once were, but they continue to persist. In 2020, five heterosexual police officers in the United Kingdom were dismissed by Hampshire Constabulary from their jobs for gross misconduct, having been found guilty of using derogatory terms such as "queers" and "horrible tranny faggots" (Parsons, 2021). The magnitude of the problem was such that Hampshire Constabulary took the unusual step of bugging the Serious and Organised Crime Unit. Recordings of conversations and interactions revealed copious examples of homophobic, sexist, and racist conversations. The investigation cast a glaring light on how other police officers in Hampshire Constabulary perceived and informally referred to the unit as a "lads' pad," a hypermasculinist work culture that, presumably, had been tolerated or gone undetected.

To summarize, available research paints a mixed picture of hypermasculinity in U.K. police organizations. Traditional police cultures can be understood to exist in mutual association with hypermasculinity and heteronormativity, wherein gay male police officers may feel exposed and vulnerable, undermined by stereotypes of gay men as not "real" men and lacking the masculine characteristics concomitant with traditional police work. Notably, some research suggests that lesbians who are open about their sexuality in police work contexts are perceived to be stereotypically masculine (e.g., emotionally and physically tough, aggressive). This may explain why some lesbian officers experience less discrimination than gay male police officers (Colvin, 2012; Galvin-White & O'Neal, 2016). Although U.K. policing reforms have promulgated the view that hypermasculine police cultures are undesirable and inappropriate for contemporary policing aimed at preventing crime and building relationships with different publics, it appears in the United Kingdom that we cannot view them as relics of the past.

## Implications for Theory and Research

Read together, the streams of literature traced above demonstrate a need for future research, which should continue to track perceptions, attitudes, and experiences of gay male police officers in the United Kingdom. Changes in the masculine constituency of police work cultures require ongoing scholarly investigation, as it cannot be taken for granted that such cultures and the masculine norms that sustain them have been transformed or that equal work opportunities have opened up for all gay male police officers to participate openly in these (re)gendered work cultures. The urgency of this research trajectory is highlighted by studies on LGBTQ+ police officers in other world regions such as the United States (Collins & Rocco, 2015, 2018; Mennicke et al., 2018). Furthermore, it remains unclear whether hypermasculine work cultures exist as isolated subcultures or are more pervasive in the United Kingdom. How gay male police officers have responded to shifts in hypermasculine police cultures constitutes a key line of empirical investigation. What is more, scholarship is needed to assess the localized impacts of diversity initiatives, policing reforms, and the government's LGBT Action Plan of 2018 on gay male police officers. Current empirical insights into how specific U.K. police organizations have responded to policing reforms and diversity initiatives are illuminating (Colvin, 2012), reminding us that localized cases are likely to be complex and contingent. This type of research is uncommon in the U.K. context, however.

Alongside these important research trajectories, another priority concerns the study of gay male police officers as a diverse group, through research that will shed light on intersections of, for example, sex, sexuality, race, ethnicity, age, and disability. One way of reading the literature on gay male police officers is that it tends to hold sexuality as the principal accountability to social difference, perhaps giving the impression that all gay male police officers might be the same. This tendency gives rise to questions about what theories we can draw on to account for how differences are multiple, intersecting, and related to historical regimes of inequality and oppression.

*Critical Perspectives on Men and Masculinities*

Although the field of police studies does not suffer from a lack of theories, the slim volume of scholarship on gay male police officers merits theoretical development. One option is to extend research on gay male police officers as gendered and sexual subjects by deriving theoretical insights from critical studies on men and masculinities. Although sexuality and gender are important categories of analysis that have commanding literatures behind them, police studies scholars have not always brought the two together to understand how sexuality is gendered. Disconnected from and critical of anti-feminist "men's movements" and activism, which remain concerned with buttressing heteronormative, white-centered, able-bodied, and often misogynistic forms of masculinity (Messner, 2016), critical studies on men and masculinities are a scholarly domain that is typically understood as a pro-feminist and politically progressive intellectual project. Sharing feminism's concern with gender, scholars in this area view masculinity as socially and culturally variable and historically patterned (Connell, 1995; Kimmel, 1994; Messner, 1997). Treating masculinity, men, and men's practices as objects of critical analysis, researchers have exposed and problematized how masculinity is privileged, rendered "natural," embedded in relations of gendered power, and produces material consequences that are the outcomes of men's practices (Connell, 1995; Kimmel, 1994; Messner, 1997). The sociological and poststructuralist arms of this subfield have been mobilized by scholars interested in organizations in their examinations of gender privilege and oppression in the workplace and their expressions of pro-feminist commitment toward eradicating the privileging of men and masculinity in organizations (Collinson & Hearn, 1996).

Analytically, we can advance research on how sexuality and gender interact with each other by using critical perspectives on masculinity to shed light on the gendering of gay male sexualities. This approach is potentially different from current studies on gay men as police officers because it forces us to ask how gay male police officers are compelled to work as particular kinds of men in specific policing contexts (Rumens & Broomfield, 2012). We may consider in much greater depth, for example, how the gendering of different types of police work can shape how gay male police officers approach identity disclosure, management, and development. Police work is diverse, and it would be unwise to assume it is gendered in the same way that stereotypes it as "unsuitable" for gay men. Additionally, directing closer attention to gender and gay male masculinities in police work environments can help us to glean detail about what sort of investments gay men make in masculinity, but also in femininity, and why. Focusing on men's practices is important, not least because it avoids identifying and categorizing "types" of masculinity, while zeroing in on how gendered power is exercised in ways that disadvantage numerous women and some men. From this approach, scholars can interrogate the relationship between gender and gay male sexualities, which must include critiques of how gay masculinities can be complicit in reproducing forms of gender privilege, heteronormativity, and misogyny.

Despite the clear benefits of deploying critical perspectives on men and masculinities to study the gendering of gay male sexualities in police organizations, the foregrounding of gender may spell a serious limitation. When gender remains a primary point of departure, that can seal off gender from other aspects of difference. If this is read as a slanted understanding about how differences shape the work experiences of gay male police officers, scholars may weigh up other available options.

*Intersectionality*

One valuable theoretical strand that police research has engaged with is intersectionality (Charles & Rouse Arndt, 2013; Hassell & Brandl, 2009; Zempi, 2020). With its scholarly pedigree in Black feminist theorizing, which paved the way for examining overlapping and multiple forms of oppression relating to gender, race, and ethnicity (Collins, 2000; Crenshaw, 1991), intersectionality is an important but still underdeveloped theoretical resource in research on LGBTQ+ police officers. Intersectionality has been variously understood as a theory, theoretical framework, and concept (Bowleg, 2012). In this context, I refer to intersectionality as a perspective, not least because, as Bowleg holds, "intersectionality has no core elements or variables to be operationalized and empirically tested" (p. 1268) As a perspective, intersectionality focuses on differences and hierarchies of oppression, which helps to avoid starting out from a position that elevates one difference over all others, or where additional "variables" of difference are bolted on. More precisely, intersectional research situates differences in a "matrix of domination" (Collins, 2000, p. vii), wherein they are (re)constructed at intersections of oppression. So far, intersectionality has been marshaled in studies on police officers and sex, sexuality, careers, and race (Charles & Rouse Arndt, 2013; Hassell & Brandl, 2009). Giwa et al. (2022) also adopt an intersectionality perspective to analyze the workplace experiences of lesbian and bisexual women police officers in Canada. Very few studies have engaged with intersectionality to examine the workplace experiences of gay male police officers.

Zempi (2020) is a notable exception in a U.K. context. Although this small-scale qualitative study does not focus exclusively on gay male police officers, it starts to show how intersecting differences can capture the distinctiveness of specific identity formations. For example, one gay male study participant reported feeling more exposed to discrimination in police work due to his dyslexia, citing the lack of support mechanisms that would enable him to do his job effectively. This kind of empirical data exhibits nuance that deserves further investigation, as it highlights how the experience of vulnerability to discrimination and patterns of inequality are not always easy to observe or predict. Indeed, differences intertwine and overlap, but determining how differences are mutually constitutive in specific police organizations and work environments requires context-sensitive research. From an intersectionality perspective, scholars can take steps to analyze how differences intersect with forms of discrimination.

For instance, the case of Detective Constable Kevin Maxwell lends it-self to analysis that adopts an intersectional perspective. In 2012, Maxwell sued the Metropolitan Police for race and sex discrimination after he was abused by colleagues while working in the counterterrorism unit at Heath-row Airport. The employment tribunal found that he had been subjected to 41 acts of discrimination. One of the most striking aspects of this case is that Maxwell positioned himself as "the future" of the Metropolitan Police, as an organizationally desirable subject who "ticked the boxes" as far as diversity agendas are concerned, being both mixed-race and gay (Peachey, 2013). Yet, as the tribunal found, Maxwell had been subjected to multiple forms of sex and race discrimination, prompting questions about how categories of differ-ence intersect with forms of discrimination, producing inequalities (Bowleg, 2012). Such analysis is warranted to address these questions, especially in the context of diversity management initiatives that have, in the United King-dom at least, been relied on to create police cultures that "value" individual differences (Colvin, 2015; Loftus, 2008, 2010). Maxwell's case highlights on-going failures in U.K. police organizations to develop organizational policies and practices that account for how differences and modes of discrimination intersect. As a perspective, intersectionality can encourage research on gay male police officers in police organizations that interrogates how intersect-ing differences are (re)constructed as organizational resources and, also, as a politics of difference that is implicated in persistent patterns of inequality.

*Queer Theory*

Another theoretical option for researchers is that of queer theories. Having already made inroads into criminology (Woods, 2014), queer theories have yet to make much of an impression in police studies. With roots in gay and lesbian studies, poststructuralism, and feminism, queer theories emerged in the early 1990s to critique what is "normal" (Halperin, 1995), in particular normative constructions of sexuality (de Lauretis, 1991). Queer studies has be-come an established academic domain characterized by theoretical diversity, transformative politics, and a commitment to disrupting and deconstructing normative regimes. The ongoing efforts of queer theorists to challenge and rupture heteronormativity have generated a well-stocked bank of theoretical resources for police studies scholars to draw upon.

Queer theory scholarship on gay male police officers could examine how the heterosexual/homosexual binary is reproduced in police work cultures, organizational structures, and practices. How organizational heteronormativity operates in specific police work contexts to sustain this binary is a key area for analysis, not least because heteronormativity in the workplace is not uniform in its nature and impact on gay male police officers. One line of inquiry is how processes of LGBTQ+ normalization in police work organizations have integrated some gay male police officers but not others. Another avenue of inquiry can galvanize queer theory research that has examined the discursive dynamics among sexuality, gender, race, and ethnicity (Eng, 2010). As such, queer theorizing on intersecting differences can broach a different set of research possibilities for how difference and identity categories are understood. For example, queer theory confronts an intersectional perspective of relatively stable social identities by highlighting their incoherencies and regulatory effects (Butler, 1990, 2004). As such, a queer theory perspective on intersectionality forces thought on how identity categories are regulated by norms (e.g., norms relating to gender, sexuality, race, ethnicity, and so on) and on the implications of articulating a commitment to destabilizing identity categories (Edelman, 2004). Researchers may adopt this queer approach to the concept of identity by asking who is represented by which identity categories and who is excluded. For which gay male police officers do identity categories present conflicts among sexual, gendered, racial, and ethnic notions of difference?

Queer theory's questioning of the ontological production of identity categories as coherent and stable can be understood as performative (Butler, 1990, 1993). Butler's notion of performativity has come to represent a distinct and popular strand of queer theorizing that invites us to think about how discourse, rather than the subject, produces the effect of a coherent and stable identity through stylized, reiterative performances. Although the subject is compelled to inhabit and repeatedly cite sexual and gender norms, they can disrupt the process of performativity by altering the way such norms are inhabited. Queer theory from a Butlerian perspective could be fruitful for analyzing how gay male police officers are compelled to cite gender and sexual norms but may vary these citations to create non-normative identities and subjectivities that are unanticipated by heteronormativity (Butler, 2004). On the same critical radar, we can investigate how gay male police officers are not able to occupy identity categories considered desirable in police organizations (e.g., through diversity monitoring mechanisms). Such an inquiry may insist on asking how gay male police officers address the normative assumptions underpinning specific identity categories and what personal costs are borne by approximating or veering from the norms that constitute identities in police organizations. Related to this would be research that explores how gay male police officers can reimagine normative notions of police work in ways that demonstrate a potentially different positioning from that of inhabiting gender norms associated with hypermasculinity.

## Conclusion

In this chapter, I have suggested that U.K. research on gay male police officers has yet to reach its full potential. This chapter has underlined the importance of this subfield within a scholarly landscape of research on LGBTQ+ sexualities and genders and police organizations. Extending and building on existing research on gay male police officers is an endeavor incumbent not only on U.K. scholars. Literature on LGBTQ+ police officers in other world regions shows similar knowledge deficits when it comes to gay male police officers, but this research also documents challenges and problems similar to those confronting gay male police officers in the United Kingdom (Collins & Rocco, 2015; Dwyer & Ball, 2020; Miller et al., 2003). Furthermore, this chapter has demonstrated the importance of analyzing differences when researching gay male police officers, which can and should encompass other facets of difference that relate to gender, race, ethnicity, and disability. From different theoretical perspectives, I have sought to raise questions that may usefully guide future scholarship so we will have a richer empirical reservoir of research to draw from. It seems important to close here by encouraging research into prospects yet to be explored about the work lives, identities, and experiences of gay male police officers around the globe.

# 11. APPLYING QUEER THEORY TO THE ROLE OF LGBTQ+ POLICE LIAISONS

Seth J. Meyer, Nicole M. Elias, and Paige L. Moore

Queer communities have long had complicated relationships with police departments and law enforcement agencies. Historically, LGBTQ+ communities faced brutality and harassment at the hands of the police, resulting in distrust and avoidance of law enforcement (Mogul et al., 2011; Owen et al., 2018). This antagonistic relationship has been influenced by various social, cultural, legal, and political aspects (Holmes, 2021). Theoretically, it is possible to trace a linear progression to a productive future from a painful past. The history of pain and mistrust among LGBTQ+ members cannot be erased when policing practices shift toward progressive notions of community policing (Dwyer, 2014b). Though modern movements have supported and affirmed LGBTQ+ communities, previous negative interactions, over-policing, and increased surveillance made LGBTQ+ people into police targets due to perceived immoral behavior and resulted in discrimination and violence at the hands of law enforcement.

Recently, organizers for multiple Pride parades have asked police organizations not to march, as their presence makes some other participants uncomfortable (Mossburg & Romine, 2022). Although some Pride organizations, such as in San Diego, have used the threat of expulsion as an opportunity to advocate for change in police departments, others have summarily banned them (Handy, 2022). Police departments are currently grappling with their histories through various internal and external efforts to build positive relationships with LGBTQ+ communities through policies and programs. One such effort to improve this tumultuous dynamic is instituting LGBTQ+ liaisons, or specialized police officers tasked with LGBTQ+ engagement, to strengthen the understanding and mutual respect between police and LGBTQ+ communities.

This chapter employs queer theory to explore how LGBTQ+ liaisons can improve relations between LGBTQ+ communities and police. Queer theory has been used to understand the relationship between police departments and LGBTQ+ communities (Colvin & Meyer, 2022; Dwyer, 2020). When combined with an expanding literature on liaison officers (Dwyer & Ball, 2013, 2020), queer theory provides an instructive framework to ask how LGBTQ+ liaisons may help mend relationships with historically marginalized and targeted SOGIE (sexual orientation, gender identity and expression) communities. To explore this question, this chapter begins with a discussion of liaison officers, followed by a distillation of key concepts of queer theory and an application of queer theory to the role of LGBTQ+ liaison officers. We conclude with policy and practice implications for police departments interested in improving their relationship with LGBTQ+ communities, which make up a growing proportion of the U.S. population.

## What Is a Liaison Officer?

Historically marginalized groups, such as the LGBTQ+ community, women, individuals living with a disability, and Black and Hispanic/Latinx people, are underrepresented in police departments. This has resulted in a mostly white, mostly male, mostly heterosexual profession now struggling to protect and serve its communities (Colvin & Meyer, 2022). Underrepresentation has led to underreporting of crimes of victimization and discrimination in marginalized communities. As a result, many police institutions have created liaison officers or their equivalent to bridge the gaps between police and communities (Mercer, 2015). The creation of police-community liaisons ensures that underserved groups feel more supported and can access the services of the police without fear of further victimization (Dwyer & Ball, 2013). These officers also strive to improve relationships between police departments and communities by serving as a voice for marginalized communities and acting as ally and advocate during policy development and implementation to address community concerns (Dario et al., 2019).

Liaison officers forge mutual relationships between different constituents (Riccucci et al., 2018). They play the role of intermediary and serve to improve relationships among different parties, sometimes with competing interests. A liaison officer should possess strong communication skills and be empathetic to both their department and its constituencies to ensure they are served as well as possible (Kunst et al., 2017). Krishnamurty et al. (2018) note that liaison officers in police agencies, schools, and the workplace are necessary to ensure that underrepresented groups such as LGBTQ+ communities, women, children, ethnic minorities, and the disabled are not excluded.

Liaison officers have demonstrated results in improving community-police relationships in various contexts. For example, Australian queer communities have engaged more with liaison officers than other law enforcement officers out of a belief that liaisons listen, understand, and respond better to community concerns (Dwyer & Ball, 2013). In the United States, where cases of racial profiling by police have led to aggressive policing, liaison officers for Black, Hispanic/Latinx, and other minority communities may lead to improved policing practices, increased police legitimacy, and fewer community-initiated reports of violence (O'Neill & Holdaway, 2007). In addition, Krishnamurty et al. (2018) note that the formation of employee resource groups in the United States has increased inclusivity for diverse workforces across different organizations as they allow space for conversations on workplace inclusivity. Therefore, liaison officers play a significant role in ensuring that various groups and their needs are listened to and responded to effectively and more equitably.

## Family Liaison Officers

Liaison police officers often work with families as a fundamental social unit and have a significant impact on reducing criminal processing system incidents. Many institutions and communities have created liaison officers, community outreach programs, advisory boards, or their equivalent to address the challenges faced by underrepresented communities (Dario et al., 2019). The creation of liaison officers at the family level ensures that underrepresented groups feel more supported and can access police and government services without fear of further victimization (Dwyer & Ball, 2013; Kunst et al., 2017; Mercer 2015). They also facilitate safe environments where children and their parents or guardians can communicate effectively to solve problems in the home before escalation (Kunst et al., 2017). This reduces delinquency and increases the probability of juveniles performing well at school (O'Neill & Holdaway, 2007).

Despite the benefits of liaison officers working with families, this approach can pose significant challenges for police liaisons when parents do not work hand-in-hand with the liaison officer (Krishnamurty et al., 2018). Family liaison officers intervene in family disputes to ensure that children do not stay in violent homes. They also assist with placing children in foster homes where the children can find stability, which will help reduce delinquency (Mercer, 2015; Riccucci et al., 2018). As domestic violence cases escalated during the COVID-19 pandemic, the presence of family liaison officers contributed to greater reporting of domestic violence and appropriate intervention strategies. As family structures become more diverse, family liaisons should have an understanding of the diversity of family structures within the LGBTQ+ community, including multiple partners and nonbiological relationships.

## Community Liaisons: Demographics and Other Interests

Historically underrepresented groups continue to be underserved and experience resource challenges, which has created the need for liaison officers to serve in their jurisdictions. Recent cases of police shootings targeting the Black community in the United States have led to distrust between Black people and the police, affecting their interactions (Kunst et al., 2017). A liaison officer, in these instances, steps into the role of facilitator between communities and law enforcement. Their role includes assisting in reporting cases of violence, which are usually underreported, as minorities are hesitant to approach law enforcement.

Although the installation of liaison officers in different institutions presents an opportunity for inclusivity, Dwyer and Ball (2013) believe that there must be an increased effort on the part of institutions to ensure that liaison officers are equipped to fulfill their roles effectively. O'Neill and Holdaway (2007) agree and believe that most liaison officers are "window dressing" on the part of institutions, as they do not serve the communities they are called on to represent. According to Mercer (2015), history can inhibit the effectiveness of institutions and their liaison officers because it has bred distrust in these institutions. The criminalization of sodomy until the 1980s, the current definition of rape limited to vaginal intercourse in many states, and systemic discrimination against Black people all influence the perceptions of minority groups toward the institutions that serve them. Domestic violence is one area with a problematic history where liaison officers are needed yet may not be effective. Riccucci et al. (2018) note that in places where liaison officers are not adequately equipped to deal with domestic violence, people who feel unsafe in their homes tend to underreport domestic violence cases.

The fractured relations in the United States between law enforcement and Black people have necessitated liaison officers to help mend ties. Yet the long history of discrimination has made mistrust difficult to mend. Not surprisingly, the effectiveness of liaison officers in Black communities has been challenging to assess. Despite community resistance, O'Neill and Holdaway (2007) advocate for liaison officers who understand the concerns of under-represented communities because they will be better equipped to assist them and build bridges. According to den Heyer (2019), liaison officers stationed in different communities who understand their communities' distinct needs have helped to bridge the gap between local populations and the police. This has been an effective form of social capital.

Compared to other demographic groups, LGBTQ+ liaisons are relatively common for community policing efforts. In Australia, police liaison programs have been one of the most effective ways of building better relationships between LGBTQ+ people and police (Dwyer & Ball, 2013). Dwyer and Ball note that Australian queer communities have engaged more with liaison officers on the force than with other officers, as they have felt their concerns are better heard. The New South Wales Police Force, for example, is known in Australia for its approach to improving relationships between police and LGBTQ+ communities. This cultural shift has illuminated the impact of police scrutiny in LGBTQ+ communities. Police continue to interact with LGBTQ+ individuals in ways that result in undue stress for LGBTQ+ people in Western contexts (Dwyer, 2011b), even if police support of LGBTQ+ people means that more victims are coming forward and criminal prosecutions of perpetrators are increasing (Tomsen, 2009).

## LGBTQ+ Liaison Officers

To build partnerships and improve community relations, police departments both large and small across the United States have appointed police liaisons, who typically act as contact points between the police and LGBTQ+ communities in the jurisdiction. These LGBTQ+ police liaisons have played an essential role in maintaining relationships with LGBTQ+ communities for decades. Liaison programs outnumber other approaches to managing relationships between the police and LGBTQ+ communities.

Gender diversity and sexual equity are international human rights goals. Significant strides have been made toward improving the connection between the police and LGBTQ+ communities, but heightened awareness about the communities' needs is still inconsistent (Dwyer & Ball, 2020). Historically, police work was marked by informing the public about the perceived immorality of queer people and communities. Agencies usually argued that the community required stringent regulation (Bronski, 2011). Recently, the public—including police organizations—has shifted its views on LGBTQ+ persons, and police have transformed their ways of engaging with LGBTQ+ communities. Police agencies have developed resources for rebuilding damaged relationships. For instance, the Seattle Police Department's Safe Place Program is a partnership with local businesses whereby the businesses agree to harbor victims of hate crimes and alert local authorities. Innovative community-police programs like this serve to build lasting community relationships.

Building relationships between LGBTQ+ communities and liaison officers is crucial for creating awareness and showing humanity to these communities. It changes how people view members of the LGBTQ+ community. Police organizations have used various strategies to increase positive interactions between LGBTQ+ communities and liaison officers, including marching in uniform in annual Pride parades. Community policing initiatives have significantly helped in achieving success. Liaison officers also support LGBTQ+ crime victims to enhance relations between the officers and the communities. According to Dwyer & Ball (2020), though, the programs have been implemented unevenly and operate differently in countries depending on policing policies and levels of investment by senior leadership.

The LGBTQ+ liaison officer's role is undertaken by police staff on either a part- or full-time basis. A liaison officer is responsible for building and maintaining vital mutual relationships that coordinate activities and facilitate communication, in this case, between LGBTQ+ communities and police officers. The officers liaise with the two groups to address specific matters of concern. LGBTQ+ liaison officers shape how police officers deliver services to LGBTQ+ communities. This invaluable role improves the confidence of LGBTQ+ people in policing services. This objective can be met by creating an effective communication channel between LGBTQ+ communities and external and internal agencies (Colvin, 2014). The process involves sharing information on LGBTQ+ matters, raising awareness about the community, and identifying hate crime rates against community members. The LGBTQ+ liaison officer works to build and maintain confidence and manages crucial incidents involving the police and LGBTQ+ communities (Colvin, 2014). The officer is also responsible for supporting policing and investigative activities. In addition, the officer should encourage crime reporting and the provision of community intelligence to LGBTQ+ communities.

LGBTQ+ communities have expressed some dissatisfaction with police liaison officers, especially due to the unavailability of the liaison officers and high turnover (Dwyer & Ball, 2014). The officers show interest in undertaking the role yet are unwilling to advance the program due to a lack of training. There is no empirical evidence to determine whether LGBTQ+ police liaison services provide extra benefits apart from general policing services. There is little information about how police officers influence LGBTQ+ members to report incidents of discrimination and victimization to the police. Assessment should be done to determine how liaison officers perceive their roles and the progress of a program toward the achievement of its objective. The complex context of building better police-LGBTQ+ relationships should also be assessed to understand how the police can influence LGBTQ+ people to trust them.

Police liaison officers should be advised to establish extensive and deep conversations and actions about dignity and respect for LGBTQ+ members in order to support the community. The valued conversations will enhance people's confidence and make them more comfortable when interacting with the police (Dwyer, 2014). Smooth interaction will foster the reporting of discrimination cases and establish a strong relationship between the police and community members. It is possible to establish a comfortable, supportive, dignifying, and respectful interaction between the two parties. More training should be provided to liaison officers on effectively improving relations between police officers and the LGBTQ+ community.

Liaison officers sometimes argue that community members consider their role to be invisible, preventing its effectiveness. Their role is to enhance the visibility of LGBTQ+ members by ensuring that they can access public services and have a good relationship with police officers. Some LGBTQ+ community members feel that liaison officers have made an effort to enhance their visibility because they experience significant legal inclusion and social equality, making them recognized in different ways that increase their acceptability and protection as members of the LGBTQ+ community (Dwyer, 2019).

Women's movements have teamed up with LGBTQ+ communities to push for reforms, equality, and acceptability in the community. They have fought for gender inclusion and have succeeded in various aspects. A synergy potential can activate when the LGBTQ+ community joins hands with women's movements to counteract harassment and gender-based discrimination and promote gender equality. Organizational resources can be useful in neutralizing oppressive actions against LGBTQ+ people and women. Inclusively framing sexuality and gender helps to destroy monosexist, cis-sexist, and heterosexist paradigms that encourage harassment and discrimination in workplaces and general public places, ultimately holding that all individuals should be treated with respect and dignity regardless of LGBTQ+ identification, color, race, disability, body shape, and cultural background. To move closer to this goal and better understand the role of liaison officers, key concepts of queer theory are explained below: queering power, heteronormativity, and advocacy through research.

## Queer Theory

Queer theory explores dichotomies in society and how they uphold power structures and work to normalize deviation (Meyer et al., 2022). Built on countering compulsory heteronormativity and sex/gender binaries (Meyer et al., forthcoming), queer theory is a valuable tool for critiquing police relations with LGBTQ+ communities, including the LGBTQ+ liaison position.

Questioning dichotomies and how they oppress queer people is called queering (Colvin & Meyer, 2022; Filax, 2006). Through the act of queering, we can examine how heterosexuality is privileged and impacts organizations and individuals (McDonald, 2015). Heteronormativity impacts the expectations of queer individuals in their public life. Similarly, cisnormativity assumes that all people fit into Christian-based binary gender norms, creating otherness for those who do not and limiting nontraditional gender expression (Darling, 2021). Though queer theory has always included transgender perspectives, it has been criticized for viewing transness as theoretical instead of transgender people as people (Benavente & Gill-Peterson, 2019; Keegan, 2020). Through queer theory, we understand how some identities and actions are othered and how that impacts the way outsiders interact with public and nonprofit organizations.

Heteronormativity and cisnormativity can have negative implications for the way that the police interact with queer people. Youths report needing to act "less queer" to avoid being harmed by law enforcement (Dwyer, 2015). Gay men who do not describe themselves as feminine still report having negative experiences with the police (Meyer, 2020), suggesting that distrust between LGBTQ+ people and police goes beyond stereotypes of femininity in men. In general, LGBTQ+ people have negative views of police compared to their heterosexual and cisgendered peers (Owen et al., 2018).

## Queering LGBTQ+ Liaisons and Its Implications

### Queering Power

Queer theory can be used to better understand the nature of policing and, specifically, police liaisons. Queer theory fits clearly within the "abolish the police" movement, with works like *The End of Policing* (Vitale, 2017) leading the intellectual charge. This viewpoint sees a movement away from policing and toward a world with a stronger safety net. This is similar to the campaign to defund the police, which advocates helping people instead of criminalizing them (The Marshall Project, n.d.).

As one of the tenets of queer theory is queering power (for example, the power dynamics between LGBTQ+ communities and the police), and given the high need that queer communities have for social services support (Meyer & Millisen, 2022), policing reforms have popular support within the queer community. Queering the power dynamics of policing means exploring the power between the police and those being policed. The unequal power dynamic leads to transgender people being arrested for "walking while trans" (Carpenter & Marshall, 2017). Indeed, this relationship leads to police reinforcing hegemonic masculinity in queer communities instead of keeping them safe. LGBTQ+ liaisons allow an officer to examine this power dynamic through asking questions such as "What are we policing?" "How do we hold power over the transgender community" and "How can we police with the transgender community instead of policing the transgender community?" Adding queer theory changes the power balance from policing over people to creating a supportive community where LGBTQ+ people can be themselves without fear of being policed.

### Heteronormativity

Queer theory highlights the complex relationships that queer people have with the police, specifically older queer people, queer people of color, and gender-nonconforming queer people, who experience poor treatment from the police (Meyer, 2020). Part of this can be connected to how police uphold heteronormativity and cisnormativity and punish those who do not fit into them. Indeed, though many LGBTQ+ individuals are aware of police liaisons in Australia, many report not using them (Dwyer et al., 2022). Police liaisons themselves report having to manage their queerness and police identity in complicated ways and worrying that their queerness might erode their ability to command respect in uniform (Dwyer & Ball, 2020). Therefore, creating a liaison program that works requires more community awareness, but it also requires internal examination of how police officers and departments uphold heteronormativity to the detriment of queer communities.

Considering the sizable literature that documents bad experiences transgender individuals have had with the police (Dwyer, 2011b; Dwyer, 2014a; Dwyer, 2014b; Dwyer, 2015; McCandless, 2018b; Naylor, 2020), a liaison should not just be someone who can communicate with the queer community but someone who looks inward and explores the culture of the local police. An LGBTQ+ liaison can help create an understanding within the department of the unique experiences of queer individuals, such as not being out to their family (or, for youth, of not having a relationship with their family), the distinctive structures of queer relationships, and the support received from nonbiological families. It is important that there be constant discussion about how heterosexism may impact how police interact on a domestic violence call where the man is being abused or when a transgender person reports being raped. Without introspection and constant conversation, the LGBTQ+ liaison position will be little more than a diversity figurehead or a way for a police department to say they tried without doing any actual work. This is important not just for an LGBTQ+ liaison but also a family police liaison to understand. By working together, LGBTQ+ and family liaisons can help support LGBTQ+ families in a respectful and equitable manner.

LGBTQ+ liaisons can work with local queer communities to improve their relationships (e.g., Holmes, 2021), but that may not be enough to build a connection between the police department and communities. This is not easy; in Charlottesville, the first Black woman police chief, who was hired to build trust in the local police department, was fired because the police officers would not change to meet the needs of the community, instead holding on to an us-versus-them mentality (Jane, 2022). These barriers make it difficult to create a system that meets the needs of minority and underrepresented groups, such as queer individuals. And although establishing a position like an LGBTQ+ liaison may be a good first step, without internal change and fair pay and time for the position, it is nothing more than a figurehead.

*Advocacy through Research*

Queer criminology, the portion of queer theory active in the criminal justice field, has a limited but robust literature (Panfil, 2018b). Queer criminology is research that examines how individuals perform or experience sex and gender within criminology or the act of queering the norms of criminology (Ball et al., 2014). This field of inquiry has examined not only the queer experience within law enforcement and crime but also the transgender experience within the field of criminology itself (Valcore et al., 2021; Walker et al., 2021). Through queer theory, the different experiences of queer offenders have been examined, providing a more holistic analysis of this vulnerable population (Asquith et al., 2017; Panfil, 2022). Queer theory also calls on researchers, such as criminologists, to be activists (Ball, 2016; Belknap, 2015). The use of critical theories, like queer theory, has allowed critical and analytical looks at how policies like hate crime laws impact lesbian and gay groups (Valcore & Dodge, 2019). Queer criminology aims to move beyond viewing LGBTQ+ people as mere variables to be added but, instead, as complex communities impacted by homophobia, transphobia, heterosexism (Buist & Lenning, 2022), over-incarceration, and police surveillance.

Queer theory has been used sparingly to create a framework for queer criminology (e.g., Asquith et al., 2017; Ball, 2016; Belknap, 2015; Panfil, 2018b; Walker et al., 2021; Valcore et al., 2021). Understanding criminology through a queer theory lens is beneficial not only for LGBTQ+ people but also for understanding how research can support all individuals who interact with the criminal legal system. Furthermore, queer criminology provides a basis for understanding vulnerable populations and approaching individuals with a holistic perspective. In the LGBTQ+ community, this means considering the impact of factors such as how exile from the family, more common for LGBTQ+ individuals than their non-LGBTQ+ peers, may lead to survival crimes (Asquith et al., 2017) or how increased surveillance and policing of minority neighborhoods (including LGBTQ+ individuals) result in higher incarceration rates and also have generation-spanning health implications for individuals and communities (Sewell & Jefferson, 2016). A queer theory approach provides researchers with tools needed to develop an understanding of LGBTQ+ individuals within larger hierarchical and societal structures that alienate and punish them and muffle their voices (Woods et al., 2013).

The addition of queer criminology to criminal justice allows for the re-examination of previous and present identity-blind policies, practices, and behaviors that have reinforced the branding of LGBTQ+ individuals as social and sexual deviants. Queer criminology opens inquiry into important questions: As raised above, are the police policing the transgender community, or are they policing with the transgender community? Are they keeping the transgender community safe from violent crimes, or are transgender individuals seen as divergent victims of crime or deviant individuals with criminal intent? These questions highlight what Gokhale (2018) referred to as the "Queer Progressive Agenda," which details that LGBTQ+ individuals have intersectional identities and experiences of oppression that resonate throughout society with all people. As such, ending the oppression and exploitation of LGBTQ+ individuals by ending practices, procedures, and policies designed to oppress liberates not only queer individuals but all humans, in alignment with the goal of international human rights. This concept supports the creation of LGBTQ+ liaisons, as these advocates and allies of the LGBTQ+ community serve to build trust, address community concerns, and enhance police legitimacy in the LGBTQ+ community (Nixon, 2021; Owen et al., 2018).

## Looking Forward: Future Policy and Research

This chapter has explored the role of LGBTQ+ liaison officers by applying queer theory. LGBTQ+ liaisons are crucial in supporting LGBTQ+ individuals and improving police relations, but additional advocacy and allyship are necessary to ensure safety and mutual respect. Historically, having an affiliation with the LGBTQ+ community has been considered in police culture to make a person unfit to be an officer (Mennicke et al., 2018), and identification with historically underrepresented groups has been deemed a threat to racial and heterosexual domination (Nixon, 2021). Despite these perceptions, the growing diversity in the United States, recent social movements, and changes in police leadership have resulted in classes of police recruits "who have displayed more accepting views of LGBTQ+ communities" and resulted in police departments becoming more accepting of officers with LGBTQ+ identities (Nixon, 2021, p. 56).

According to a 2022 Gallup poll, 7.1% of adults (an increase from 5.6% in 2020) in the United States identified as LGBTQ+ (Jones, 2022). This upward trend is expected to increase to around 20% of Generation Z adults identifying as part of the LGBTQ+ community. These statistics show that although many current policies reflect cis-heteronormative beliefs, LGBTQ+ individuals are a growing population in the United States, and police policies and practices must reflect this growing diversity and be updated when inconsistent with community values.

Studies of LGBTQ+ police personnel indicate that discrimination in police departments against LGBTQ+ community members and police officers persist, if less overtly so (Cuoto, 2018; Nixon, 2021). The application of queer theory has the potential to promote the internal change needed to topple the hegemonic masculinity and heteronormativity that plagues police departments and makes these organizations unsafe for queer individuals. With increased funding for social services to support individuals, diversion programs, and community safety instead of the prison-industrial complex, police departments can be fully reimagined as agencies that support queer individuals for the future safety of all communities instead of the few.

Though police departments have largely neglected to apply queer theory in policies and programs, successful reform has occurred during times of heightened political unrest (Sinclair et al., 2021). This includes policies and programs designed to right past wrongs through the application of a restorative justice lens (McKenna & Holtfreter, 2021) and designed to letting individuals with lived experiences of unjust policing participate in all aspects of the policy-making process (McIntosh & Wright, 2019). As such, the values of advocacy, allyship, and ensuring that community leaders have a place at the table during policy-making have served not only to improve relationships with communities but also to strengthen police legitimacy among community residents.

Applying the tenets of queer theory to the role of LGBTQ+ liaison officers shows there is significant and promising work to be done in both theory and practice. Future research should explore how queer theory and queerness can help policing be a more equitable profession. Decision makers in police departments should consider the structural inequities that have led to the distrust that LGBTQ+ and other vulnerable populations have toward the police and determine what internal change is needed to support communities rather than just police them. Ultimately, there is no quick and easy solution to mending the troubled past of LGBTQ+ and police relations. However, applying queer theory to make more concerted research and practice efforts is a promising first step.

# 12. BLURRING THE BINARIES
## The Experiences of Genderqueer Police Officers

Angela Dwyer, Leah M. Rouse, and Heather Panter

Research demonstrates that police interactions with lesbian and gay (LG) people are marked by discrimination because historical thinking about them as morally deviant continues to inform police thinking (Dwyer & Tomsen, 2016). Quasi-military, masculinist police cultures (Charles & Rouse Arndt, 2013) mean that transgender people are even worse off, being more likely to be arrested (Stotzer, 2014); harassed by police (Grant et al., 2011; Hodge & Sexton, 2020), particularly if they are a person of color (Galvan & Barzargan, 2012; Graham, 2014; Nichols, 2010); and murdered, with police misgendering and deadnaming them during investigation (DeJong et al., 2021). Unfortunately, these types of experiences also infiltrate the lives of LG police officers. Police workplace cultures have improved somewhat in recent decades (Charles & Rouse Arndt, 2013; Hamilton et al., 2019), but with police attitudes continuing to echo ideas about moral perversity (Moton et al., 2020; Myers et al., 2004), LG officers experience discrimination around recruitment, termination, and promotion (Barratt et al., 2014; Galvin-White & O'Neal, 2016; Hodge & Sexton, 2020; Jones & Williams, 2015; Mennicke et al., 2018; Miller & Lilley, 2014; Rennstam & Sullivan, 2018).

Unsurprisingly, the experiences of transgender police officers are markedly worse. Transgender officers routinely have police colleagues who utter transphobic pejoratives, exclude them from girls or guys talk after their gender affirmation, and vandalize their property (Panter, 2017, 2018). They can be excluded from recruitment because they are deemed unable to search women or men and therefore incapable of fulfilling basic policing duties (Little et al., 2002), and if they do manage to be recruited, and affirm their gender in-service, they are demoted, subjected to inappropriate psychological assessment (Mallory et al., 2013), misgendered, or moved into clerical or administrative positions so that the public does not see them.

Although research documenting the experiences of lesbian, gay, and even transgender police officers is increasing, the experiences of police officers who identify as bisexual or genderqueer are relatively unknown. There is some knowledge about bisexual police officers (Jones & Williams, 2015), but it is limited, and beyond the scope of the chapter, which focuses on genderqueer officers. For all we know at this point, genderqueer people (like transgender people) are not even able to be recruited by police organizations, simply because police searches are to be carried out by someone of the same sex and genderqueer people fail to fit in this binary sex-segregated protocol. Genderqueer people may be elided from police recruitment simply because they may not "exist" on police recruitment forms—there is usually no tick box for genderqueer. They may also fail to "fit" with binary sex-segregated fitness test requirements organized around a lower fitness level for female recruits and a higher level of fitness for male recruits. Genderqueer people may be automatically excluded from being recruited by police organizations for all these reasons because police organizational structures implicitly and explicitly discourage them from being part of policing. However, as we argue, we can only surmise about their experiences in policing because the research we need to understand them does not exist.

With more young people now identifying as genderqueer (GLAAD, 2017), and police organizations being pressured to diversify more than ever, we focus here on issues affecting genderqueer officers within and around policing organizations. This chapter preliminarily unpacks some of these issues to better understand how binarized notions of gender impact the lives of genderqueer police officers. Each of us coauthors has experiences and scholarship relevant to this discussion. Rouse has worked as an officer and a psychologist in, and conducted research with, police organizations run by both mainstream and First Nations U.S. policing structures and has observed how the latter organizations tend not to be organized around binary sex-segregated notions of gender. Panter and Dwyer have both done research involving interviews with police officers wherein a few identified as gender-queer. For this chapter, we draw together our limited experiences and data to elaborate on what it means to be genderqueer in the thoroughly gendered world of policing.

First, we highlight the lack of research on the experiences of genderqueer people with police. Second, based on the limited knowledge we have, we propose a series of suppositions about the experiences genderqueer police officers might have in binary-gendered policing organizations. Third, we bend the "rules" of doing qualitative research by analyzing the experiences of three genderqueer police officers we interviewed in past research projects where the experiences of these officers could not be analyzed in their own right because there were so few of them. Fourth, we elaborate on how the practices of some police organizations managed by First Nations people have notions of gender that are more fluid. We conclude with considerations for what policing organizations might rethink in order to ensure the safety and well-being of genderqueer officers in the future.

## What We Know about Genderqueer Police Interactions and Workplace Experiences

The policing experiences of genderqueer people generally tend to be over-looked in, or omitted from, research on policing. There are a few reasons for this. First, mainstream research on policing—focused either on police interactions in the community or on those employed as police—often omits questions about sexuality and gender diversity. Research focuses instead on vulnerabilities like social class and gender (Buist et al., 2018)—and when the focus is gender, it assumes a male-female binary (Valcore & Pfeffer, 2018). Second, when gender diversity is included in research projects, it tends to be an additional variable rather than being the principal focus; and when researchers have collected their data and find too few gender-diverse people to analyze as a group, they omit the results (James et al., 2016). Third, when queer criminological researchers do focus on LGBTQ+ people's experiences of policing, these projects most often do so in terms of the broader acronym, with data about genderqueer people's experiences collapsed into the cate-gory of transgender for analysis (James et al., 2016). Again, the responses of genderqueer people may not be enough to warrant attention if researchers did not undertake targeted recruitment to ensure an adequate number of genderqueer participants in the research sample.

To our knowledge, at the time of writing, no research has explicitly focused only on the policing experiences of genderqueer people, although a recent study included interviews with some genderqueer people in a broader sample (Osborn, 2022a). This is considerably problematic given that estimates suggest that, by 2025, Millennials will represent 75% of the workforce, and they are more than twice as likely to identify as genderqueer or genderfluid than previous generations (GLAAD, 2017). This suggests an urgent need to disaggregate these data and better understand the lived experiences of genderqueer people, both generally and for those working in criminal processing systems.

The scant evidence we do have suggests that, like gay and lesbian people, genderqueer people have not had positive policing experiences, but this evidence is based on research wherein genderqueer identities were collapsed under a "transgender" umbrella. The Transgender Survey of 2015 collected the most comprehensive existing data about the lived experiences of transgender people in the United States and found that 70% of nonbinary/genderqueer people had never or sometimes been treated with respect by police (James et al., 2016). These data were almost an identical match to data collected specifically from nonbinary people in the United Kingdom (Valentine, 2015). Interestingly, this project collected significant data from genderqueer participants (45%), but this was not reported. Nonetheless, 69% of respondents in this survey reported not feeling comfortable with disclosing their status as nonbinary when they were seeking police support. These statistics are concerning, given that we know so little about how genderqueer offenders are treated because "strictly binary, sex-based classification renders them invisible" (Walker et al., 2018, p. 226).

The little we know about police-genderqueer interactions is significant in comparison with what we know about genderqueer police officers: in this area, we know nothing. Research on the experiences of genderqueer people as workers in police organizations does not exist. There may be a range of reasons why this is so, but we suspect one chief reason is that genderqueer police officers do not yet feel safe enough to make their genderqueer identity known to the police organizations they work for.

## What We Might Surmise about Genderqueer People Working as Police

It seems likely that a fear of discrimination, and people hiding their genderqueer identities, might characterize the experiences of genderqueer people working in criminal processing systems. However, we can only surmise that genderqueer police officers may experience discomfort around disclosing their gender identity to work colleagues as we have no research to verify this. As such, our remaining discussion of existing literature consists of three suppositions we might make about what the research could tell us about the experiences of genderqueer people and police officers. We do this so that we can then test these suppositions against the limited data we collected from genderqueer police officers in past research projects with differing methodological approaches and aims.

*Supposition One: Police Culture Would Be a Challenge for Genderqueer Police*

We surmise that the binary sex-segregated organizational structure of Western police organizations, and the masculinist police culture that permeates these organizations (Moton et al., 2020), intimates that genderqueer police officers may be subject to harassment and discrimination from fellow officers and police managers. Police organizations are saturated with, and iteratively reproduce, socialized expectations of what it means to be a "man" in line with notions of hegemonic masculinity (Connell & Messerschmidt, 2005). These expectations are heteronormative (i.e., sexual relationships are between members of opposite sexes) and cisnormative (i.e., the outward appearance of a person assigned male at birth should be masculine), and the practices from these expectations marginalize any men deemed nonmasculine or nonheterosexual, while also sustaining and legitimizing the subordination of women. Nonbinary people in the work of Osborn (2022b) noted how they "felt particularly unsafe in spaces dominated by straight cisgender men" (p. 65), such as police organizations are. We have no evidence about how genderqueer police officers might be perceived in police organizations, but we can surmise they would have challenging and harmful experiences based on the negative experiences of gay, lesbian, bisexual, and transgender police officers. Previous research demonstrates immense pressure for LG officers to conform to feminine or masculine appearance and behavioral expectations (Myers et al., 2004). This has been corroborated by research focused on the experiences of transgender and gender-diverse workers generally (Boncori et al., 2019).

*Supposition Two: Genderqueer Police Would Be Harassed by Police Colleagues*

We surmise that genderqueer police officers would experience harassment and discrimination from their police colleagues, and likely they also encounter ignorance, as have police officers identifying as transgender (Panter,

2017, 2018). Research suggests that discrimination and harassment of gay and lesbian police officers has decreased somewhat in recent time (Jones & Williamson, 2015), but these advances have happened in the context of heteronormative and cisnormative expectations of hegemonic masculinity. Research also shows the substantially harmful experiences of transgender police officers in this organizational context (Panter, 2018), evidence suggesting that genderqueer police officers likely have to contend with similar forms of harassment and discrimination because their identity as a genderqueer person does not "fit" with sex-segregated policing structures and environments. We know that gay- and lesbian-identifying police leaders can act as important mentors and supports for other gay and lesbian police officers, but research intimates that harassment and discrimination can prevail in situations where police managers have discretion to make decisions around personal matters (Colvin, 2012; Jones, 2015). Just as gay male police officers need to manage personal risk by being hypervigilant about whom they disclose their identity to (Collins & Rocco, 2015), genderqueer officers might also manage these risks by masking their gender identity and aligning their appearance and behaviors with their sex assigned at birth. Research already shows that genderqueer people are managing the risks of disclosing their identity to colleagues and managers in other organizations (Boncori et al., 2019).

*Supposition Three: Genderqueer Officers Would Experience Discomfort in Sex-Segregated Police Spaces and Operations*

We surmise that police uniforms, central to policing's "blue identities" (Charles & Rouse Arndt, 2013; Mendoza & Parks-Stamm, 2019) and a key influencer of collective and individual perceptions (Johnson et al., 2014), would present a considerable challenge for genderqueer police officers. Research demonstrates that police uniforms have an especially significant role in how officers feel ambitious, authoritative, trustworthy, and powerful (Mendoza & Parks-Stamm, 2019), as well as providing them with essential tactical tools for doing policing. We suggest that the key concern for genderqueer police officers would be how the uniforms are typically sex-segregated and characteristically masculine in their shape and styling. Police officers undertaking gender-affirmation processes might be provided with a choice to wear the male or female uniform of their police organization, but they may find themselves being pushed to wear the uniform that aligns with their sex assigned at birth or their sex as affirmed.

Research highlights how genderqueer people tend toward fluidity with expression of their gender identities rather than being inclined toward one in a binary presentation of masculine or feminine (James et al., 2016). This means genderqueer people may prefer flexibility in moving between uniform styles rather than being locked into one sex-specific style of uniform, or they may prefer a non-sexed/gendered style of uniform. Police uniform policies, and more traditional-thinking police leaders on uniform committees, may not allow this fluidity and instead insist on sex-segregated uniform styling. This has been evidenced in research with transgender police officers who were punished for uniform violations involving hair, fingernail length, and makeup (Panter 2018). Resistance can even come from members of the public, with one nonbinary police officer noting in a newspaper interview that they had received "interesting comments" from people, shaped by cisnormative expectations about how police officers should be gendered in their appearance, including being asked if they had lost a bet (Reyna-Rodriguez, 2019).

We further surmise that other job structures and processes organized around sex segregation would create challenges for genderqueer officers, particularly bathrooms, online and paper-based forms, change and locker rooms, and search procedures. Research on nonbinary people found that they felt significantly vulnerable to harm in sex-segregated public bathrooms, with participants reporting having delayed going to the toilet for many hours because they feared their appearance would not "pass" in either a female or a male public restroom: "Using the male restroom, or even the women's restroom, was just like completely not okay for me" (Osborn, 2022b, p. 64). We surmise that genderqueer police officers are equally likely to feel vulnerable and uncomfortable in sex-segregated bathrooms in police organizations, in addition to other sex-segregated processes. Substantial and costly changes would be needed to ensure that bathrooms, forms, change and locker rooms, and search procedures were reorganized in ways that were not sex-segregated. This is a challenging process to undertake, considering that even mixed-gender double-crewing responses have been seen to be more effective (gender double-crewing is where police respond to call outs in a pair of one male and one female officer; New Zealand Police Association, 2021), and sometimes these arrangements are mandated. The very fabric of doing police work is organized in sex-segregated ways, and the underlying assumption is that these ways of working are most effective and safe.

Finally, we surmise that the binary understandings of gender that implicitly inform police culture would be challenging to navigate for genderqueer officers. Even casual talk between police colleagues around the water cooler or a break room table, in conversations touching on relationships or what officers did over the weekend, can be heavily heteronormative and cisnormative. For instance, genderqueer officers may be considered "unfit" by their colleagues to undertake police tasks like police searches, and even the public may object, simply because genderqueer officers fail to meet expectations for sex-segregated procedures. Members of the public are entitled to request a person of the same gender to undertake invasive, intimate searches, meaning that genderqueer officers could be pushed to align themselves with a binary gender to be considered "fit" to conduct these searches. Some evidence supports this, with research finding that transgender people seeking police work have been rejected because they failed to meet the requirement for sex-segregated search protocols (Little et al., 2002).

## Experiences of Genderqueer Officers in Our Research

As noted above, the authors of this chapter have interviewed police officers who identify as lesbian, gay, bisexual, and transgender in research projects. While undertaking this research, we also interviewed officers who identify as genderqueer, yet we have not been able to analyze these interviews because there were too few of them in our respective projects to enable generalizable discussion or analysis across multiple participants. Given the lack of research capturing genderqueer narratives, we bend the rules of "good" research and attempt to highlight the issues raised in three interviews with genderqueer officers. We do this with a view to indicating what the key concerns are for these officers, while also pointing out the urgent need for further research and significant cultural change within police organizations. Most importantly, we do this as a way of honoring the stories these officers shared with us. We structure our discussion of them in terms of "testing" the three suppositions that we elaborated above.

Protecting the anonymity of these interviewees is crucial and a matter of genuine safety. In all cases, we researchers made more extensive efforts than usual to allay the very real, lived, and reiterated (in the interviews) fears of these participants and to ensure them that we would keep their identities confidential. As such, we mention here only that the interviewees held different ranks (constable, sergeant) in policing organizations in different Western countries (United Kingdom, United States, Australia). They had all worked for their policing organization for 10–15 years. None of the three officers identified as non-white. We refer to the three interviewees according to the gender identity category they mentioned during their interview. The interviewees each had their own way of identifying as a genderqueer person, namely, as genderqueer, gender-blur, or gender-neutral.

*Police Culture and Disclosure as a Challenge for Genderqueer Police*

The influence of police culture was clearly indicated by our genderqueer interviewees, but the culture had shaped their experiences in a range of different ways. One of the key measures of police culture they discussed was disclosure: if genderqueer officers could disclose their status safely and comfortably to anyone they worked with, this seemed to indicate that their workplace police culture was supportive of genderqueer police officers. Unfortunately, comments from the interviewees evidenced that the culture of their organizations was not safe or comfortable enough for disclosure most of the time. They articulated a range of fears they had around this, including "fear of gossip in the workplace" (gender-blur). Generally, the interviewees described more significant impacts after they had begun to make changes to their appearance (such as "increased hair length and slowed beard removal" [gender-blur]) and throughout the process of affirming their gender, including "extended discriminations," which "eventually impacted my confidence, concentration, financial state/saving, health and well-being" (gender-blur).

The culture of their employing police organizations was not at a point where genderqueer police officers could disclose their identities without experiencing significant negative impact. This was highlighted in comments from the gender-neutral officer when they talked about whether there were other genderqueer officers in their organization:

> I actually think we do have one. I can't confirm this, but from my understanding, we do have one officer that openly identifies as gender neutral in [police organization redacted]. Yeah, look, like I said, that's only hearsay. I haven't met this person—I've only been told by other people. And again, the rumor mill can be quite horrible at times. That was my understanding, so I don't know if it is, or it isn't, the case.

The existence of other genderqueer officer colleagues in 2020, the year the interview took place, was tentative and grounded in hearsay and rumor rather than knowledge that another officer had disclosed their genderqueer status to police colleagues and leaders.

Interviewees discussed that they had learned how and where to disclose diverse identities from previously disclosing sexuality diversity; disclosure of any form of less-than-visible diversity evidently had impacted the lived experiences of officers. Sometimes these disclosures were initiated by the officer themselves, but at other times confidential information about their genderqueer status was shared with others without their consent (gender-blur). The genderqueer officer interviewed reflected on this in relation to when they made the decision to have top surgery:

> At that point, I then had to disclose to the manager at work . . . which because of my previous experience and how, um . . . my sexuality . . . I felt it would be used against me. I thought, "Great I survived being a gay woman and now I am going to come across as someone who is genderqueer, which most people won't understand." Um . . . so I am going to be very, very careful about this . . . I am going to be very cautious about who I tell, which led me to probably be a little bit isolated on my team. (genderqueer)

Not disclosing the important life event of top surgery to police colleagues led to their feeling isolated from their team, a significant impact for this genderqueer officer in a policing environment heavily reliant on teams. This isolation, emerging out of a generalized mistrust of their policing colleagues, provides a glimpse of the police cultures these officers work in. A police culture where they were able to disclose their identity without fear had not yet been achieved by their employing organizations.

Mistrust was a key issue, and this materialized mostly around disclosure of their genderqueer identity. The gender-blur officer had a particularly challenging trajectory in this respect: from disclosing during private conversations between individual officers, all the way through to a high-ranking officer "holding court" and publicly disclosing their genderqueer identity at a social event with many officers present. Disclosure of confidential information about their genderqueer status was experienced as "a huge betrayal," and it made them feel "shocked, disgusted, and sick and sweaty" and overall "so vulnerable" (gender-blur). The officer was repeatedly challenged on why they had longer hair, why they were seeking a different uniform, why they had changed their name, and why they had longer fingernails. All these things were discussed with officers in managerial positions in the police organization before the genderqueer officer proceeded with gender affirmation, yet other officers in their work area continually challenged them. Even when the changes being undertaken aligned with organizational policies, other officers made derogatory statements about the appearance of the officer. For instance, after informing police managers about growing their hair longer, an inspector in their work area asked why their hair was longer, and they were told their appearance made other officers think that they were "a mess and could not do the job" (gender-blur). Other officers threatened to cut their hair, and they were summoned to explain the changes to their hair with the superintendent, even though "my hair was not contrary to the dress code policy" (gender-blur). They were also "instructed to write reports about my hair intentions." Eventually, the harassment evolved to "complete blanking" and "strategic avoidance" by senior officer managers, culminating in the officer begging to be moved to another department. Staggeringly, just two months after this move, in what could be described only as an astonishing betrayal of trust by the organization, the key officer involved in the harassment and discrimination toward the gender-blur officer was moved into the same area they had been moved to. In an organization where legitimacy hinges entirely upon police officers completing their work in ways that align with an unspoken expectation of trust (Jackson et al., 2012), the experiences of this officer represent glaring examples of breaching trust.

When agreed-upon disclosures were made by genderqueer police officers, they were heavily managed by police supervisors. For instance, the gender-queer officer talked about the need to do this after "a two-year journey to try and access hormones":

> at that point, myself and my training department sat down with my team and said "Right, this is what is happening . . . this is where I am coming from. Anybody got any questions . . . um . . . feel free to ask away within certain boundaries. If you have questions later on . . . you want to ask, then feel free to ask . . . you can meet me personally, or you can put it to my supervisor, and I will do my best to address any concerns you got." My team was basically, ya know, more concerned to whether I was going to carry on being part of the team than anything else [laughter]. (genderqueer)

This officer had a positive experience with disclosing their genderqueer identity to other police colleagues, but this did not happen just once. Like the experiences of disclosure for other transgender, and even sexuality-diverse people, disclosure was a reiterative process marked by caution and hyper-vigilance:

> For me it is always gonna be a little bit different because I identify as genderqueer. So, I always got the question of: do I say something or don't I? And experience has taught me, it is not relevant—just do the job. In fact, I had a very interesting experience because my supervisor . . . when she asked me, "Do I call you 'he' or 'she?'" I said, "If you are going to make me choose a binary, then I will go as 'she'" because I was quite a butch girl before and I don't see myself as a guy, so you can make me the butchest girl you have ever known [laughter]. (genderqueer)

Disclosure was not a singular or linear process for the genderqueer officer—it was a reiterative process of careful decision-making depending on officers involved.

Importantly, although disclosure was a decision made by two officers interviewed (genderqueer and gender-blur), it was impossible for the gender-neutral officer. Police culture in their organization meant that disclosing their status as a genderqueer person was too challenging. The gender-neutral officer explained that they chiefly "identify as gay . . . there are some other categories I use, but in a work sense I only use that. On the rest, it gets too hard for everyone to work to understand, so I don't bother with it at work." The officer had learned about what types of queer identities are more acceptable in the culture of their police organization, and this meant the officer had made the decision not to disclose their genderqueer identity:

> I actually identify as gender neutral, but I just don't bring that into the workplace because it's just too hard for people to understand. Yeah, like I don't think I could tell anyone at work that I was taking some form of hormone replacement therapy; they just wouldn't understand. So, I just leave it completely—it's just, it is what it is. (gender-neutral)

General interactions in their workplace were what indicated to them that disclosing a genderqueer identity was "just too hard." For instance, when asked about their experiences of discrimination in their workplace, they noted "nothing major through work" but went on say, "in more recent times with a lot of the talk about gender, I've had people having conversations around me, and I've tried to like steer them in the right way, but that's, that's not directed at me or anything" (gender-neutral). These conversations were evidence enough for this officer that colleagues were not in a place where they were ready to understand and accept a genderqueer colleague.

Comments from the genderqueer interviewees highlighted that what is needed is "a society change" to create a safe police workplace for genderqueer officers and that more time was needed to make this achievable. The gender-neutral officer suggested that, over time, things might change within the organization that would make it possible to be an "out" genderqueer officer, but that would take considerable time: "I think it's just a thing that it's just gonna come over time as generationally it becomes more accepted. Even how it has been for gay people, it's become more and more accepted as times passed on." However, the gender-neutral officer clarified that the culture in their organization was not at that point of change and understanding yet. When asked about whether they could ask a person what pronouns they used, the gender-neutral officer answered, "I don't think we're quite in a space where people are used to using non-gendered pronouns on a regular basis, especially in this job." Individual police colleagues they worked with really mattered; if other police colleagues chose not to change their thinking, then culture change in police organizations was not possible. As the genderqueer officer suggested, "you can have all the best policies in the world . . . as I have learned . . . but it comes down to personnel, and they can decide to ignore those policies and take it into their own hands." A police organization might be taking steps to change police culture, but individual officers still had the discretion to ignore those changes.

## Genderqueer Police Experienced Ignorance from Police Colleagues

In contrast with the discrimination and violence experienced by transgender officers (Panter, 2017), genderqueer officers mainly experienced ignorance around gender diversity. The exception to this was the gender-blur officer, who, short of experiencing violence, experienced significant and ongoing discrimination. Interviewees mentioned discriminatory experiences of other genderqueer officers they had heard about, such as one being referred unnecessarily for a psychiatric assessment and another being subject to nonconsensual disclosure of their identity among medical professionals. This is not to say that genderqueer officers do not experience discrimination and violence more broadly—it is just that this was not the case for the three officers we interviewed. Many comments in the interviews reflected how the ignorance of police colleagues produced awkward, uncomfortable, emotionally harmful, and traumatic experiences for genderqueer officers. This is highlighted well by comments from two interviewees:

I can come into this section, and I probably have out of 50 people, maybe 10 that would fully understand it [gender diversity] if I was lucky. I don't see it being fixed anytime soon. I think you've still got some people with their own ideas. I had a full-blown argument with someone the other day about them being pissed off about the use of bathrooms and trans people using bathrooms, so it's just dependent on the people. (gender-neutral)

This is to a certain extent why I don't always declare that I am gender-queer . . . because it is hard enough for people to get their heads around the fact that people go from A to Z . . . without people like me who go from A to Q and stop along the way. (genderqueer)

Ignorance about gender diversity was regularly navigated by the gender-neutral police officer, and these interactions were stressful and emotionally draining. They reflected on this further into their interview when they discussed their role as an LGBTQ+ police liaison officer and the types of support they provided to other officers. They talked about how "the main thing" they provided support about was "struggl[ing] to understand your transgender or gender-neutral spaces in recent times." They noted this is vastly different from police understandings about sexuality diversities: "I don't really get anyone coming and asking, 'I don't understand gay people at all.' I think everyone has got somewhat of a grasp on that, but it's just all this new, everyone's got their own opinions, and some of them are very old school." Police understood sexuality diversity in their employing organization, but an understanding of "new" ideas about gender diversity was significantly lacking. Later in the interview, the gender-neutral officer explained that police officers who joined their organization from other jurisdictions, particularly jurisdictions with more cultural and gender diversity overall, are more comfortable talking about gender diversity and have more developed understandings of the issues:

Funnily enough, I find a lot of ex [other jurisdiction] coppers, like the people that are from the [other jurisdiction] come and join the service. Obviously, there's a lot more diversity in [other jurisdiction], so they bring that diversity with them. They're a lot more easy to talk to about it. (gender-neutral)

The genderqueer officers understood well when officers had more knowledge about gender diversity, or when officers were ignorant of the issues, and were more comfortable talking to officers with better knowledge about it.

## Genderqueer Officers Experienced Discomfort in Sex-Segregated Police Spaces and Operations

A range of issues related to the sex-segregated nature of police spaces and operations came up in the interviews. Some of these were straightforward structural issues needing to be addressed. For instance, the gender-neutral officer said, "we have literally a tick box that's male or female on a charge record—there's no other box you can tick," and they mentioned later in the interview that this would be an area for improvement. Searching people was also brought up, with the genderqueer officer speaking at length about historical changes around the legalities of searches by transgender police officers. They noted, for example, how some police organizations managed this in the beginning by issuing transgender people "a search exemption certificate; so if you went into the custody block and someone said, 'Search that guy,' you would bring out your little certificate and go, 'But I can't. I can't search that guy because, ya know, I am exempt.'" The genderqueer officer went on to argue with their organization that having an exemption certificate was in fact discriminatory, using the example of a transgender man in their police workplace: "you are constantly expecting him to excuse himself from searches. He is constantly being outed to colleagues who don't know that he is trans at all . . . it is degrading." Importantly, the interviewee also noted that this system could further isolate transgender police officers who have not acquired a Gender Identity Certificate (a document in the United Kingdom showing that a person has undertaken procedures to affirm their gender) because they are not undergoing medical gender affirmation:

> So if you got a trans member of your team, and you think he can never bloody search anyone because he doesn't have his paperwork, then that is a real pain in the ass, and he is not pulling his weight. He is gonna feel isolated and be judged against him. (genderqueer)

The genderqueer officer ended this discussion by arguing that an officer should be allowed to negotiate and establish "mutual consent for searches," where both the officer and the person being searched are aware of the circumstances of the search and they both consent to it. In support of the argument, the genderqueer officer offered some compelling examples:

> You have a white supremacist who you have locked up for being racist. If he is gonna be searched by a B&E [black and ethnic] officer, you may find he is not really happy with that. How are you going to deal with that? . . .

You have locked up someone from the BNP [British National Party] or the National Front. You have a quite camp officer that might be gay, or might not be gay, but everyone else thinks they are gay, and he says, "No way am I being searched by him." How will you deal with that? . . . There has to be a better flexibility in it. (genderqueer)

This discussion highlights the messy, complex environment of police searches when the identities of police officers do not match with the sex-segregated procedure. Ironically, implementing even more stringent, inflexible processes to maintain the clear "line" between the sexes in these processes can serve to further marginalize genderqueer officers.

What featured prominently in the interviews, though, was how sex-segregated practices in police organizations most often became discriminatory because police managers had the discretion to intervene and manipulate these practices. This theme is highlighted well by the experiences of the gender-blur officer. For instance, the length of their hair was repeatedly the subject of disparaging comments: "each time my hair got too long," one inspector "insisted that I got it cut, and for a few months, and for just an easier life, I complied without grumble" (gender-blur). As was noted above, even though their hair did not breach the policy for hair length, their hair was the subject of comments because it disrupted cisgender ideas about how a binary-sexed body should display gender identity: "I would not recommend growing your hair in my force or being anything different than whatever pre-decided boxes you are expected to be in to progress nicely" (gender-blur).

The gender-blur officer spoke of having similar experiences concerning uniforms. Their police organization went through an update of the uniforms, and the officer "made [for me] the huge decision to request female 'blacks' uniform. After a clear and confidential conversation explaining my wishes/needs, this was issued without incident . . . as the force's dress code policy supports such." However, a month later the problematic inspector stated that uniform stores had questioned the request, and the officer had to provide "further and extensive personal details" so that the uniform request could be processed. Another month following this request, the officer was informed by people they knew that "uniform stores are telling people you are having a sex change," and they learned that the people working in uniform stores had told other people their confidential information. As was the case with hairstyle, the gender-blur officer was discriminated against by decision makers involved in issuing sex-segregated uniforms. Even though organizational policy meant that this process should have been simple, the (in)discretion and decision-making of police colleagues created further discrimination for this officer, which for them felt like "being back to school and there being a bully in the playground and you're not sure when he's going to pick on you next, but you know there will be a next time, and it will hurt" (gender-blur).

*Suggestions for Improvement*

Genderqueer officers made multiple suggestions for improving their own circumstances and those of other genderqueer officers in the future. Passing mentions were made of initiatives related to changing police organizational structures, such as the need to "update all their forms to begin with . . . once that's finalized to get some further training on where we go from there" (gender-neutral). However, the chief focus of discussion was what the gender-neutral officer called "big hurdles" when it came to changing police culture over time. In their discussion of this, this officer oscillated "between gay men and, I would think, anyone that was openly transgender. I think that would be the two big hurdles" in changing police culture to the point where these officers would feel comfortable and safe to disclose their identities in the workplace. Unsurprisingly, the other initiative mentioned for culture change was initial, further, and ongoing training with all police officers. The gender-neutral officer elaborated this point well: training needed to cover "how you navigate dealing with persons who identify as transgender or gender neutral in the future." The genderqueer officer stated that initiatives focused on police cultural change were imperative because "it is always going to be difficult for trans people to be treated equally because people can't relate to that difference when their gender identity . . . and their gender presentation doesn't stack up . . . [T]o try understanding when that doesn't is very difficult."

Diversifying the workforce of their employing organization was also recognized as a way of improving police culture to make it safe and comfortable for genderqueer police in the future. They suggested that police organizations employ more transgender and genderqueer police officers. For instance, the gender-neutral officer claimed their police organization "could really help gay males or transgender people" by "hir[ing] more" gay and transgender people, but the possibility of doing this was contingent on a range of different factors. For instance, the gender-neutral officer went on to state that ultimately "you've gotta have them [transgender and gay people] wanting to join and be right for the job. . . . [Y]ou got to find and attract those people to this, this career." This officer was skeptical about the capacity of their police organization to recruit transgender or gay people. The comments of the genderqueer officer were different from those of the gender-neutral officer, because they were not focused specifically on the need to recruit more diverse people, but their comments nonetheless reflected on how people who have lived experience with diversities will be more open to gender diversity:

> I remember trying to explain to a guy . . . "I don't identify as a guy or a girl, and I know that sounds weird," and he goes, "No, not really." He said, "I am half Black and I am half white, and I always have had an issue with one community that don't accept me. The Black community never accept me, and the white community doesn't accept me, so I am sort of stuck in the middle." He said, "I kind of know where you are coming from," and I haven't thought of it that way. (genderqueer)

Although the officers mentioned different types of initiatives that might be useful for pushing cultural change forward in their police organizations, their interviews were also characterized by a sense of defeat and perhaps even exhaustion. For instance, the gender-neutral officer stated that "how they [police managers/organizations] get them [police officers] across that, I don't know."

## Gender in First Nations Police Organizations

Police organizations of the United States, United Kingdom, and Australia are structured around Western mainstream values and conceptualizations. This is an epistemology influenced by Judeo-Christian values of gender and sexuality, which are inherently tied to conceptualizations about power dynamics and social order. However, sovereign First Nations of the Americas are also in the West, and these cultures and languages are not marked by binary constructs of gender, sexuality, and roles. First Nations cultures and origin stories articulate an array of what the mainstream refers to as genders:

> Gender in [First Nations'] worldview and languages does not recognize a binary, with most having three or four genders framed via Creation and Original Instructions teachings. First Nations languages tend to be heavily verb-based and describe the relationships among entities. These relationships are articulated in traditional teachings that relate role and purpose for an individual, community, or Nation. Role is generally not ascribed by gender or biological sex, but by one's purpose—a more

spiritual and interpersonal template. Similar groups have been identified in the literature on masculinities (e.g., Gilmore's, 1990, comments on the Tahitians and Semai). The psychological literature addressing First Nations groups, Native Hawaiians, Pacific Islanders, and many other traditionalist Indigenous groups demonstrates significant parallels by worldview. (Rouse, 2016, p. 320)

Within First Nations groups, the roles related to what constitutes mainstream policing are different as well. Although the structures vary widely, an overall better conceptualization of the role of law enforcement within First Nations' worldview would be that of the protector, rather than the enforcer. The primary responsibility of the protector is to act as a role model of good community and individual conduct, a mentor and teacher.

Although an overview of the legal and administrative history organizing First Nations' governance post-colonization and their police departments is beyond the scope of this chapter, some mention is critical. First Nations communities have all been highly disrupted by the colonizing impact of European countries. Communities that have been able to retain traditional teachings, language, and culture are logically more likely to have traditional orientations in their "policing" structures, as are those organized by First Nations communities themselves rather than by the influence of mainstream governance structures like the United States Bureau of Indian Affairs.

Consider as one example the tribal police department with which Rouse is currently a coordinating psychologist contracted by the agency. The agency is seated within what mainstream anthropology refers to as the tribe's matriarchal, matrilineally oriented nation, a nation that has access to traditional cultural practices and guidance, and also first-language resources and teachers. In mainstream terms, the tribe's policing agency employs 6 women and 12 men. One of three agency leaders is a woman. These numbers, even within the gender binary construct, are significantly more balanced than within the mainstream profession, which has women making up 13% of sworn personnel (Crooke, 2013). Two members of the agency have identified as genderfluid, one of the three consulting psychologists as lesbian, and one as intersex. Given the small size of the agency, these numbers are remarkable and seem to indicate something different is happening here to make way for such diversity of expression and role (whether gender or protector/enforcer).

The Navajo, or Diné, Nation Police Department is one of the largest tribal police departments in the United States and employs 183 men and 48 women in sworn positions, at the time of writing this chapter, which again is remarkably more diverse in terms of binary gender than the mainstream rate (*Women encouraged to join*, 2017). No information is available on gender diversity among its sworn personnel, but given the prominent role of fluid gender, and the matriarchal, matrilineal nature of the Diné culture, it would stand to reason that diversity abounds there too:

> The Diné have generally treated intersex and gender-variant individuals similarly, with both as normative. Although a complete relating of the teachings is not appropriate for this chapter or any other written format, Diné Creation and Instructions stories relate the transient and purposeful nature of all existence, with a central character being Changing Woman.[1] Changing Woman embodies all that is "male" and "female" and the *hózhó* (balance–harmony–beauty) of all within nature. From a traditional Indigenous perspective, physical presentation is viewed as malleable, cyclical, and transient. (Rouse, 2016, p. 321–322)

Though even First Nations policing agencies have their modern-day origins in mainstream structures and worldview, many have retained culturally congruent values and structures within these systems. This is not to say, however, that these systems cannot be influenced by the colonization effect on their communities and the individuals within the agencies (e.g., individuals having little acculturation to their nation's original teachings). Some agencies also employ non–tribal members and non–First Nations personnel, and all agencies must deal with mainstream law enforcement. Thus, even when a tribe prioritizes traditional roles, other influences can creep in. For example, the following story was shared by a nonbinary-identified sworn member of a tribal agency: "We were all standing around talking about a call, and the supervisor who was a tribal member and sent to the call said he refused to address the individual as 'they.' He stood right next to me."

Though First Nations policing agencies may not offer the ideal world for accommodating diversity, they do offer an excellent opportunity for exploration. Within many First Nations, people construed as gender-nonconforming by the mainstream are in fact normative within Indigenous worldviews and often hold critical roles within societal structures and the spiritual worldview. Perhaps the idea of diversity training in policing can draw upon these worldview constructs as alternative ways of performing the duties of policing, and organizing the agencies' related structures, rather than focusing on individuals. This is another core difference between mainstream and First

Nations' worldviews, the latter being much more focused on the good of all and being a good relative and less on having people conform. There are many ways to express being a good relative.

## Conclusion

This chapter examined the experiences of genderqueer officers in the United States, United Kingdom, and Australia. It highlighted the lack of empirical attention paid to genderqueer people in queer criminology and within policing studies in general. As such, this chapter outlined (despite scant literature) what studies have shown regarding police interactions with genderqueer people. Further, from a theoretical perspective, this chapter examined the obstacles that exist for genderqueer people within police culture(s) in which heteronormative and cisnormative expectations are rigidly maintained and regulated and which form an occupational barrier toward positive acceptance within policing. Occupational and socialization barriers exist within sex-segregated police spaces, gendered uniforms, and administrative work policies regarding genderqueer police.

Unlike other research that examined genderqueer experiences collectively with other transgender people, this chapter focused solely on genderqueer occupational experiences in policing. Relying on three interviews, this study identified issues with genderqueer disclosure (coming out to colleagues) and the fears surrounding identity disclosure. Further, occupational uniform and dress code policies were cited as issues that resulted in administrative punishment. For example, genderqueer officers described challenges they had faced with how they present themselves at work, which conflict with their identity development. Their experiences show how uniform and dress code policies are used administratively by police managers as a tool to enforce heteronormative and cisnormative conformity within policing. Moreover, the exclusion and isolation felt by genderqueer officers was mentioned when they recounted incidents of workplace bias (apart from administrative punishments), particularly in sex-segregated police spaces or in sex-segregated job roles such as police searches. All these things meant that the experiences of genderqueer officers are elided and erased in doing the work of policing.

What do policing organizations need to do to move forward so that binarized notions of gender are overcome? Remedies like gender-neutral toilets would begin to make police spaces more comfortable for genderqueer officers, but this would only be the beginning. A complete rethinking of how police processes and structures are built would also be required to ensure that genderqueer officers feel comfortable working in policing organizations. We would argue for the need to Indigenize policing, focusing on First Nations' values of being a good relative and recognizing gender fluidity rather than the construct of diversity.

We suggest several occupational improvements that should occur within policing to encourage more socialized acceptance of genderqueer people: making changes to current uniform and dress code policies to support genderqueer people, introducing gender-neutral toilets, reassessing gendered policies, taking steps to improve cultural perceptions by recruiting more genderqueer officers for effective representation, and decolonizing and undoing cisnormative practices within police training. We recommend that further studies examine best practices for implementing these suggested changes while also considering a range of intersectional components when examining genderqueer identities within policing. We need to know what genderqueer police experience on the job so that we can begin to unpack these lived experiences and make their voices count in policy development in police organizations.

*Note*

1. The Diné term is intentionally not included here to respect the way such knowledge is meant to be conveyed, which is not in writings such as this chapter. Further, the being is not considered fully woman or man but rather the wholeness that is humanity and other beings.

# CONCLUSION

Roddrick Colvin, Angela Dwyer, and Sulaimon Giwa

With the ever-increasing tensions emerging around police and vulnerable populations, this volume exemplifies a relatively fledgling imperative task: to sustain a critical research focus on the relations between LGBTQ+ people and police. The recent surge in projects focused on these interactions in criminology has adeptly highlighted that they can be challenging, violent, and discriminatory, and mutual mistrust heavily influences this (Calhoun, 2017; Colvin, 2014; Dario et al., 2019; Dwyer, 2011a, 2014a; Dwyer et al., 2015; Guadalupe-Diaz, 2016; Hodge & Sexton, 2020; Leonard & Fileborn, 2018; Mallory et al., 2015; McCandless, 2018b; Miles-Johnson, 2015; Owen et al., 2018; Pickles, 2020; Williams & Robinson, 2004). The growing anti-police sentiment among LGBTQ+ communities around the world exacerbates these problematic relationships (Holmes, 2021), as does the unresolved tension in social movements between those who want to exclude police organizations from participating in Pride and other celebratory events and those who support their participation (Giwa et al., 2021; Gregoire, 2022).

Our purpose in compiling this volume was this: make the first attempt to draw together a diverse range of voices on the topic of police-LGBTQ+ relations using varied empirical and conceptual approaches. With contributions covering a spectrum of perspectives, from community activists and leaders, police officers, and social work practitioners, we sought to think through these relations in a broader context. The volume therefore covers an expansive and contentious territory, but this is necessary to delve deeply and move beyond what is already known about this topic. Undertaking this project has highlighted some key areas on which to focus future research inquiries.

## Future Research Focus on Intersectionality

The primary point emerging is the importance of a sustained focus on, and broadening of, an intersectional consideration of these issues. The chapters in parts 1 and 2 of this volume strongly demonstrate the need to decenter the Westernized, Global North ways of thinking about LGBTQ–police relations and to move instead toward a more thorough consideration of the issues by drawing on Global South knowledges and approaches. Chapters in the volume highlight without doubt that the experiences of LGBTQ+ people worsen when the person that police interact with is also a person of color, and/or a person with disability, and/or a person with limited resources, and/or a person experiencing a mental health crisis. These and many other forms of vulnerability may coalesce in the lived experiences of LGBTQ+ people, meaning their experience with police can be heavily influenced by these factors.

The need to persist with a focus on intersectionality is most clearly illustrated by the research in this volume showing how ethnicity and race continue to negatively influence LGBTQ–police interactions. The policing experiences of LGBTQ+ people of color are characterized by mistrust, discrimination, harassment, and violence. Parts 1 and 2 demonstrate how imperative it is that future research continue to parse out the uniquely challenging experiences of LGBTQ+ people of color. Unpacking these experiences and making them known to police organizations around the world is of especial urgency in the current social context, where we are witnessing a resurgence in white supremacist activities that seem to be targeting LGBTQ+ rights movements and activism. Further to this aim, research needs to focus on the Global South and the state of LGBTQ–police relations in developing nations where human rights are less prioritized in everyday policing practices (Giwa et al. 2020) and where the conditions for people in prisons and police custody are evidently adverse.

## Future Research Focus on Evaluating Policing Cultures and Practices

The chapters of this volume indicate an imperative need for further research exploring police organizational cultures and the policing methods and practices that emerge out of these cultures. The research showcased demonstrates well the ongoing challenges faced not only by LGBTQ+ people interacting with police organizations but also by LGBTQ+ people working within these organizations. It highlights the need for researchers to maintain their examination of current policing methods and practices, especially when most of them that impact the lives of LGBTQ+ people, and vulnerable people generally, are devised by people working within police organizations, both civilian and sworn, and typically without consulting LGBTQ+ people. If future policing practices are going to be in any way safer, researchers need to document and understand more fully the impact that police cultures have on decision-making affecting the lives of LGBTQ+ people, both those working for police organizations and those living outside them.

The impact of police culture is another reason why we need to maintain a research focus on individual LGBTQ+ experiences with police. Research must further unpack and document intersectional vulnerabilities and how they influence policing interactions because police organizations are often under-resourced in ways that would enable significant revision of ingrained hypermasculine police cultures. This is especially important in the context of the expanding militarization of police organizations, the increasing reliance on lethal weaponry, and the further embedding of the idea of police officer as warrior. Although police organizations arguably exist to serve and protect, there is not enough emphasis on developing the skills of police officers that would make the basic protection of vulnerable people possible. Shifts in police culture and practice are happening alongside movements away from ideas that police officers are de-escalation and negotiation experts. Research evidence demonstrates that de-escalation, verbal negotiation, and social support should characterize respectful responses to vulnerable people in crisis in public spaces. With police cultures drifting farther away from these forms of police practice, it is imperative that research challenge how policing is done with vulnerable people, including LGBTQ+ people. Research also needs to substantiate that police organizations are making progress inside the organization in addition to outward-facing work that forges better relationships with LGBTQ+ communities.

## Where to from Here?

We suggest that the chapters in this volume point out the need for a fundamental shift in how we examine police work, police culture, and the policies and practices that police cultures develop. If indeed we are to create police organizations that serve and protect LGBTQ+ people in future, there is substantial work to be done by researchers. There is much still to document about every identity of the LGBTQ+ acronym and the distinctive challenges they face when interacting with police in private and public spaces. We need to better understand the deep injustices manifested in the behavior of police officers, often trained with a warrior mindset, when interacting with LGBTQ+ people who are experiencing multiple forms of vulnerability. We need new and innovative ways of conceptualizing and documenting these interactions to ensure that we fully understand what is required of police organizations that can protect LGBTQ+ people.

Most importantly, academics, activists, and community leaders (and we hope police officers and leaders!) must maintain conversations about these issues to ensure that new research influences how police policy and practice develops in the future. While there are increasingly vehement calls from LGBTQ+ communities to walk away from, and reject engagement with, police organizations, the chapters in this volume show the imperative need to do the opposite. We suggest that leaving it to police organizations to devise policies and practices that impact LGBTQ+ people is the riskier path, especially when recruitment processes for police organizations deliberately filter out most people who have lived experience of complex vulnerability. We must maintain critical and challenging conversations across the chasm of mistrust to ensure that safe and dignifying experiences might be a future possibility for LGBTQ+ people, both inside and outside police organizations. We argue that this is the only way to make progress toward illuminating a more comprehensive path whereby the challenges of LGBTQ+ people can be ably addressed.

# Contributors

**Roberto L. Abreu** is an assistant professor of counseling psychology and the director of the ¡Chévere! Lab in the Department of Psychology at the University of Florida. A recent publication: Abreu, R. L., Gonzalez, K. A., Capielo Rosario, C., Lockett, G. M., Lindley, L., & Lane, S. (2021). "We are our own community": Immigrant Latinx transgender people community experiences. *Journal of Counseling Psychology, 68*(4), 390–403.

**Dhanya Babu** is a doctoral student in the Department of Criminal Justice of John Jay College of Criminal Justice, City University of New York. Her research revolves around gender-based violence experienced by LGBTQ+ persons of color. Her most recent work was published in the *Journal of Black Sexuality and Relationships*.

**Koree S. Badio** is a graduate student at the University of Florida in the Department of Psychology. A recent publication: Freitag, S., Mekawi, Y., Badio, K. S., Holmes, E. V., Youngbood, A., & Lamis, D. A. (2022). The roles of culture, race, and ethnicity in suicide. In M. Pompili (Ed.), *Suicide risk assessment and prevention* (pp. 757–778). Springer Nature.

**Kwan-Lamar Blount-Hill** is an assistant professor at Arizona State University. His research is about social identity and its influence on perceptions and experiences of justice and justice-concerned systems and processes. He is a former police officer, firefighter, and licensed attorney.

Roddrick Colvin is a professor of public administration and the director of the School of Public Affairs at San Diego State University. His current research interests include public employment equity, police officers' shared perceptions and decision-making, and LGBTQ civil rights. His research has appeared in a number of scholarly journals, including the *Review of Public Personnel Administration*, *Police Quarterly*, and *Women and Criminal Justice*. He is the author of the book *Gay and Lesbian Cops: Diversity and Effective Policing* (Lynne Rienner Publishers, 2012).

Alexa DeGagne is an associate professor in the program of Women's and Gender Studies at Athabasca University. Her current research, funded by the Social Sciences and Humanities Research Council, examines the changing relationships between 2SLGBTQ (Two-Spirit, lesbian, gay, bisexual, transgender, queer) communities and police organizations across Canada.

Angela Dwyer is an associate professor in police studies and emergency management in the School of Social Sciences, College of Arts, Law, and Education, University of Tasmania, and the deputy director of the Tasmanian Institute of Law Enforcement Studies. She is the cochair of the Division of Queer Criminology (American Society of Criminology) and the secretary of Equality Tasmania, a state-based organization that lobbies for legislative change to protect the lives of LGBTIQ Tasmanians. She is also part of Just Equal, a national advocacy organization lobbying for similar legislative change in Australia. She is a leading scholar on how sexuality, gender, and sex diversity influence policing and criminal justice experiences and how young people from vulnerable groups experience policing. She has broad expertise with qualitative and quantitative research methods, including interviews, focus groups, surveys, observation, document analysis, and discourse analysis. She is the lead editor of *Queering Criminology* with Dr. Matthew Ball and Dr. Thomas Crofts, published by Palgrave Macmillan, 2016.

Nicole M. Elias is an associate professor in the Department of Public Management of John Jay College of Criminal Justice, City University of New York, and the founding codirector of Women in the Public Sector at John Jay College. Her research focuses on equity in public administration and policy, with an emphasis on the ethics of administration, management of human resources in public organizations, and public policy impacts on different populations.

Sulaimon Giwa is an associate professor in the School of Social Work with a cross-appointment in the Department of Sociology (police studies) at Memorial University of Newfoundland and Labrador. He is the endowed chair in criminology and criminal justice at St. Thomas University and is an antiracism, equity, diversity, and inclusion trainer and consultant. Dr. Giwa's professional experience includes research and policy work, antiracist community and organizational change, and direct practice in diverse contexts, including policing and corrections. He has worked with coalition movements against police racial profiling for over a decade, having led the first effort to acknowledge and address racial profiling in policing in Ottawa, Canada. Dr. Giwa's applied research program and professional activities centralize critical race transformative pedagogies and theories as frameworks and analytic tools for social justice and equity.

**Tyson Marlow** graduated with a BS in psychology from the University of Florida in 2020. He is currently completing a master's degree in human development counseling on the Clinical Mental Health Counseling track at Vanderbilt University.

**Julio A. Martin** is a doctoral student in the Department of Psychology, counseling psychology area, at the University of Florida. A recent publication: Comer, J. S., Golik, A., & Martin, J. (2019). Learning from the past: Understanding children's mental health after 9/11 and the Boston Marathon bombing. In S. Tyano, C. W., Hoven, & L. Amsel (Eds.), *An international perspective on disasters and children's mental health* (pp. 73–91). Springer Nature.

**Sean A. McCandless** works as an associate professor at the University of Texas at Dallas. His research centers on how accountability for social equity is achieved. He is published in numerous journals and edited volumes.

**Seth J. Meyer** is an assistant professor of public administration and nonprofit management in the Political Science Department at Bridgewater State University. His research focuses on social equity, specifically around the LGBTQ+ and Jewish communities. He also does research on organizational behavior in nonprofit organizations.

**Paige L. Moore** is a doctoral research and teaching assistant in the School of Public and International Affairs at North Carolina State University. Her background as a research professional has focused on identifying and examining innovative solutions to social problems through research, analysis, and practice.

**Lauren Moton** is a senior research associate at the Marron Institute of New York University. Informed by Black feminist and queer criminology, her scholarship broadly examines the intersection of victimization, marginalized identity, and criminal legal systems. Her work can be found in *Race and Justice*, *Victims & Offenders*, the *Journal of Criminal Justice*, and others.

**Max Osborn** is an assistant professor of sociology and criminology at Villanova University. Their research focuses on institutional harm toward marginalized populations, particularly LGBTQ+ people, and on consequences of victimization. Max's work can be found in outlets including *Feminist Criminology, Journal of Gay and Lesbian Social Services*, and *Psychological Medicine*.

**Heather Panter** is a senior lecturer and program leader at Liverpool John Moores University. Prior to entering academia she was a police detective in Atlanta, Georgia. As an academic, her research involves the comparative cross-examination of police cultures within the United States and the United Kingdom in respect to officers' cognitive and social perceptions of LGBTQ+ identities. A portion of this research was published in her first book titled *Transgender Cops: The Intersection of Gender and Sexuality Expectations in Police Cultures* (Routledge, 2018).

**Leah M. Rouse** is board certified in counseling psychology and is a licensed psychologist in the state of Wisconsin. Her research interests include trauma psychology, suicidology, and mental health issues facing law enforcement, military populations, cancer patients/survivors, and American Indian communities. She privileges contextual and qualitative perspectives in research and practice.

**Nick Rumens** is a professor in business and management at Oxford Brookes University, United Kingdom. Engaging with queer theories, his research has been published in a wide range of scholarly journals including *Organization Studies, Human Relations*, and *Human Resource Management Journal*. His latest book is *Queer Business: Queering Organization Sexualities* (Routledge, 2017).

**Mitchell D. Sellers** is a research specialist at the American Association of Nurse Practitioners. He taught courses on American politics, public policy, and research methodology. His current projects analyze the role of nurse practitioners in the health care system.

**Emma L. Turley** is a senior lecturer in criminology at Central Queensland University and a chartered psychologist with the British Psychological Society. Emma is a critical psychologist who has a broad range of interdisciplinary research interests that span criminology and psychology. Her specialist areas of interest include gender, social justice, inequalities, LGBTQI+ issues, feminism, sexualities, and the digital world.

# References

Abreu, R. L., Gonzalez, K. A., Capielo Rosario, C., Lindley, L., & Lockett, G. M. (2021). "What American dream is this?": The effect of Trump's presidency on immigrant Latinx transgender people. *Journal of Counseling Psychology, 68*(6), 657–669. https://doi.org/10.1037/cou0000541

Abreu, R. L., Gonzalez, K. A., Capielo Rosario, C., Lockett, G. M., Lindley, L., & Lane, S. (2021). "We are our own community": Immigrant Latinx transgender people community experiences. *Journal of Counseling Psychology, 68*(4), 390–403. https://doi.org/10.1037/cou0000546

Abreu, R. L., Gonzalez, K. A., Lindley, L., Capielo Rosario, C., Lockett, G. M., & Teran, M. (2023). "Why can't I have the office jobs?": Immigrant Latinx transgender peoples' experiences with seeking employment. *Journal of Career Development, 50*(1), 20–36. https://doi.org/10.1177/08948453211062951

Acker, J. (1990). Hierarchies, jobs, bodies: A theory of gendered organizations. *Gender & Society, 4*(2), 139–158. https://doi.org/10.1177/089124390004002002

Ahlers, C. J., Schaefer, G. A., Mundt, I. A., Roll, S., Englert, H., Willich, S. N., & Beier, K. M. (2011). How unusual are the contents of paraphilias? Paraphilia-associated sexual arousal patterns in a community-based sample of men. *Journal of Sexual Medicine, 8*(5), 1362–1370. https://doi.org/10.1111/j.1743-6109.2009.01597.x

Ahmed, S. (2017). *Archaeology of Babel: The colonial foundation of the humanities.* Stanford University Press.

Alison, L., Santtila, P., Kenneth Sandnabba, N., & Nordling, N. (2001). Sado-masochistically oriented behavior: Diversity in practice and meaning. *Archives of Sexual Behavior, 30*(1), 1–12. https://doi.org/10.1023/A:1026438422383

Allport, G. W. (1958). *The nature of prejudice: Abridged.* Doubleday.

Alters, S., & Schiff, W. (2006). *Essential concepts for healthy living* (4th ed.). Jones and Bartlett.

Ambler, J. K., Lee, E. M., Klement, K. R., Loewald, T., Comber, E. M., Hanson, S. A., Cutler, B., Cutler, N., Sagarin, B. J. (2017). Consensual BDSM facilitates role-specific altered states of consciousness: A preliminary study. *Psychology of Consciousness, 4*(1), 75–91. https://doi.org/10.1037/cns0000097

American Civil Liberties Union. (2022). *Mass incarceration.* https://www.aclu.org/issues/smart-justice/mass-incarceration

American Psychiatric Association. (2013). *Diagnostic and statistical manual of mental disorders: DSM-5* (5th ed.).

Amnesty International. (2005). *USA: Stonewalled; Police abuse and misconduct against lesbian, gay, bisexual and transgender people in the U.S.* https://policycommons.net/artifacts/355882/usa/1316955/

Asher, J., & Horowitz, B. (2020, June 19). How do the police actually spend their time? *New York Times.* https://www.nytimes.com/2020/06/19/upshot/unrest-police-time-violent-crime.html

Asquith, N. L., Dwyer, A., & Simpson, P. (2017). A queer criminal career. *Current Issues in Criminal Justice, 29*(2), 167–180. https://doi.org/10.1080/10345329.2017.12036094

Associated Press. (2021, May 17). *NYC Pride parade bans police; gay officers "disheartened."* NBC News. https://www.nbcnews.com/feature/nbc-out/nyc-pride-parade-bans-police-gay-officers-disheartened-n1267565

Australian Law Reform Commission. (2018). *Pathways to justice—inquiry into the incarceration rate of Aboriginal and Torres Strait Islander peoples* [ALRC report 133]. https://www.alrc.gov.au/publication/pathways-to-justice-inquiry-into-the-incarceration-rate-of-aboriginal-and-torres-strait-islander-peoples-alrc-report-133/

Avery, D. (2021, June 1). *Ohio's 1st lesbian sheriff on her rocky journey to becoming "proud and fearless."* NBC News. https://www.nbcnews.com/feature/nbc-out/ohio-s-1st-lesbian-sheriff-her-rocky-journey-becoming-proud-n1269156

Babbie, E. (2010). *The practice of social research* (12th ed.). Wadsworth.

Ball, M. (2016). Queer criminology as activism. *Critical Criminology, 24*(4), 473–487. https://doi.org/10.1007/s10612-016-9329-4

Ball, M. (2019). Unsettling queer criminology: Notes towards decolonization. *Critical Criminology, 27*(1), 145–161. https://doi.org/10.1007/s10612-019-09440-0

Ball, M., Buist, C. L., & Woods, J. B. (2014). Introduction to the special issue on queer/ing criminology: New directions and frameworks. *Critical Criminology, 22*(1), 1–4. https://doi.org/10.1007/s10612-013-9231-2

Ball, M., & Dwyer, A. (2018). Queer criminology and the global south: Setting queer and southern criminologies into dialogue. In K. Carrington, R. Hogg, J. Scott, & M. Sozzo (Eds.), *The Palgrave handbook of criminology and the global south* (pp. 121–138). Palgrave Macmillan.

Banerjie, A. (2019). Beyond decriminalisation: Understanding queer citizenship through access to public spaces in India. *NUJS Law Review, 12*, 1–15.

Barik, S. (2021, July 18). Transgender persons' attempt to break new ground in Odisha. *The Hindu.* https://www.thehindu.com/news/national/other-states/transgender-persons-attempt-to-break-new-ground-in-odisha/article35390729.ece

Barker, M., Gupta, C., & Iantaffi, A. (2007). The power of play: The potentials and pitfalls in healing narratives of BDSM. In D. Langdridge & M. Barker (Eds.), *Safe, sane and consensual contemporary perspectives on sadomasochism* (pp. 197–216). Palgrave Macmillan.

Barlow, D. E., & Barlow, M. H. (2018). *Police in a multicultural society: An American story.* Waveland Press.

Barratt, C. L., Bergman, M. E., & Thompson, R. J. (2014). Women in federal law enforcement: The role of gender role orientations and sexual orientation in mentoring. *Sex Roles, 71*(1–2), 21–32. https://doi.org/10.1007/s11199-014-0388-2

Barrie, D. G., & Broomhall, S. (2012). *A history of police and masculinities, 1700–2010.* Routledge. https://doi.org/10.4324/9780203141427

Bartle, J. (2018) *Where should the law draw the line between consent and culpability in sadomasochism?* The Conversation. https://theconversation.com/where-should-the-law-draw-the-line-between-consent-and-culpability-in-sadomasochism-91229

Bauer, G. R., Hammond, R., Travers, R., Kaay, M., Hohenadel, K. M., & Boyce, M. (2009). "I don't think this is theoretical; this is our lives": How erasure impacts health care for transgender people. *Journal of the Association of Nurses in AIDS Care, 20*(5), 348–361. https://doi.org/10.1016/j.jana.2009.07.004

Bayerl, P. S., Horton, K. E., & Jacobs, G. (2018). How do we describe our professional selves? Investigating collective identity configurations across professions. *Journal of Vocational Behavior, 107*, 168–181. https://doi.org/10.1016/j.jvb.2018.04.006

Beliso–De Jesús, A. M. (2020). The jungle academy: Molding white supremacy in American police recruits. *American Anthropologist, 122*(1), 143–156. https://doi.org/10.1111/aman.13357

Belkin, A., & McNichol, J. (2002). Pink and blue: Outcomes associated with the integration of open gay and lesbian personnel in the San Diego Police Department. *Police Quarterly, 5*(1), 63–95. https://doi.org/10.1177/1098611102129198020

Belknap, J. (2015). Activist criminology: Criminologists' responsibility to advocate for social and legal justice. *Criminology, 53*(1), 1–22. https://doi.org/10.1111/1745-9125.12063

Benavente, G., & Gill-Peterson, J. (2019). The promise of trans critique: Susan Stryker's queer theory. *GLQ, 25*(1), 23–28. https://doi.org/10.1215/10642684-7275222

Benjamin, H. (1966). *The transsexual phenomenon.* Julian Press.

Beresford, S. (2016). Lesbian spanners: A re-appraisal of UK consensual sado-masochism laws. *Liverpool Law Review, 37*(1–2), 63–80. https://doi.org/10.1007/s10991-016-9182-2

Bergman, S. (2020). *Pride in Hamilton: An independent review into the events surrounding Hamilton Pride 2019.* Cooper, Sandler, Shime & Bergman LLP. https://criminal-lawyers.ca/wp-content/uploads/2020/06/Pride-in-Hamilton-Report-June-8.pdf

Bernstein, M., & Kostelac, C. (2002). Lavender and blue: Attitudes about homosexuality and behavior toward lesbians and gay men among police officers. *Journal of Contemporary Criminal Justice, 18*(3), 302–328. https://doi.org/10.1177/1043986202018003006

Bernstein, M., Kostelac, C., & Gaarder, E. (2003). Understanding "heterosexism": Applying theories of racial prejudice to homophobia using data from a southwestern police department. *Race, Gender & Class, 10*(4), 54–74.

Bernstein, M., & Swartwout, P. (2012). Gay officers in their midst: Heterosexual police employees' anticipation of the consequences for coworkers who come out. *Journal of Homosexuality, 59*(8), 1145–1166. https://doi.org/10.1080/00918369.2012.673945

Bernstein, N. (2010, January 9). Officials hid truth of immigrant deaths in jail. *New York Times.* https://www.nytimes.com/2010/01/10/us/10detain

Bettcher, T. M. (2007). Evil deceivers and make-believers: On transphobic violence and the politics of illusion. *Hypatia, 22*(3), 43–65. https://doi.org/10.1111/j.1527-2001.2007.tb01090.x

Bilge, S. (2013). Intersectionality undone: Saving intersectionality from feminist intersectionality studies. *Du Bois Review, 10*(2), 405–424.

Blackmer, C. E. (2019). Pinkwashing. *Israel Studies, 24*(2), 171–181.

Blessett, B. (2020). Rethinking the administrative state through an intersectional framework. *Administrative Theory & Praxis, 42*(1), 1–5. https://doi.org/10.1080/10841806.2018.1517526

Blount-Hill, K.-L., St. John, V., Moton, L. N., & Ajil, A. (2022). In their experience: A review of racial and sexual minority experience in academe and proposals for building an inclusive criminology. *Race and Justice, 12*(3), 457–480. https://doi.org/10.1177/21533687221087352

Bolman, L. G., & Deal, T. E. (2017). *Reframing organizations: Artistry, choice, and leadership* (6th ed.). Wiley.

Boncori, I., Sicca, L. M., & Bizjak, D. (2019). Transgender and gender non-conforming people in the workplace: Direct and invisible discrimination. In S. Nachmias & V. Caven (Eds.), *Inequality and organizational practice: Vol. 1. Work and welfare* (pp. 141–160). Palgrave Macmillan.

Borges, S. (2018). Home and homing as resistance: Survival of LGBTQ Latinx migrants. *Women's Studies Quarterly, 46*(3–4), 69–84. https://doi.org/10.1353/wsq.2018.0032

Bowleg, L. (2012). The problem with the phrase *women and minorities*: Intersectionality—an important theoretical framework for public health. *American Journal of Public Health, 102*(7), 1267–1273. https://doi.org/10.2105/AJPH.2012.300750

Bradley, B. (2021, June 5). Hamilton's LGBTQ communities have long fought a lack of support from police and the city. Now they are headed to the human rights tribunal. *Toronto Star.* https://www.thestar.com/news/canada/2021/06/05/hamiltons-lgbtq-communities-have-long-fought-a-lack-of-support-from-police-and-the-city-now-they-are-headed-to-the-human-rights-tribunal.html

Brandl, S. G., & Stroshine, M. S. (2013). The role of officer attributes, job characteristics, and arrest activity in explaining police use of force. *Criminal Justice Policy Review, 24*(5), 551–572. https://doi.org/10.1177/0887403412452424

Bronski, M. (2011). *A queer history of the United States* (Vol. 1). Beacon Press.

Brown, A., Barker, E. D., & Rahman, Q. (2020). A systematic scoping review of the prevalence, etiological, psychological, and interpersonal factors associated with BDSM [Annual Review of Sex Research special issue]. *Journal of Sex Research, 57*(6), 781–811. https://doi.org/10.1080/00224499.2019.1665619

Brown, C., Dashjian, L. T., Acosta, T. J., Mueller, C. T., Kizer, B. E., & Trangsrud, H. B. (2012). The career experiences of male-to-female transsexuals. *Counseling Psychologist, 40*(6), 868–894. https://doi.org/10.1177/0011000011430098

Brown, R. A. (2019). Policing in American history. *Du Bois Review, 16*(1), 189–195. https://doi.org/10.1017/S1742058X19000171

Brunet, J. R. (2015). Social equity in criminal justice. In N. J. Johnson & J. H. Svara (Eds.), *Justice for all: Promoting social equity in public administration* (pp. 165–186). Routledge.

Budge, S. L., Tebbe, E. N., & Howard, K. A. S. (2010). The work experiences of transgender individuals: Negotiating the transition and career decision-making processes. *Journal of Counseling Psychology, 57*(4), 377–393. https://doi.org/10.1037/a0020472

Buist, C. L., & Lenning, E. (2016). *Queer criminology: New directions in critical criminology.* Routledge.

Buist, C. L., & Lenning, E. (2022). *Queer criminology* (2nd ed.). Taylor & Francis.

Buist, C. L., Lenning, E., & Ball, M. (2018). Queer criminology. In W. S. DeKeseredy & M. Dragiewicz (Eds.), *Routledge handbook of critical criminology* (pp. 96–106). Routledge.

Bullough, V. L. (2002). *Before Stonewall: Activists for gay and lesbian rights in historical context.* Routledge. https://doi.org/10.4324/9781315801681

Burke, M. E. (1993). *Coming out of the blue: British police officers talk about their lives in "the job" as lesbians, gays, and bisexuals.* Cassell.

Burke, M.E. (1994). Homosexuality as deviance: The case of the gay police officer. *British Journal of Criminology, 34*(2), 192–203. https://doi.org/10.1093/oxfordjournals.bjc.a048402

Burke, M. E. (1995). Identities and disclosures: The case of lesbian and gay police officers: Marc Burke examines the conflicts that can arise. *Psychologist, 8*(12), 543–547.

Butler, J. (1990) *Gender trouble.* Routledge

Butler, J. (1993). *Bodies that matter: On the discursive limits of "sex."* Routledge. https://doi.org/10.4324/9780203760079

Butler, J. (2004). *Undoing gender.* Taylor & Francis. https://doi.org/10.4324/9780203499627

Cain, P. A. (1993). Litigating for lesbian and gay rights: A legal history. *Virginia Law Review, 79*(7), 1551–1641. https://doi.org/10.2307/1073382

Calhoun, C. (2017). "Bullseye on their back": Police profiling and abuse of trans and gender non-conforming individuals and solutions beyond the Department of Justice guidelines. *Alabama Civil Rights and Civil Liberties Review, 8*(1): 127–144.

Capers, I. B. (2008). Cross dressing and the criminal. *Yale Journal of Law & the Humanities, 20*(1), 1.

Carlström, C. (2021). Spiritual experiences and altered states of consciousness—parallels between BDSM and Christianity. *Sexualities, 24*(5–6), 749–766. https://doi.org/10.1177/1363460720964035

Carpenter, L. F., & Marshall, B. (2017). Walking while trans: Profiling of transgender women by law enforcement, and the problem of proof. *William & Mary Journal of Women and the Law, 24*(1), 5–38.

Carrington, K., Guala, N., Puyol, M. V., & Sozzo, M. (2020). How women's police stations empower women, widen access to justice and prevent gender violence. *International Journal for Crime, Justice and Social Democracy, 9*(1), 42–67. https://doi.org/10.5204/ijcjsd.v9i1.1494

Carter, D. (2010). *Stonewall: The riots that sparked the gay revolution*. St. Martin's Press.

CBC News. (2017, November 2). *Number of visible minorities in Hamilton has doubled over last 2 decades*. https://www.cbc.ca/news/canada /hamilton/hamilton-2016-census-visible-minorities-doubled-1.4383573.

CBC News. (2019, June 20). *Chief says police would have deployed differently if they were welcome at Pride*. https://www.cbc.ca/news/canada/hamilton /girt-pride-protest-1.5182014?fbclid=IwAR0EONmyrwTuDNU15Dp8HY b0ewvmDNXYeUCzpZgPaVpI5IbGChaVid0V2jg

Cerezo, A. (2016). The impact of discrimination on mental health symptomatology in sexual minority immigrant Latinas. *Psychology of Sexual Orientation and Gender Diversity, 3*(3), 283–292. https://doi.org/10.1037 /sgd0000172

Charbonneau, E., & Riccucci, N. M. (2008). Beyond the usual suspects: An analysis of the performance measurement literature on social equity indicators in policing. *Public Performance & Management Review, 31*(4), 604–620. https://doi.org/10.2753/PMR1530-9576310405

Charbonneau, E., Riccucci, N. M., Van Ryzin, G. G., & Holzer, M. (2009). The self-reported use of social equity indicators in urban police departments in the United States and Canada. *State & Local Government Review, 41*(2), 95–107. https://doi.org/10.1177/0160323X0904100203

Charles, M. W., & Rouse Arndt, L. M. (2013). Gay- and lesbian-identified law enforcement officers: Intersection of career and sexual identity. *Counseling Psychologist, 41*(8), 1153–1185. https://doi.org/10.1177/0011000012472376

Charmaz, K. (2006). *Constructing grounded theory: A practical guide through qualitative analysis*. Sage.

Chemerinsky, E. (2015). *Constitutional law: Principles and policies* (5th ed.). Wolters Kluwer.

Cherney, A. (1999). Gay and lesbian issues in policing. *Current Issues in Criminal Justice, 11*(1), 35–52. https://doi.org/10.1080/10345329.1999.12036146

Chojnacki, J. T., & Gelberg, S. (1994). Toward a conceptualization of career counseling with gay/lesbian/bisexual persons. *Journal of Career Development, 21*(1), 3–10. https://doi.org/10.1007/BF02107099

Cisneros, N. (2016). Resisting "massive elimination": Foucault, immigration, and the GIP. In P. Zurn & A. Dilts (Eds.), *Active intolerance: Michel Foucault, the Prisons Information Group, and the future of abolition* (pp. 241–257). Palgrave Macmillan.

Cleghorn, M., Holman, A., Ratelle, N., Teubner, C., & Troyer, C. (2018). Employment discrimination against LGBT persons. *Georgetown Journal of Gender and the Law, 19*(2), 367+.

Coffey, A., & Atkinson, P. (1996). *Making sense of qualitative data: Complementary research strategies*. Sage.

Collins, J. C., & Rocco, T. S. (2015). Rules of engagement as survival consciousness: Gay male law enforcement officers' experiential learning in a masculinized industry. *Adult Education Quarterly, 65*(4), 295–312. https://doi.org/10.1177/0741713615585163

Collins, J. C., & Rocco, T. S. (2018). Queering employee engagement to understand and improve the performance of gay male law enforcement officers: A phenomenological exploration. *Performance Improvement Quarterly, 30*(4), 273–295. https://doi.org/10.1002/piq.21255

Collins, P. H. (2000). *Black feminist thought: Knowledge, consciousness, and the politics of empowerment.* Routledge.

Collinson, D. L., & Hearn, J. R. (1996). *Men as managers, managers as men: Critical perspectives on men, masculinities and management*s. Sage. https://doi.org/10.4135/9781446280102

Colvin, R. A. (2007). The rise of transgender-inclusive laws: How well are municipalities implementing supportive nondiscrimination public employment policies? *Review of Public Personnel Administration, 27*(4), 336–360. https://doi.org/10.1177/1077800407301777

Colvin, R. (2009). Shared perceptions among lesbian and gay police officers: Barriers and opportunities in the law enforcement work environment. *Police Quarterly, 12*(1), 86–101. https://doi.org/10.1177/1098611108327308

Colvin, R. A. (2012). *Gay and lesbian cops: Diversity and effective policing.* Lynne Rienner. https://doi.org/10.1515/9781588269348

Colvin, R. (2014). Policing the lesbian and gay community: The perceptions of lesbian and gay police officers. In D. Peterson & V. R. Panfil (Eds.), *Handbook of LGBT communities, crime, and justice* (pp. 183–205). Springer.

Colvin, R. (2015). Shared workplace experiences of lesbian and gay police officers in the United Kingdom. *Policing, 38*(2), 333–349. https://doi.org/10.1108/PIJPSM-11-2014-0121

Colvin, R. (2020). The emergence and evolution of lesbian and gay police associations in Europe. *European Law Enforcement Research Bulletin, 19*, 51–69.

Colvin, R. & Meyer, S. (2022) Applying queer theory to public administration: Reimagining police officer recruitment. In K. A. Bottom, J. Diamond, P. T. Dunning, & I. C. Elliott (Eds.), *Handbook of teaching public administration* (pp. 309–318). Edward Elgar.

Colvin, R., & Moton, L. (2021). Lesbian police officers: A review of television portrayals and their lived experiences. *Public Integrity, 23*(3), 253–268. https://doi.org/10.1080/10999922.2020.1794267

Commuri, C. (2017). *Sticky policy narratives: A case study of India's "criminal tribes"* [Conference paper]. International Conference on Public Policy, Singapore.

Connell, R. (1995). *Masculinities.* University of California Press.

Connell, R. W., & Messerschmidt, J. W. (2005). Hegemonic masculinity: Rethinking the concept. *Gender & Society, 19*(6), 829–859. https://doi .org/10.1177/0891243205278639

Connolly, P. H. (2006). Psychological functioning of bondage/domination/ sado-masochism (BDSM) practitioners. *Journal of Psychology and Human Sexuality, 18*(1), 79–120. https://doi.org/10.1300/J056v18n01_05

Conway, M., Pizzamiglio, M. T., & Mount, L. (1996). Status, communality, and agency: Implications for stereotypes of gender and other groups. *Journal of Personality and Social Psychology, 71*(1), 25–38. https://doi.org /10.1037/0022-3514.71.1.25

Copple, J. E., & Dunn, P. M. (2017). *Gender, sexuality, and 21st century policing: Protecting the rights of the LGBTQ+ community.* Community Oriented Policing Services, U.S. Department of Justice.

Côté, P.-B., & Blais, M. (2021). "The least loved, that's what I was": A qualitative analysis of the pathways to homelessness by LGBTQ+ youth. *Journal of Gay & Lesbian Social Services, 33*(2), 137–156. https://doi.org/10.1080 /10538720.2020.1850388

Couto, J. L. (2018). Hearing their voices and counting them in: The place of Canadian LGBTQ police officers in police culture. *Journal of Community Safety and Well-Being, 3*(3), 84–87.

Craig, E. (2007). Trans-phobia and the relational production of gender. *Hastings Women's Law Journal, 18*(2), 137–172.

Crenshaw, K. (1989). Demarginalizing the intersection of race and sex: A Black feminist critique of antidiscrimination doctrine, feminist theory and antiracist politics. *University of Chicago Legal Forum, 1989*(1), 139–167.

Crenshaw, K. (1991). Mapping the margins: Intersectionality, identity politics, and violence against women of color. *Stanford Law Review, 43*(6), 1241–1299. https://doi.org/10.2307/1229039

Crocker, J., & Lutsky, N. (1986). Stigma and the dynamics of social cognition. In S. C. Ainlay, G. Becker, & L. M. Coleman (Eds.), *The dilemma of difference* (pp. 95–121). Springer.

Crooke, C. (2013). Women in law enforcement. *COPS: The E-newsletter of the COPS Office, 6*(7): https://cops.usdoj.gov/html/dispatch/07–2013 /women_in_law_enforcement.asp

Crosby, A. A., & Monaghan, J. (2018). *Policing indigenous movements: Dissent and the security state.* Fernwood.

Cross, F. L., Rivas-Drake, D., & Aramburu, J. (2022). Latinx immigrants raising children in the land of the free: Parenting in the context of persecution and fear. *Qualitative Social Work, 21*(3), 559–579. https://doi.org /10.1177/14733250211014578

Dallas Police Department. (2021). *LGBTQ+ liaison officers.* https://dallas police.net/communitys/glbtliaisonofficer

Dario, L. M., Fradella, H. F., Verhagen, M., & Parry, M. M. (2019). Assessing LGBT people's perceptions of police legitimacy. *Journal of Homosexuality, 67*(7), 885–915. https://doi.org/10.1080/00918369.2018.1560127

Darling, M. J. T. (2021). Living on the margins beyond gender binaries: What are the challenges to securing rights. *Public Integrity, 23*(6), 573–594. https://doi.org/10.1080/10999922.2020.1825180

Daum, C. W. (2015). The war on solicitation and intersectional subjection: Quality-of-life policing as a tool to control transgender populations. *New Political Science, 37*(4), 562–581. https://doi.org/10.1080/07393148.2015.1089030

Davidson, S. (2016). Gender inequality: Nonbinary transgender people in the workplace. *Cogent Social Sciences, 2*(1). https://doi.org/10.1080/23311886.2016.1236511

Davies, A., & Thomas, R. (2003). Talking cop: Discourses of change and policing identities. *Public Administration* [London], *81*(4), 681–699. https://doi.org/10.1111/j.0033-3298.2003.00367.x

Davis, A. Y. (1974). *Angela Davis: An autobiography.* Random House.

de Lauretis, T. (1991). Queer theory: Lesbian and gay sexualities; An introduction. *Differences, 3*(2), iii–xviii. https://doi.org/10.1215/10407391-3-2-iii

DeJong, C. (2005). Gender differences in officer attitude and behavior: providing comfort to citizens. *Women & Criminal Justice, 15*(3–4), 1–32. https://doi.org/10.1300/J012v15n03_01

DeJong, C., Holt, K., Helm, B., & Morgan, S. J. (2021). "A human being like other victims": The media framing of trans homicide in the United States. *Critical Criminology, 29*(1), 131–149. https://doi.org/10.1007/s10612-021-09559-z

den Heyer, G. (2019). New Zealand police cultural liaison officers: Their role in crime prevention and community policing. In J. F. Albrecht, G. den Heyer, & P. Stanislas (Eds.), *Policing and minority communities* (pp. 235–254). Springer.

Devor, A. H. (2004). Witnessing and mirroring: A fourteen stage model of transsexual identity formation. *Journal of Gay & Lesbian Psychotherapy, 8*(1–2), 41–67. https://doi.org/10.1300/J236v08n01_05

DeVylder, J., Fedina, L., & Link, B. (2020). Impact of police violence on mental health: A theoretical framework. *American Journal of Public Health, 110*(11), 1704–1710. https://doi.org/10.2105/AJPH.2020.305874

Diaz, J. (2021, February 3). *New York repeals "walking while trans" law.* NPR. https://www.npr.org/2021/02/03/963513022/new-york-repeals-walking-while-trans-law

Dick, P., & Cassell, C. (2002). Barriers to managing diversity in a UK constabulary: The role of discourse. *Journal of Management Studies, 39*(7), 953–976. https://doi.org/10.1111/1467-6486.00319

Dispenza, F., Watson, L. B., Chung, Y. B., & Brack, G. (2012). Experience of career-related discrimination for female-to-male transgender persons: A qualitative study. *Career Development Quarterly, 60*(1), 65–81. https://doi.org/10.1002/j.2161-0045.2012.00006.x

Doan, P. L., & Higgins, H. (2011). The demise of queer space? Resurgent gentrification and the assimilation of LGBT neighborhoods. *Journal of Planning Education and Research, 31*(1), 6–25. https://doi.org/10.1177/0739456X10391266

Dolamore, S., & Naylor, L. A. (2018). Providing solutions to LGBT homeless youth: Lessons from Baltimore's Youth Empowered Society. *Public Integrity, 20*(6), 595–610. https://doi.org/10.1080/10999922.2017.1333943

Douglas, H. (2019). Policing domestic and family violence. *International Journal for Crime, Justice and Social Democracy, 8*(2), 31–49. https://doi.org/10.5204/ijcjsd.v8i2.1122

Downing, L. (2013). Safewording! Kinkphobia and gender normativity in *Fifty Shades of Grey*. *Psychology and Sexuality, 4*(1), 92–102. https://doi.org/10.1080/19419899.2012.740067

Drake, D. S., & Matuszak, M. (2018). Inspiring and nurturing LGBTQI youth. In W. Swan (Ed.), *The Routledge handbook of LGBTQIA administration and policy* (pp. 213–243). Routledge.

Drescher, J. (2015). Out of DSM: Depathologising homosexuality. *Behavioural Science 5*(4), 565–575.

du Plessis, C., Winterbotham, S., Fein, E. C., Brownlow, C., du Preez, J., McKenna, B., Chen, P., Beel, N., & du Plessis, G. (2021). I'm still in the blue family: Gender and professional identity construction in police officers. *Journal of Police and Criminal Psychology, 36*, 386–396.

Duggan, L. (2002). The new homonormativity: The sexual politics of neoliberalism. *Materializing Democracy, 10*, 175–194.

Dunkley, C. R., & Brotto, L. A. (2020). The role of consent in the context of BDSM. *Sexual Abuse, 32*(6), 657–678. https://doi.org/10.1177/1079063219842847

Dwyer, A. (2007). Visibly invisible: Policing queer young people as a research gap. In B. Curtis (Eds.), *TASA 2007 conference proceedings: Public sociologies; lessons and trans-Tasman comparisons* (pp. 1–9). Sociological Association of Australia.

Dwyer, A. (2008). Policing queer bodies: Focusing on queer embodiment in policing research as an ethical question. *Law and Justice Journal, 8*(2), 414–428.

Dwyer, A. (2011a). "It's not like we're going to jump them": How transgressing heteronormativity shapes police interactions with LGBT young people. *Youth Justice, 11*(3), 203–220. https://doi.org/10.1177/1473225411420526

Dwyer, A. (2011b). Policing lesbian, gay, bisexual and transgender young people: A gap in the research literature. *Current Issues in Criminal Justice, 22*(3), 415–433. https://doi.org/10.1080/10345329.2011.12035896

Dwyer, A. (2012). Policing visible sexual/gender diversity as a program of governance. *International Journal for Crime, Justice and Social Democracy, 1*(1), 14–26.

Dwyer, A. (2014a). "We're not like these weird feather boa–covered AIDS-spreading monsters": How LGBT young people and service providers think riskiness informs LGBT youth–police interactions. *Critical Criminology, 22*(1), 65–79. https://doi.org/10.1007/s10612-013-9226-z

Dwyer, A. (2014b). Pleasures, perversities, and partnerships: The historical emergence of LGBT-police relationships. In D. Peterson & V. R. Panfil (Eds.), *Handbook of LGBT communities, crime, and justice* (pp. 148–164). Springer. https://doi.org/10.1007/978-1-4614-9188-0_8.

Dwyer, A. (2015). Teaching young queers a lesson: How police teach lessons about non-heteronormativity in public spaces. *Sexuality & Culture, 19*(3), 493–512. https://doi.org/10.1007/s12119-015-9273-6

Dwyer, A. (2019). Queering policing: What is best practice with LGBTQ communities? *Current Issues in Criminal Justice, 31*(3), 383–398. https://doi.org/10.1080/10345329.2019.1640172

Dwyer, A. (2020). Queering police administration: How policing administration complicates LGBTIQ-police relations. *Administrative Theory & Praxis, 42*(2), 172–190. https://doi.org/10.1080/10841806.2019.1659047

Dwyer, A., & Ball, M (2013). *GLBTI police liaison services: A critical analysis of existing literature* [Conference presentation]. 6th Annual Australian and New Zealand Critical Criminology Conference, University of Tasmania. https://hdl.handle.net/102.100.100/524131

Dwyer, A., & Ball, M. J. (2020). "You'd just cop flak from every other dickhead under the sun": Navigating the tensions of (in)visibility and hypervisibility in LGBTI police liaison programs in three Australian states. *Journal of Contemporary Criminal Justice, 36*(2), 274–292. https://doi.org/10.1177/1043986219894420

Dwyer, A., Ball, M., & Barker, E. (2015). Policing diverse sexualities and genders in rural spaces. *Rural Society, 24*(3), 227–243.

Dwyer, A., Ball, M., Lee, M., Crofts, T., & Bond, C. (2020). Barriers stopping LGBTI people from accessing LGBTI police liaison officers: Analysing interviews with community and police. *Criminal Justice Studies, 33*(3), 256–275. https://doi.org/10.1080/1478601X.2020.1786280

Dwyer, A., Bond, C. E. W., Ball, M., Lee, M., & Crofts, T. (2022). Support provided by LGBTI police liaison services: An analysis of a survey of LGBTIQ people in Australia. *Police Quarterly, 25*(1), 33–58. https://doi.org/10.1177/10986111211038048

Dwyer, A., & Colvin, R. A. (2022). Queer(y)ing the experiences of LGBTQ workers in criminal processing systems. In C. Buist & L. K. Semprevivo (Eds.), *Queering criminology in theory and praxis* (pp. 56–69). Bristol University Press.

Dwyer, A., & Panfil, V. (2017). "We need to lead the charge—talking only to each other is not enough": The Pulse Orlando mass shooting and the futures of queer criminologies. *Criminologist: The Official Newsletter of the American Society of Criminology, 42*(3), 1–7.

Dwyer, A., & Tomsen, S. (2016). The past is the past? The impossibility of erasure of historical LGBTIQ policing. In M. Ball, A. Dwyer, & T. Crofts (Eds.), *Queering criminology* (pp. 36–53). Palgrave Macmillan.

Edelman, L. (2004). *No future: Queer theory and the death drive.* Duke University Press. https://doi.org/10.1215/9780822385981

Elias, N., & Colvin, R. (2020). A third option: Understanding and assessing non-binary gender policies in the United States. *Administrative Theory & Praxis, 42*(2), 191–211.

Eng, D. L. (2010). *The feeling of kinship: Queer liberalism and the racialization of intimacy.* Duke University Press. https://doi.org/10.1515/9780822392828

Epp, C. R., Maynard-Moody, S., & Haider-Markel, D. (2017). Beyond profiling: The institutional sources of racial disparities in policing. *Public Administration Review, 77*(2), 168–178. https://doi.org/10.1111/puar.12702

Faccio, E., Sarigu, D., & Iudici, A. (2020). What is it like to be a BDSM player? The role of sexuality and erotization of power in the BDSM experience. *Sexuality & Culture, 24*(5), 1641–1652. https://doi.org/10.1007/s12119-020-09703-x

Faderman, L. (1991). *Odd girls and twilight lovers: A history of lesbian life in twentieth-century America.* Penguin.

Farr, P. (2016). *Queer victims: Reports of violence by LGBTQI survivors result in violent assaults by police* [Master's thesis, Arizona State University]. ASU Library KEEP. https://keep.lib.asu.edu/items/154773

Fenley, V. M. (2020). Layer of inequity: The challenge of homelessness. In M. E. Guy & S. A. McCandless (Eds.), *Achieving social equity: From problems to solutions* (pp. 67–81). Melvin & Leigh.

Fennell, J. (2018). "It's all about the journey": Skepticism and spirituality in the BDSM subculture. *Sociological Forum, 33*(4), 1045–1067. https://doi.org/10.1111/socf.12460

Fernandez, B., & Gomathy, N. B. (2005). Voicing the invisible: Violence faced by lesbian women in India. In A. Narrain & G. Bhan (Eds.), *Because I have a voice: Queer politics in India* (pp. 155–163). Yoda Press.

Filax, G. (2006). Politicising action research through queer theory. *Educational Action Research, 14*(1), 139–145. https://doi.org/10.1080/09650791600585632

Fish, J. N. (2020). Future directions in understanding and addressing mental health among LGBTQ youth. *Journal of Clinical Child and Adolescent Psychology, 49*(6), 943–956. https://doi.org/10.1080/15374416.2020 .1815207

Fiske, S. T., Cuddy, A. J. C., Glick, P., & Xu, J. (2002). A model of (often mixed) stereotype content: Competence and warmth respectively follow from perceived status and competition. *Journal of Personality and Social Psychology, 82*(6), 878–902. https://doi.org/10.1037/0022-3514.82.6.878

Fitzsimmons, T. (2018, June 23). *Police at Pride? Gay cops, LGBTQ activists struggle to see eye-to-eye*. NBC News. https://www.nbcnews.com/feature /nbc-out/police-pride-gay-cops-lgbtq-activists-struggle-see-eye-eye- n886031

Foucault, M. (1977). *Discipline and punish: The birth of the prison* (A. Sheridan, Trans.). Pantheon Books.

Foucault, M. (1978). *The history of sexuality: Vol. 1. An introduction* (R. Hurley, Trans.). Pantheon Books.

Foucault, M. (2003). *Society must be defended: Lectures at the Collège de France, 1975–76* (M. Bertani & A. Fontana, Eds.) (D. Macey, Trans.). Picador.

Friedrich, R. J. (1980). Police use of force: Individuals, situations, and organizations. *Annals of the American Academy of Political and Social Science, 452*(1), 82–97. https://doi.org/10.1177/000271628045200109

Gade, D. M., & Wilkins, V. M. (2013). Where did you serve? Veteran identity, representative bureaucracy, and vocational rehabilitation. *Journal of Public Administration Research and Theory, 23*(2), 267–288. https://doi.org /10.1093/jopart/mus030

Gagné, P., Tewksbury, R., & McGaughey, D. (1997). Coming out and crossing over: Identity formation and proclamation in a transgender community. *Gender & Society, 11*(4), 478–508. https://doi.org/10.1177 /089124397011004006

Gallup. (2021, May 26). *Mixed views among Americans on transgender issues*. https://news.gallup.com/poll/350174/mixed-views-among-americans -transgender-issues.aspx

Galvan, F. H., & Bazargan, M. (2012). *Interactions of transgender Latina women with law enforcement*. Williams Institute.

Galvin-White, C. M., & O'Neal, E. N. (2016). Lesbian police officers' interpersonal working relationships and sexuality disclosure: A qualitative study. *Feminist Criminology, 11*(3), 253–284. https://doi.org/10.1177 /1557085115588359

Guadalupe-Diaz, X. (2016). Disclosure of same-sex intimate partner violence to police among lesbians, gays, and bisexuals. *Social Currents, 3*(2), 160–171.

Gaynor, T. S. (2018a). Social construction and the criminalization of identity: State-sanctioned oppression and an unethical administration. *Public Integrity, 20*(4), 358–369. https://doi.org/10.1080/10999922.2017.1416881

Gaynor, T. S. (2018b). Bias in the U.S. criminal justice system. In A. Farazmand (Ed.), *Global encyclopedia of public administration, public policy, and governance* (pp. 1–5). Springer.

Gaynor, T. S., & Blessett, B. (2014). Inequality at the intersection of the Defense of Marriage Act and the Voting Rights Act: A review of the 2013 Supreme Court decisions. *Administrative Theory & Praxis, 36*(2), 261–267. https://doi.org/10.1080/10841806.2014.11029956

Gaynor, T. S., & Blessett, B. (2022). Predatory policing, intersectional subjection, and the experiences of LGBTQ people of color in New Orleans. *Urban Affairs Review, 58*(5), 1305–1339. https://doi.org/10.1177/10780874211017289

Gerber, G. L. (2009). Status and the gender stereotyped personality traits: Toward an integration. *Sex Roles, 61*(5–6), 297–316. https://doi.org/10.1007/s11199-008-9529-9

Gerety, R. M. (2020, December 28). An alternative to police that police can get behind. *The Atlantic.* https://www.theatlantic.com/politics/archive/2020/12/cahoots-program-may-reduce-likelihood-of-police-violence/617477/

Gillespie, W. (2008). Thirty-five years after Stonewall: An exploratory study of satisfaction with police among gay, lesbian, and bisexual persons at the 34th annual Atlanta Pride festival. *Journal of Homosexuality, 55*(4), 619–647.

Giwa, S. (2018). Community policing in racialized communities: A potential role for police social work. *Journal of Human Behavior in the Social Environment, 28*(6), 710–730. https://doi.org/10.1080/10911359.2018.1456998

Giwa, S., Colvin, R. A., Karki, K. K., Mullings, D. V., & Bagg, L. (2021). Analysis of "yes" responses to uniformed police marching in Pride: Perspectives from LGBTQ+ communities in St. John's, Newfoundland and Labrador, Canada. *SAGE Open, 11*(2). https://doi.org/10.1177/21582440211023140

Giwa, S., Colvin, R. A., Ricciardelli, R., & Warren, A. P. (2022). Workplace experiences of lesbian and bisexual female police officers in the Royal Newfoundland Constabulary. *Women & Criminal Justice, 32*(1–2), 93–110. https://doi.org/10.1080/08974454.2021.1962480

Giwa, S., & Greensmith, C. (2012). Race relations and racism in the LGBTQ community of Toronto: Perceptions of gay and queer social service providers of color. *Journal of Homosexuality, 59*(2), 149–185. https://doi.org/10.1080/00918369.2012.648877

Giwa, S., & Jackman, M. C. (2020). *Missing persons investigation and police interaction with racialized people who identify as LGBTQ2S+*. A paper prepared for the Independent Civilian Review of Missing Persons Investigations. Toronto Police Services Board.

Giwa, S. A. O., Logie, C. H., Karki, K. K., Makanjuola, O. F., & Obiagwu, C. E. (2020). Police violence targeting LGBTIQ+ people in Nigeria: Advancing solutions for a 21st century challenge. *Greenwich Social Work Review, 1*(1), 36–49. https://doi.org/10.21100/gswr.vli1.1108

GLAAD. (2017, March 30). *Accelerating acceptance: GLAAD study reveals twenty percent of millennials identify as LGBTQ.* https://www.glaad.org/blog/new-glaad-study-reveals-twenty-percent-millennials-identify-lgbtq

Goffman, E. (1963). *Stigma: Notes on the management of spoiled identity.* Prentice-Hall.

Gohkale, D. (2018). The interSEXion: A vision for a queer progressive agenda. In M. Adams et al. (Eds.), *Readings for diversity and social justice* (4th ed., pp. 388–391). Routledge.

Goldberg, N. G., Mallory, C., Hasenbush, A., Stemple, L., & Meyer, I. H. (2019). Police and the criminalization of LGBT people. In T. R. Lave & E. J. Miller (Eds.), *The Cambridge handbook of policing in the United States* (pp. 374–391). Cambridge University Press.

Gomez, M. M. (2013). Prejudice-based violence. In C. Motta & M. Sáez (Eds.), *Gender and sexuality in Latin America—cases and decisions* (pp. 279–323). Springer.

Gooden, S. T. (2015). *Race and social equity: A nervous area of government.* Routledge. https://doi.org/10.4324/9781315701301

Goodison, S. E., Barnum, J. D., Jackson, B. A., Sitar, S. I., Vermeer, M. J. D., & Woods, D. (2020). *The law enforcement response to homelessness: Identifying high-priority needs to improve law enforcement strategies for addressing homelessness.* RAND Corporation.

Goodman, R. (2001). Beyond the enforcement principle: Sodomy laws, social norms, and social panoptics. *California Law Review, 89*(3), 643–740. https://doi.org/10.2307/3481180

Goodmark, L. (2009). Autonomy feminism: An anti-essentialist critique of mandatory interventions in domestic violence cases. *Florida State University Law Review, 37*(1), 1–48.

Gorman, E. H. (2005). Gender stereotypes, same-gender preferences, and organizational variation in the hiring of women: Evidence from law firms. *American Sociological Review, 70*(4), 702–728. https://doi.org/10.1177/000312240507000408

Gossett, C., & Huxtable, J. (2017). Existing in the world: Blackness at the edge of trans visibility. In R. Gossett, E. A. Stanley, & J. Burton (Eds.), *Trap door: Trans cultural production and the politics of visibility* (pp. 39–55). MIT Press.

Government Equalities Office. (2018) *LGBT Action Plan: Improving the lives of lesbian, gay, bisexual and transgender people*. https://assets.publishing.service.gov.uk/government/uploads/system/uploads/attachment_data/file/721367/GEO-LGBT-Action-Plan.pdf

Government Equalities Office. (2019). *LGBT Action Plan: Annual progress report, 2018 to 2019*. https://dera.ioe.ac.uk/id/eprint/33740/

Graham, L. F. (2014). Navigating community institutions: Black transgender women's experiences in schools, the criminal justice system, and churches. *Sexuality Research & Social Policy, 11*(4), 274–287. https://doi.org/10.1007/s13178-014-0144-y

Grant, J. M., Mottet, L. A., Tanis, J., Harrison, J., Herman, J. L., & Keisling, M. (2011). *Injustice at every turn: A report of the transgender discrimination survey*. National Center for Transgender Equality and National Gay and Lesbian Task Force.

Greensmith, C., & Giwa, S. (2013). Challenging settler colonialism in contemporary queer politics: Settler homonationalism, Pride Toronto, and Two-Spirit subjectivities. *American Indian Culture and Research Journal, 37*(2), 129–148.

Greeson, M. R., Campbell, R., & Fehler-Cabral, G. (2014). Cold or caring? Adolescent sexual assault victims' perceptions of their interactions with the police. *Violence and Victims, 29*(4), 636–651. https://doi.org/10.1891/0886-6708.VV-D-13-00039

Gregoire, P. (2022, November 24). NSW police has no place at Mardi Gras, says Pride in Protest's Mikhael Burnard. *Sydney Criminal Lawyers* [Blog]. https://www.sydneycriminallawyers.com.au/blog/nsw-police-has-no-place-at-mardi-gras-says-pride-in-protests-mikhael-burnard/

Griggs, C. (1998). *S/he: Changing sex and changing clothes*. Bloomsbury. https://doi.org/10.2752/9781847888846

Groenke, G. (2019). *Law and society: The criminalization of Latinx in the United States* [Master's thesis, City University of New York]. CUNY Academic Works. https://academicworks.cuny.edu/gc_etds/3421

Grzanka, P. R., Gonzalez, K. A., & Spanierman, L. B. (2019). White supremacy and counseling psychology: A critical–conceptual framework. *Counseling Psychologist, 47*(4), 478–529. https://doi.org/10.1177/0011000019880843

Guadalupe-Diaz, X. (2016). Disclosure of same-sex intimate partner violence to police among lesbians, gays, and bisexuals. *Social Currents, 3*(2), 160–171.

Hail-Jares, K., Vichta-Ohlsen, R., Butler, T. M., & Byrne, J. (2023). Queer homelessness: The distinct experiences of sexuality and trans-gender diverse youth. *Journal of LGBT Youth, 20*(4), 757–782. https://doi.org/10.1080/19361653.2021.1990817

Halperin, D. M. (1995). *Saint Foucault: Towards a gay hagiography*. Oxford University Press.

Hamilton, K. M., Park, L. S., Carsey, T. A., & Martinez, L. R. (2019). "Lez be honest": Gender expression impacts workplace disclosure decisions. *Journal of Lesbian Studies, 23*(2), 144–168. https://doi.org/10.1080/10894160.2019.1520540

Hammers, C. (2019). Reworking trauma through BDSM. *Signs: Journal of Women in Culture and Society, 44*(2), 491–514. https://doi.org/10.1086/699370

Handy, S. (2022, July 7). *Uniformed police officers to march in San Diego Pride parade*. CBS 8. https://www.cbs8.com/article/news/local/uniformed-police-officers-in-san-diego-pride/509-c9f41903-84de-4761-a83c-99f4ceae3409

Hanmer, J., Radford, J., & Stanko, E. (1989). *Women, policing, and male violence: International perspectives*. Routledge. https://doi.org/10.4324/9780203514771

Harmon, R. A. (2019). Justifying police practices: The example of arrests. In T. R. Lave & E. J. Miller (Eds.), *The Cambridge handbook of policing in the United States* (pp. 163–177). Cambridge University Press.

Hassell, K. D., & Brandl, S. G. (2009). An examination of the workplace experiences of police patrol officers: The role of race, sex, and sexual orientation. *Police Quarterly, 12*(4), 408–430. https://doi.org/10.1177/1098611109348473

Haviv, N. (2016). Reporting sexual assaults to the police: The Israeli BDSM community. *Sexuality Research & Social Policy, 13*(3), 276–287. https://doi.org/10.1007/s13178-016-0222-4

Hazard Jr., G. C. (1995). Law, morals, and ethics. *Southern Illinois University Law Journal, 19*, 447–458.

Headley, A. M. (2020). Race, ethnicity, and social equity in policing. In M. E. Guy & S. A. McCandless (Eds.), *Achieving social equity: From problems to solutions* (pp. 82–97). Melvin and Leigh.

Headley, A. M., & Wright, J. E. (2020). Is representation enough? Racial disparities in levels of force and arrests by police. *Public Administration Review, 80*(6), 1051–1062. https://doi.org/10.1111/puar.13225

Hébert, A., & Weaver, A. (2014). An examination of personality characteristics associated with BDSM orientations. *Canadian Journal of Human Sexuality, 23*(2), 106–115. https://doi.org/10.3138/cjhs.2467

Heidensohn, F. (1992). *Women in control? The role of women in law enforcement*. Clarendon Press.

Heifetz, R. A., Linsky, M., & Grashow, A. (2009). *The practice of adaptive leadership: Tools and tactics for changing your organization and the world*. Harvard Business Review Press.

Herbert, S. (2006). Tangled up in blue: Conflicting paths to police legitimacy. *Theoretical Criminology, 10*(4), 481–504. https://doi.org/10.1177/1362480606068875

Herek, G. M. (2009). Sexual stigma and sexual prejudice in the United States: A conceptual framework. *Contemporary Perspectives on Lesbian, Gay, and Bisexual Identities, 54*, 65–111. https://doi.org/10.1007/978-0-387-09556-1_4

Herek, G. M. (2010). Sexual orientation differences as deficits: Science and stigma in the history of American psychology. *Perspectives on Psychological Science, 5*(6), 693–699. https://doi.org/10.1177/1745691610388770

Hereth, J. (2022). *Overrepresentation of people who identify as LGBTQ+ in the criminal legal system.* Safety and Justice Challenge. https://safetyandjusticechallenge.org/resources/overrepresentation-of-people-who-identify-as-lgbtq-in-the-criminal-legal-system/

Hinchy, J. (2019). *Governing gender and sexuality in colonial India: The hijra, c. 1850–1900.* Cambridge University Press. https://doi.org/10.1017/9781108592208

History.com Editors. (2017, May 31). *Stonewall riots.* History.com. https://www.history.com/topics/gay-rights/the-stonewall-riots

Hodge, J., & Sexton, L. (2020). Examining the blue line in the rainbow: The interactions and perceptions of law enforcement among lesbian, gay, bisexual, transgender and queer communities. *Police Practice and Research, 21*(3): 246–263.

Hoffman, P. B., & Hickey, E. R. (2005). Use of force by female police officers. *Journal of Criminal Justice, 33*(2), 145–151. https://doi.org/10.1016/j.jcrimjus.2004.12.006

Holmes, A. (2021). Marching with pride? Debates on uniformed police participating in Vancouver's LGBTQ pride parade. *Journal of Homosexuality, 68*(8), 1320–1352. https://doi.org/10.1080/00918369.2019.1696107

Holt, K. (2016). Blacklisted: Boundaries, violations, and retaliatory behavior in the BDSM community. *Deviant Behavior, 37*(8), 917–930. https://doi.org/10.1080/01639625.2016.1156982

Holvoet, L., Huys, W., Coppens, V., Seeuws, J., Goethals, K., & Morrens, M. (2017). Fifty shades of Belgian gray: The prevalence of BDSM-related fantasies and activities in the general population. *Journal of Sexual Medicine, 14*(9), 1152–1159. https://doi.org/10.1016/j.jsxm.2017.07.003

Home Office. (2021). *National statistics: Police workforce, England and Wales.* https://www.gov.uk/government/statistics/police-workforce-england-and-wales-31-march-2021/police-workforce-england-and-wales-31-march-2021

Hong, S. (2017). Does increasing ethnic representativeness reduce police misconduct? *Public Administration Review, 77*(2), 195–205. https://doi.org/10.1111/puar.12629

Hooker, J. (2020). LGBTQ persons, allies, and the pursuit of social equity. In M. E. Guy and S. A. McCandless (Eds.), *Achieving social equity: From problems to solutions* (pp. 28–40). Melvin and Leigh.

Howells, L. (2019). *Protesters decry Hamilton police after arrest connected to Pride violence*. CBC News. https://www.cbc.ca/news/canada/hamilton /protesters-decry-hamilton-police-after-arrest-connected-to-pride -violence-1.5186650?fbclid=IwAR2VltL19qNYpJsYwzKiQ6YTPIrNklj 40RmvUm1mGYBYS9vscl5C5bteAZI

Human Rights Campaign. (2020). *State of equality index*. Accessed November 29, 2021. https://www.hrc.org/resources/state-equality-index

Human Rights Campaign. (2021). *Municipal equality index*. Accessed November 29, 2021. https://www.hrc.org/resources/municipal-equality -index

Human Rights Watch. (2016). *World report 2016: Events of 2015*. Policy Press.

Ingram, H., Schneider, A. L., & DeLeon, P. (2019). Social construction and policy design. In P. A. Sabatier (Ed.), *Theories of the policy process* (2nd ed., pp. 93–126). Routledge.

International Commission of Jurists. (2017). *Unnatural offences: Obstacles to justice in India based on sexual orientation and gender identity*.

Irazábal, C., & Huerta, C. (2016). Intersectionality and planning at the margins: LGBTQ youth of color in New York. *Gender, Place and Culture, 23*(5), 714–732. https://doi.org/10.1080/0966369X.2015.1058755

Irving, D. (2021). Rethinking how police respond to homelessness. *RAND* [Blog]. https://www.rand.org/blog/rand-review/2021/03/rethinking-how -police-respond-to-homelessness.html

Jackson, J., Bradford, B., Stanko, B., & Hohl, K. (2012). *Just authority? Trust in the police in England and Wales*. Willan.

Jackson, P. A. (2000). An explosion of Thai identities: Global queering and re-imagining queer theory. *Culture, Health & Sexuality, 2*(4), 405–424. https://doi.org/10.1080/13691050050174422

Jagose, A. (2009). Feminism's queer theory. *Feminism & Psychology, 19*(2), 157–174. https://doi.org/10.1177/0959353509102152

Jain, D., Aher, A., Shaikh, S., Sarkar, A., & Tronic, B. (2020). Negotiating violence: Everyday queer experiences of the law. *Violence and Gender, 7*(4), 141–149. https://doi.org/10.1089/vi0.2020.0002

Jain, D., & Rhoten, K. M. (2020). Epistemic injustice and judicial discourse on transgender rights in India: Uncovering temporal pluralism. *Journal of Human Values, 26*(1), 30–49. https://doi.org/10.1177 /0971685819890186

Jain, D., & Tronic, B. (2019). Conflicting abortion laws in India: Unintended barriers to safe abortion for adolescent girls. *Indian Journal of Medical Ethics, 4*(4), 310–317. https://doi.org/10.20529/IJME.2019.059

James, S. E., Herman, J., Keisling, M., & Mottet, L. & Anafi, M. (2016.) *2015 US transgender survey: Version 1*. Inter-university Consortium for Political and Social Research. https://doi.org/10.3886/ICPSR37229.v1

Jane, A. (2022, August 13). *Charlottesville's first black woman police chief fired as officers refused to comply*. The Root. https://www.theroot.com /charlottesvilles-first-Black-woman-police-chief-fired-a-1849409335

Jelen, T. G. (2017). Public attitudes toward abortion and LGBTQ issues: A dynamic analysis of region and partisanship. *SAGE Open, 7*(1). https:// doi.org/10.1177/2158244017697362

Johnson, K., Lennon, S. J., & Rudd, N. (2014). Dress, body and self: Research in the social psychology of dress. *Drugs, 1*(1), 1. https://doi.org/10.1186 /s40691-014-0020-7

Johnson, N. J., & Svara, J. H. (2015). *Justice for all: Promoting social equity in public administration*. Routledge.

Johnson, R. G., Rivera, M. A., & Lopez, N. (2018). A public ethics approach focused on the lives of diverse LGBTQ homeless youth. *Public Integrity, 20*(6), 611–624. https://doi.org/10.1080/10999922.2017.1342217

Jones, E. (2019, September 23). What did Halifax's new police chief Dan Kinsella learn in Hamilton? *Halifax Examiner*. https://www.halifaxexaminer .ca/uncategorized/what-did-halifaxs-new-police-chief-dan-kinsella -learn-in-hamilton/.

Jones, J. M. (2022, February 17). *LGBT identification in U.S. ticks up to 7.1%*. Gallup. https://news.gallup.com/poll/389792/lgbt-identification-ticks -up.aspx

Jones, M. (2015). Who forgot lesbian, gay, and bisexual police officers? Findings from a national survey. *Policing, 9*(1), 65–76. https://doi.org/10.1093 /police/pau061

Jones, M., & Williams, M. L. (2015). Twenty years on: Lesbian, gay and bisexual police officers' experiences of workplace discrimination in England and Wales. *Policing & Society, 25*(2), 188–211. https://doi.org/10.1080 /10439463.2013.817998

Joseph, S. (2005). *Social work practice and men who have sex with men*. Sage.

Jozifkova, E. (2013). Consensual sadomasochistic sex (BDSM): The roots, the risks, and the distinctions between BDSM and violence. *Current Psychiatry Reports, 15*(9), 392–392. https://doi.org/10.1007/s11920-013-0392-1

Jubb, N., Camacho, G., D'Angelo, A., Hernández, K., Macassi, I., Meléndez, L., & Yáñez, G. (2010). *Women's police stations in Latin America: An entry point for stopping violence and gaining access to justice*. CEPLAES, IDRC.

Katzenstein, P. J. (1996). *The culture of national security: Norms and identity in world politics*. Columbia University Press.

Keegan, C. M. (2020). Against queer theory. *TSQ, 7*(3), 349–353. https://doi .org/10.1215/23289252-8552978

Keehnen, O. (2008, October 20). Behind the wall: LGBT police. *Windy City Times.* https://windycitytimes.com/m/APPredirect.php?AID=19143

Keiser, L. R. (2011). Representative bureaucracy. In R. F. Durant (Ed.), *The Oxford handbook of American bureaucracy.* https://doi.org/10.1093/oxfordhb/9780199238958.003.0030

Kennedy, A. C., & Prock, K. A. (2018). "I still feel like I am not normal": A review of the role of stigma and stigmatization among female survivors of child sexual abuse, sexual assault, and intimate partner violence. *Trauma, Violence, & Abuse, 19*(5), 512–527. https://doi.org/10.1177/1524838016673601

Kennelly, J. (2011). Policing young people as citizens-in-waiting: Legitimacy, spatiality and governance. *British Journal of Criminology, 51*(2), 336–354. https://doi.org/10.1093/bjc/azr017

Kennelly, J. (2015). "You're making our city look bad": Olympic security, neoliberal urbanization, and homeless youth. *Ethnography, 16*(1), 3–24. https://doi.org/10.1177/1466138113513526

Khan, U., 2016. Take my breath away: Competing contexts between domestic violence, kink and the criminal justice system in *R. v. J.A. Oñati Socio-legal Series, 6* (6), 1405–1425. https://ssrn.com/abstract=2891048

Kieran, R., & Sheff, E. (2016). How did it hurt? Distinguishing between intimate partner violence and BDSM relationships. In P. Karian (Ed.), *Critical & experiential: Dimensions in gender and sexual diversity.* Resonance Press.

Kimble, S. (2015). Lesbian, gay, bisexual, and transgender youth (and adult) homelessness. In W. Swan (Ed.), *Gay, lesbian, bisexual, and transgender civil rights: A public policy agenda for uniting a divided America* (pp. 229–250). Routledge.

Kimmel, M. S. Globalization and its mal(e)contents: The gendered moral and political economy of terrorism. In M. S. Kimmel, J. Hearn, & R.W. Connell (Eds.), *Handbook of studies on men and masculinities* (pp. 414–431). Sage.

Kinsey, A. C., Pomeroy, W. B., Martin, C. E., Bancroft, J., & Gebhard, P. H. (1953). *Sexual behavior in the human female.* Indiana University Press.

Klages, M. (2017). *Literary theory: The complete guide.* Bloomsbury.

Krettenauer, T., & Lefebvre, J. P. (2021). Beyond subjective and personal: Endorsing pro-environmental norms as moral norms. *Journal of Environmental Psychology, 76.* https://doi.org/10.1016/j.jenvp.2021.101644

Krishna, A. (2013). Making it in India: Examining social mobility in three walks of life. *Economic and Political Weekly, 48*(49), 38–49.

Krishna, A. (2014). Examining the structure of opportunity and social mobility in India: Who becomes an engineer? *Development and Change, 45*(1), 1–28. https://doi.org/10.1111/dech.12072

Krishnamurty, K., Scully, M., & Carberry, E. J. (2018). Employee resource groups in the workplace: Their prevalence, composition, and concerns. In *Proceedings of the 48th Atlantic Schools of Business Conference, Université de Moncton, 2018* (pp. 274–284).

Kumar, P. (2017). Radicalizing community development: The changing face of the queer movement in Hyderabad City. *Community Development Journal, 52*(3), 470–487. https://doi.org/10.1093/CDJ/BSX026

Kumar, P. (2020). Mapping queer "celebratory moment" in India: Necropolitics or substantive democracy? *Community Development Journal, 55*(1), 159–176. https://doi.org/10.1093/cdj/bsz031

Kumar, S., Heath, A., & Oliver, H. (2002). Determinants of social mobility in India. *Economic and Political Weekly, 37*(29), 2983–2987.

Kunst, M. J. J., Saan, M. C., Bollen, L. J. A., & Kuijpers, K. F. (2017). Secondary traumatic stress and secondary posttraumatic growth in a sample of Dutch police family liaison officers. *Stress and Health, 33*(5), 570–577.

Lam, K. (2019, February 8). LGBT police officers say they've faced horrible discrimination, and now they're suing. *USA Today.* https://www.usatoday.com/story/news/2019/02/08/lgbt-law-enforcement-officers-sue-over-workplace-discrimination/2404755002/

Langdridge, D., & Barker, M. (2007). Situating sadomasochism. In D. Langdridge & M. Barker (Eds.). *Safe, sane and consensual contemporary perspectives on sadomasochism* (pp. 3–9). Palgrave Macmillan.

Leonard, W., & Fileborn, B. (2018). *Policing for same sex attracted and sex and gender diverse (SSASGD) young Victorians.* Monograph series no. 110. La Trobe University, Melbourne. https://www.police.vic.gov.au/sites/default/files/2019-01/Policing-for-SSASGD-Young-People---ARCSHS.pdf

Lewis, A. P. (2009). Discourses of change: Policing, sexuality, and organizational culture. *Asia Pacific Journal of Marketing and Logistics, 4*(3), 208–230. https://doi.org/10.1108/17465640911002518

Little, C., Stephens, P., & Whittle, S. (2002). The praxis and politics of policing: Problems facing transgender people. *Law and Justice Journal, 2*(2), 226–243.

Loftus, B. (2008). Dominant culture interrupted: Recognition, resentment and the politics of change in an English police force. *British Journal of Criminology, 48*(6), 756–777. https://doi.org/10.1093/bjc/azn065

Loftus, B. (2010). Police occupational culture: Classic themes, altered times. *Policing & Society, 20*(1), 1–20. https://doi.org/10.1080/10439460903281547

Lombardi, E. L., Wilchins, R. A., Priesing, D., & Malouf, D. (2002). Gender violence: Transgender experiences with violence and discrimination. *Journal of Homosexuality, 42*(1), 89–101. https://doi.org/10.1300/J082v42n01_05

Lubitow, A., Carathers, J., Kelly, M., & Abelson, M. (2017). Transmobilities: Mobility, harassment, and violence experienced by transgender and gender nonconforming public transit riders in Portland, Oregon. *Gender, Place and Culture, 24*(10), 1398–1418. https://doi.org/10.1080/0966369X .2017.1382451

Ludwig, J. E. (2017). BDSM and sexual assault in the rules of evidence: A proposal. *New York University Review of Law and Social Change, 43*, 11–39.

Lum, C., Telep, C. W., Koper, C. S., & Grieco, J. (2012). Receptivity to research in policing. *Justice Research and Policy, 14*(1), 61–95. https://doi.org/10.3818 /JRP.14.1.2012.61

Lyons, P. M., DeValve, M. J., & Garner, R. L. (2008). Texas police chiefs' attitudes toward gay and lesbian police officers. *Police Quarterly, 11*(1), 102–117. https://doi.org/10.1177/1098611107302655

Lyons, T., Krüsi, A., Pierre, L., Kerr, T., Small, W., & Shannon, K. (2017). Negotiating violence in the context of transphobia and criminalization: The experiences of trans sex workers in Vancouver, Canada. *Qualitative Health Research, 27*(2), 182–190. https://doi.org/10.1177/1049732315613311

Maccio, E. M., & Ferguson, K. M. (2016). Services to LGBTQ runaway and homeless youth: Gaps and recommendations. *Children and Youth Services Review, 63*, 47–57. https://doi.org/10.1016/j.childyouth.2016.02.008

Machado, M. A., & Lugo, A. M. (2022). A behavioral analysis of two strategies to eliminate racial bias in police use of force. *Behavior Analysis in Practice, 15*(4), 1221–1231. https://doi.org/10.1007/s40617-021-00551-1

Macpherson, W., Cook, T., Sentamu, J., & Stone, R. (1999). *The Stephen Lawrence inquiry: Report of an inquiry by Sir William Macpherson of Cluny*, CM 4262-I. Stationery Office.

Make the Road New York. (2012). *Transgressive policing: police abuse of LGBTQ communities of color in Jackson Heights*. https://maketheroadny .org/wp-content/uploads/2018/02/MRNY_Transgressive_Policing_Full _Report_10.23.12B.pdf

Mallory, C., Hasenbush, A., & Sears, B. (2013). *Discrimination against law enforcement officers on the basis of sexual orientation and gender identity: 2000 to 2013*. Williams Institute.

Mallory, C., Hasenbush, A., & Sears, B. (2015). Addressing harassment and discrimination by law enforcement against LGBT police officers and community members to improve effective policing. *LGBTQ Policy Journal, 5*, 79–87.

Marcus, S. (2005). Queer theory for everyone: A review essay. *Signs: Journal of Women in Culture and Society, 31*(1), 191–218. https://doi.org/10.1086 /432743

The Marshall Project. (n.d.). *The future of policing*. https://www.themarshall project.org/2020/10/23/the-future-of-policing

Maslov, A. (2016). *Measuring the performance of the police: The perspective of the public.* Research report 2015-R034. Public Safety Canada / Sécurité publique Canada.

Masters, W. H., Johnson, V. E., & Kolodny, R. C. (1995). *Human sexuality* (5th ed.). HarperCollins.

Mathew, P. (2016, November 9). *Transgender woman dies in Chennai, she was found burnt outside a police station.* News Minute. https://www.thenewsminute.com/article/transgender-woman-dies-chennai-she-was-found-burnt-outside-police-station-52639

Maynard, R. (2017). *Policing black lives: State violence in Canada from slavery to the present.* Fernwood.

McCandless, S. (2018a). Improving community relations: How police strategies to improve accountability for social equity affect citizen perceptions. *Public Integrity, 20*(4), 370–385. https://doi.org/10.1080/10999922.2017.1416880

McCandless, S. (2018b). LGBT homeless youth and policing. *Public Integrity, 20*(6), 558–570. https://doi.org/10.1080/10999922.2017.1402738

McCandless, S., & Blessett, B. (2022). Dismantling racism and white supremacy in public service institutions and society: Contextualizing the discussion and introducing the symposium. *Administrative Theory & Praxis, 44*(2), 91–104.

McCandless, S., & Elias, N. M. (2021). Beyond Bostock: Implications for LGBTQ+ theory and practice. *Administrative Theory & Praxis, 43*(1), 1–15. https://doi.org/10.1080/10841806.2020.1840903

McCandless, S., & Vogler, G. M. (2020). "Habermasville": Police-community intersections and communicative rationality. *Administrative Theory & Praxis, 42*(4), 443–458. https://doi.org/10.1080/10841806.2019.1678350

McCarthy, D. J. (2013). Gendering "soft" policing: Multi-agency working, female cops, and the fluidities of police culture/s. *Policing & Society, 23*(2), 261–278. https://doi.org/10.1080/10439463.2012.703199

McDonald, J. (2015). Organizational communication meets queer theory: Theorizing relations of "difference" differently. *Communication Theory, 25*(3), 310–329. https://doi.org/10.1111/comt.12060

McElvain, J. P., & Kposowa, A. J. (2008). Police officer characteristics and the likelihood of using deadly force. *Criminal Justice and Behavior, 35*(4), 505–521. https://doi.org/10.1177/0093854807313995

McIntosh, I., & Wright, S. (2019). Exploring what the notion of "lived experience" offers for social policy analysis. *Journal of Social Policy, 48*(3), 449–467.

McKenna, N. C., & Holtfreter, K. (2021). Trauma-informed courts: A review and integration of justice perspectives and gender responsiveness. *Journal of Aggression, Maltreatment & Trauma, 30*(4), 450–470.

McLean, C. (2021). The growth of the anti-transgender movement in the United Kingdom. The silent radicalization of the British electorate. *International Journal of Sociology, 51*(6), 473–482.

McNeil, J., Bailey, L., Ellis, S., Morton, J., & Regan, M. (2012). *Trans mental health study 2012.* Scottish Transgender Alliance. http://www.scottish trans.org/wp-content/uploads/2013/03/trans_mh_study.pdf

Meier, K. J. (1975). Representative bureaucracy: An empirical analysis. *American Political Science Review, 69*(2), 526–542. https://doi.org/10.2307/1959084

Mello, F., & Arredondo, V. (2020). *Students push UC to abolish police departments.* Cal Matters. https://calmatters.org/education/2020/06/students -push-uc-to-abolish-police-departments/

Mendoza, S. A., & Parks-Stamm, E. J. (2020). Embodying the police: The effects of enclothed cognition on shooting decisions. *Psychological Reports, 123*(6), 2353–2371. https://doi.org/10.1177/0033294119860261

Mennicke, A., Gromer, J., Oehme, K., & MacConnie, L. (2018). Workplace experiences of gay and lesbian criminal justice officers in the United States: A qualitative investigation of officers attending a LGBT law enforcement conference. *Policing & Society, 28*(6), 712–729. https://doi.org/10.1080 /10439463.2016.1238918

Mercer, E. (2015). Out in force: The new struggle against sexually oriented policing. *Inquiries Journal, 7*(3). http://www.inquiriesjournal.com/a?id=1007

Messerschmidt, J. W. (1996). Managing to kill: Masculinities and the space shuttle Challenger explosion. *Masculinities, 3*(4), 1–22.

Messner, M. A. (1997). *Politics of masculinities: Men in movements.* Rowman & Littlefield.

Messner, M. A. (2016). Forks in the road of men's gender politics: Men's rights vs feminist allies. *International Journal for Crime, Justice and Social Democracy, 5*(2), 6–20. https://doi.org/10.5204/ijcjsd.v5i2.301

Meyer, D. (2020). "So much for protect and serve": Queer male survivors' perceptions of negative police experiences. *Journal of Contemporary Criminal Justice, 36*(2), 228–250. https://doi.org/10.1177/1043986219894430

Meyer, S., & Millison, J. (2022). Queer up your work: Adding sexual orientation and gender identity to public and nonprofit research. *Journal of Public and Nonprofit Affairs, 8*(1), 145–156.

Meyer, S., & Reeves, E. (2021). Policies, procedures and risk aversity: Police decision-making in domestic violence matters in an Australian jurisdiction. *Policing & Society, 31*(10), 1168–1182. https://doi.org/10.1080 /10439463.2020.1869234

Meyer, S. J., Dale, E. J., & Willis, K. K. M. (2022). "Where my gays at?" The status of LGBTQ people and queer theory in nonprofit research. *Nonprofit and Voluntary Sector Quarterly, 51*(3), 566–586. https://doi.org/10.1177 /08997640211021497

Meyer, S. J., Dale, E. J., & Willis, K. K. (forthcoming). *Burn it to the ground: Queer theory, (hetero)normativities, and binaries in nonprofit organizations.*

Miles-Johnson, T. (2013a). Confidence and trust in police: How sexual identity difference shapes perceptions of police. *Current Issues in Criminal Justice, 25*(2), 685–702. https://doi.org/10.1080/10345329.2013.12035990

Miles-Johnson, T. (2013b). LGBTI variations in crime reporting: How sexual identity influences decisions to call the cops. *SAGE Open, 3*(2). https://doi .org/10.1177/2158244013490707

Miles-Johnson, T. (2015). "They don't identify with us": Perceptions of police by Australian transgender people. *International Journal of Transgenderism, 16*(3), 169–189. https://doi.org/10.1080/15532739.2015.1080647

Miles-Johnson, T. (2016a). Perceptions of group value: How Australian transgender people view policing. *Policing & Society, 26*(6), 605–626. https:// doi.org/10.1080/10439463.2014.996563

Miles-Johnson, T. (2016b). Policing diversity: Examining police resistance to training reforms for transgender people in Australia. *Journal of Homosexuality, 63*(1), 103–136. https://doi.org/10.1080/00918369.2015.1078627

Miles-Johnson, T. (2019). Policing diverse people: How occupational attitudes and background characteristics shape police recruits' perceptions. *SAGE Open, 9*(3), https://doi.org/10.1177/2158244019865362.

Miller, S. L. (1999). *Gender and community policing: Walking the talk.* Northeastern University Press.

Miller, S. L., Forest, K. B., & Jurik, N. C. (2003). Diversity in blue: Lesbian and gay police officers in a masculine occupation. *Men and Masculinities, 5*(4), 355–385. https://doi.org/10.1177/0095399702250841

Miller, S. L., & Lilley, T. G. (2014). Proving themselves: The status of LGBQ police officers. *Sociology Compass, 8*(4), 373–383. https://doi.org/10.1111 /soc4.12149

Mills, S., Dion, M., Thompson-Blum, D., Borst, C., & Diemert, J. (2019). *Mapping the void: Two-spirit and LGBTQ+ experiences in Hamilton.* McMaster University and the AIDS Network.

Minero, L. P., Domínguez Jr., S., Budge, S. L., & Salcedo, B. (2022). Latinx trans immigrants' survival of torture in US detention: A qualitative investigation of the psychological impact of abuse and mistreatment. *International Journal of Transgender Health, 23*(1–2), 36–59.

Mishra, R. (2021, March 1). In a first, Chhattisgarh police hire 13 transgenders as constables. *Hindustan Times.* https://www.hindustantimes.com/india -news/in-a-first-chhattisgarh-police-hire-13-transgenders-as-constables -101614610481859.html

Mogul, J., Ritchie, A., & Whitlock, K. (2011). *Queer (in)justice: The criminalization of LGBT people in the United States.* Beacon Press.

Monica, P. (2011). Beyond the pleasure principle: The criminalization of consensual sadomasochistic sex. *Texas Journal of Women and the Law, 11*(1), 51–92.

Moosavi, L. (2019). Decolonising criminology: Syed Hussein Alatas on crimes of the powerful. *Critical Criminology, 27*(2), 229–242. https://doi.org /10.1007/s10612-018-9396-9

Moran, L., & Skeggs, B. (2003). *Sexuality and the politics of violence and safety.* Taylor & Francis.

Moran, L. J., & Sharpe, A. N. (2004). Violence, identity, and policing: The case of violence against transgender people. *Criminal Justice, 4*(4), 395–417. https://doi.org/10.1177/1466802504048656

Moser, C. (2006). Demystifying alternative sexual behaviors. *Sexuality, Reproduction & Menopause, 4*(2), 86–90. https://doi.org/10.1016/j.sram .2006.08.007

Moser, C., & Kleinplatz, P. J. (2006). DSM-IV-TR and the paraphilias: An argument for removal. *Journal of Psychology and Human Sexuality, 17*(3–4), 91–109. https://doi.org/10.1300/J056v17n03_05

Moser, C., & Kleinplatz, P. J. (2007). Themes of SM expression. In D. Langdridge & M. Barker (Eds.), *Safe, sane and consensual contemporary perspectives on sadomasochism* (pp. 35–54). Palgrave Macmillan.

Mossburg, C., & Romine, T. (2022, May 24). *San Francisco's mayor to opt out of Pride parade over ban on police participating in uniform.* CNN. https:// www.cnn.com/2022/05/24/us/san-francisco-pride-police-uniform/index .html

Moton, L., Blount-Hill, K., & Colvin, R. A. (2020). Squaring the circle: Exploring lesbian experience in a heteromale police profession. In C. Coates & M. Walker-Pickett (Eds.), *Women, minorities, and criminal justice: A multicultural intersectionality approach* (pp. 243–255). Kendall Hunt.

Mountz, S. E. (2016). That's the sound of the police: State-sanctioned violence and resistance among LGBT young people previously incarcerated in girls' juvenile justice facilities. *Affilia, 31*(3), 287–302. https://doi.org /10.1177/0886109916641161

Murphy-Oikonen, J., & Egan, R. (2022). Sexual and gender minorities: Reporting sexual assault to the police. *Journal of Homosexuality, 69*(5), 773–795. https://doi.org/10.1080/00918369.2021.1892402

Myers, K. A., Forest, K. B., & Miller, S. L. (2004). Officer friendly and the tough cop: Gays and lesbians navigate homophobia and policing. *Journal of Homosexuality, 47*(1), 17–37. https://doi.org/10.1300/J082v47n01_02

Nadal, K. L., Quintanilla, A., Goswick, A., & Sriken, J. (2015). Lesbian, gay, bisexual, and queer people's perceptions of the criminal justice system: Implications for social services. *Journal of Gay & Lesbian Social Services, 27*(4), 457–481. https://doi.org/10.1080/10538720.2015.1085116

NALSA v. Union of India. (2014). AIR 2014 SC 1863.

Narrain, S. (2004). Sexuality and the law. *Frontline, 20*(26), 20. https://frontline.thehindu.com/the-nation/article30220469.ece

Nash, C. J., & Gorman-Murray, A. (2014). LGBT neighbourhoods and "new mobilities": Towards understanding transformations in sexual and gendered urban landscapes. *International Journal of Urban and Regional Research, 38*(3), 756–772. https://doi.org/10.1111/1468-2427.12104

Nataraj, S. (2017). Criminal "folk" and "legal" lore: The kidnap and castrate narrative in colonial India and contemporary Chennai. *South Asian History and Culture, 8*(4), 523–541. https://doi.org/10.1080/19472498.2017.1371508

National Academies of Sciences, Engineering, and Medicine. (2022). *Reducing inequalities between lesbian, gay, bisexual, transgender, and queer adolescents and cisgender, heterosexual adolescents: Proceedings of a workshop*. National Academies Press. https://doi.org/10.17226/26383

National Association for the Advancement of Colored People. (2021). *Criminal justice fact sheet*. https://naacp.org/resources/criminal-justice-fact-sheet

National Center for Transgender Equality (2019). *Failing to protect and serve: Police department policies towards transgender people*. https://transequality.org/sites/default/files/docs/resources/FTPS_FR_v3.pdf

National Center for Transgender Equality. (n.d.). *ID documents center*. https://transequality.org/documents

National Coalition for Sexual Freedom. (2022). *Consent legal cases*. https://ncsfreedom.org/consent-legal-cases-3/.

National Conference of State Legislatures. (2022). *Legislative responses for policing-state bill tracking database*. https://www.ncsl.org/civil-and-criminal-justice/legislative-responses-for-policing-state-bill-tracking-database

Navtej Singh v. Union of India. (2018). AIR 2018 SC 4321.

Naylor, L. A. (2020). *Social equity and LGBTQ rights: Dismantling discrimination and expanding civil rights*. Routledge.

Neocleous, M. (2000). *The fabrication of social order: A critical theory of police power*. Pluto Press.

New Zealand Police Association. (2021). *Double-crewing "more productive."* https://www.policeassn.org.nz/news/double-crewing-more-productive#/

Newmahr, S. (2011). *Playing on the edge: Sadomasochism, risk, and intimacy*. Indiana University Press.

Newman, T. (2023). *Sex and gender: Meanings, definition, identity, and expression*. Medical News Today. https://www.medicalnewstoday.com/articles/232363

Nichols, A. (2010). Dance Ponnaya, dance! Police abuses against transgender sex workers in Sri Lanka. *Feminist Criminology, 5*(2), 195–222. https://doi .org/10.1177/1557085110366226

Nimbi, F. M., Ciocca, G., Limoncin, E., Fontanesi, L., Uysal, Ü. B., Flinchum, M., Tambelli, R., Jannini, E. A., & Simonelli, C. (2020). Sexual desire and fantasies in the LGBT+ community: Focus on lesbian women and gay men. *Current Sexual Health Reports, 12*, 153–161.

Nixon, T. T. (2021). *Pride in policing: Perspectives of LGBTQ police officers* [Doctoral dissertation, University of Alabama at Birmingham].

Nolan, T. C. (2006). Outcomes for a transitional living program serving LGBTQ youth in New York City. *Child Welfare, 85*(2), 385–406.

Nordling, N., Sandnabba, N. K., Santtila, P., & Alison, L. (2006). Differences and similarities between gay and straight individuals involved in the sadomasochistic subculture. *Journal of Homosexuality, 50*(2–3), 41–57. https://doi.org/10.1300/J082v50n02_03

Norman-Major, K. (2018). Thinking outside the box: Using multisector approaches to address the wicked problem of homelessness among LGBTQ youth. *Public Integrity, 20*(6), 546–557. https://doi.org/10.1080/10999922 .2017.1325999

North Shore. (2019, June). *Hamilton Pride 2019 reportback.* https://north -shore.info/2019/06/19/hamilton-pride-2019-reportback/

Northouse, P. (2022). *Leadership: Theory and practice* (9th ed.). Sage.

Office of the Correctional Investigator. (n.d.). *Annual report, 2019–2020.* https://oci-bec.gc.ca/sites/default/files/2023-06/annrpt20192020-eng.pdf

Office of the Independent Police Review Director. (2019). *Service complaint investigative report.* https://pub-hamilton.escribemeetings.com/filestream .ashx?DocumentId=224797

O'Neill, M., & Holdaway, S. (2007). Examining "window dressing": The views of black police associations on recruitment and training. *Journal of Ethnic and Migration Studies, 33*(3), 483–500. https://doi.org/10.1080 /13691830701234780

Osborn, M. (2022a). *LGBTQIA+ individuals' encounters with police: Contextual factors, help-seeking, and service needs* [Doctoral dissertation, City University of New York].

Osborn, M. (2022b). "Nobody ever correctly recognizes me": Nonbinary presentation, visibility, and safety across contexts. In M. T. Segal & V. Demos (Eds.), *Gender visibility and erasure* (pp. 51–69). Emerald.

Owen, S. S., Burke, T. W., Few-Demo, A. L., & Natwick, J. (2018). Perceptions of the police by LGBT communities. *American Journal of Criminal Justice, 43*(3), 668–693. https://doi.org/10.1007/s12103-017-9420-8

Padrón, K. (2015). *Legal injuries: Deportability and US immigration policy in the lives of transLatina immigrants* [Doctoral dissertation, University of Minnesota].

Palmer, N. A., & Kutateladze, B. L. (2022). What prosecutors and the police should do about underreporting of anti-LGBTQ hate crime. *Sexuality Research & Social Policy, 19*(3), 1190–1204. https://doi.org/10.1007/s13178-021-00596-5

Panfil, V. R. (2018a). LGBTQ populations of color, crime, and justice: An emerging but urgent topic. In R. Martínez Jr., M. E. Hollis, & J. I. Stowell (Eds.), *The handbook of race, ethnicity, crime, and justice* (pp. 415–433). John Wiley & Sons.

Panfil, V. R. (2018b). Young and unafraid: Queer criminology's unbounded potential. *Palgrave Communications, 4*(1), 110. https://doi.org/10.1057/s41599-018-0165-x

Panfil, V. R. (2022). "Everybody needs their story to be heard": Motivations to participate in research on LGBTQ criminal offending. *Deviant Behavior, 43*(6), 647–665. https://doi.org/10.1080/01639625.2021.1902756

Panter, H. (2017). Pre-operative transgender motivations for entering policing occupations. *International Journal of Transgenderism, 18*(3), 305–317. https://doi.org/10.1080/15532739.2017.1281194

Panter, H. (2018). *Transgender cops: The intersection of gender and sexuality expectations in police cultures.* Routledge. https://doi.org/10.4324/9781315403700

Paoline, E. A., & Terrill, W. (2004). Women police officers and the use of coercion. *Women & Criminal Justice, 15*(3–4), 97–119.

Parent, M. C., DeBlaere, C., & Moradi, B. (2013). Approaches to research on intersectionality: Perspectives on gender, LGBT, and racial/ethnic identities. *Sex Roles, 68*(11–12), 639–645. https://doi.org/10.1007/s11199-013-0283-2

Parsons, V. (2021, January 8). *Bigoted police officers fired after secret tapes revealed enough homophobic, racist and sexist slurs "to last a lifetime."* Pink News. https://www.thepinknews.com/2021/01/08/hampshire-police-homophobia-sexism-racism/

Peachey, P. (2013, June 17). Kevin Maxwell: "I was meant to be the future. I ticked the boxes." *Independent.* https://www.independent.co.uk/news/people/profiles/kevin-maxwell-i-was-meant-to-be-the-future-i-ticked-the-boxes-8662615.html

People's Union for Civil Liberties–Karnataka. (2001). *Human rights violations against sexual minorities in India: A PUCL-K fact-finding report about Bangalore.*

Pew Research Center. (2022). *Religious landscape study: Views about homosexuality by state.* https://www.pewresearch.org/religion/religious-landscape-study/compare/views-about-homosexuality/by/state/

Pfeffer, C. A. (2014). "I don't like passing as a straight woman": Queer negotiations of identity and social group membership. *American Journal of Sociology, 120*(1), 1–44. https://doi.org/10.1086/677197

Phillips-Osei, W. (2018). *Cracking down on cages: Feminist and prison abolitionist considerations for litigating solitary confinement in Canada.* [Master of Laws research paper, Western Law].

Pickles, J. (2020). Policing hate and bridging communities: A qualitative evaluation of relations between LGBT+ people and the police within the North East of England. *Policing & Society, 30*(7), 741–759. https://doi.org/10.1080/10439463.2019.1588269

Pike, D., & Rollings, J. (2016). *LGBTQ+ speak out! Making Hamilton a queer and trans positive city.* Social Planning and Research Council of Hamilton. https://sprchamilton.ca/wp-content/uploads/2016/06/SpeakOUT_2016_WEB.pdf

Polewski, L. (2019, June 14). *Hamilton Pride celebration will not include police recruitment booth.* Global News. https://globalnews.ca/news/5392798/hamilton-pride-no-police-presence/

Praat, A. C., & Tuffin, K. F. (1996). Police discourses of homosexual men in New Zealand. *Journal of Homosexuality, 31*(4), 57–73. https://doi.org/10.1300/J082v31n04_03

Pride Hamilton Board. (2019, June 16). *2019 Pride Hamilton event a success despite protestors.* https://static.wixstatic.com/ugd/3f1d0c_377f7a0347f84e459b18244968ed2e35.pdf?fbclid=IwAR1rCslVOBUmGNcBZ7uVFngM42G3QpBN7nHXuA9xnggJqbHR48RS1I328CM

Quintana, N. S., Rosenthal, J., & Krehely, J. (2010). *On the streets: The federal response to gay and transgender homeless youth.* Center for American Progress. https://www.americanprogress.org/issues/lgbt/reports/2010/06/21/7983/on-the-streets/

R v. Brown (1994) 1 AC 212 (HL) (Lord Templeman).

Rabe-Hemp, C. E. (2009). POLICEwomen or PoliceWOMEN? Doing gender and police work. *Feminist Criminology, 4*(2), 114–129. https://doi.org/10.1177/1557085108327659

Radulova, L. (2014). Victoria police issue "apology" 20 YEARS after Tasty nightclub raid. *Daily Mail.* https://www.dailymail.co.uk/news/article-2716303/Victoria-police-apologise-7-hour-strip-search-463-clubbers-TWENTY-years-incident.html

Randazzo, T. J. (2005). Social and legal barriers: Sexual orientation and asylum in the United States. In E. Luibhéid & L. Cantú Jr. (Eds.), *Queer migrations: Sexuality, US citizenship, and border crossings* (pp. 30–60). University of Minnesota.

Ream, G. L., & Forge, N. R. (2014). Homeless lesbian, gay, bisexual, and transgender (LGBT) youth in New York City: Insights from the field. *Child Welfare, 93*(2), 7–22.

Reck, J. (2009). Homeless gay and transgender youth of color in San Francisco: "No one likes street kids"—even in the Castro. *Journal of LGBT Youth, 6*(2–3), 223–242. https://doi.org/10.1080/19361650903013519

Reddy, S. (2010). Shifting public/private boundaries: Young women's sexuality within the context of HIV and AIDS in South Africa. *Agenda* [Durban], *24*(83), 88–94. https://doi.org/10.1080/10130950.2010.9676295

Rennstam, J., & Sullivan, K. R. (2018). Peripheral inclusion through informal silencing and voice: A study of LGB officers in the Swedish police. *Gender, Work, and Organization, 25*(2), 177–194. https://doi.org/10.1111/gwa0 .12194

Revathi, A. (2010). *Truth about me: A hijra life story*. Penguin Books

Reyna-Rodriguez, V. (2019). Non-binary police officer finds inclusivity at ISUPD. *Iowa State Daily*. https://www.iowastatedaily.com/diversity/iowa -state-university-police-department-non-binary-police-officer-lgbtqia -and-diversity/article_87ed6c84-0b16-11ea-a394-a301e5cfd246.html

Riccucci, N. M., Van Ryzin, G. G., & Jackson, K. (2018). Representative bureaucracy, race, and policing: A survey experiment. *Journal of Public Administration Research and Theory, 28*(4), 506–518. https://doi.org /10.1093/jopart/muy023

Riccucci, N. M., Van Ryzin, G. G., & Lavena, C. F. (2014). Representative bureaucracy in policing: Does it increase perceived legitimacy? *Journal of Public Administration Research and Theory, 24*(3), 537–551. https://doi .org/10.1093/jopart/muu006

Rich, A. (1980). Compulsory heterosexuality and lesbian existence. *Signs: Journal of Women in Culture and Society, 5*(4), 631–660. https://doi.org /10.1086/493756

Richters, J., Altman, D., Badcock, P. B., Smith, A. M., De Visser, R. O., Grulich, A. E., Rissel, C., & Simpson, J. M. (2014). Sexual identity, sexual attraction and sexual experience: The second Australian Study of Health and Relationships. *Sexual Health, 11*(5), 451–460. https://doi.org/10.1071 /SH14117

Richters, J., De Visser, R. O., Rissel, C. E., Grulich, A. E., & Smith, A. M. A. (2008). Demographic and psychosocial features of participants in bondage and discipline, "sadomasochism" or dominance and submission (BDSM): Data from a national survey. *Journal of Sexual Medicine, 5*(7), 1660–1668. https://doi.org/10.1111/j.1743-6109.2008.00795.x

Ridinger, R. (2006). Negotiating limits: The legal status of SM in the United States. In P. Kleinplatz & J. Moser (Eds.), *Sadomasochism: Powerful pleasures* (pp. 189–216). Harrington Park Press.

Ritchie, A. J. (2013). The pertinence of *Perry* to challenging the continuing criminalization of LGBT people. *New York University Review of Law and Social Change, 37*(1), 63–69.

Ritchie, A. J. (2017). *Invisible no more: Police violence against black women and women of color.* Beacon Press.

Ritchie, A. J., & Jones-Brown, D. (2017). Policing race, gender, and sex: A review of law enforcement policies. *Women & Criminal Justice, 27*(1), 21–50. https://doi.org/10.1080/08974454.2016.1259599

Robinson, B. A. (2020a). *Coming out to the streets: LGBTQ youth experiencing homelessness.* University of California Press. https://doi.org/10.2307/j.ctv182js8v

Robinson, B. A. (2020b). The lavender scare in homonormative times: Policing, hyper-incarceration, and LGBTQ youth homelessness. *Gender & Society, 34*(2), 210–232. https://doi.org/10.1177/0891243220906172

Robinson, B. A. (2021). "They peed on my shoes": Foregrounding intersectional minority stress in understanding LGBTQ youth homelessness. *Journal of LGBT Youth, 20*(4), 783–799. https://doi.org/10.1080/19361653.2021.1925196

Rouse, L. M. (2016). American Indians, Alaska Natives, and the psychology of men and masculinity. In Y. J. Wong & S. R. Wester (Eds.), *APA handbook of men and masculinities* (pp. 319–337). American Psychological Association. https://doi.org/10.1037/14594-015

Rubin, G. (1984). Thinking sex: Notes for a radical theory of the politics of sexuality. In C. Vance (Ed.), *Pleasure and danger: Exploring female sexuality* (pp. 267–319). Routledge & Kegan Paul.

Rumens, N. (2018). *Queer business: Queering organization sexualities.* Routledge. https://doi.org/10.4324/9781315747781

Rumens, N., & Broomfield, J. (2012). Gay men in the police: Identity disclosure and management issues. *Human Resource Management Journal, 22*(3), 283–298. https://doi.org/10.1111/j.1748-8583.2011.00179.x

Russell, E. K. (2019). *Queer histories and the politics of policing.* Routledge.

Ryan, H. (2019). *When Brooklyn was queer.* St. Martin's Press.

Sagarin, B. J., Lee, E. M., Erickson, J. M., Casey, K. G., & Pawirosetiko, J. S. (2019). Collective sex environments without the sex? Insights from the BDSM community. *Archives of Sexual Behavior, 48*(1), 63–67. https://doi.org/10.1007/s10508-018-1252-1

Sand, L. (2019). Removing judgement: Discussing BDSM in adult sexuality education. *American Journal of Sexuality Education, 14*(2), 258–267. https://doi.org/10.1080/15546128.2019.1584869

Saria, V. (2019). Begging for change: Hijras, law and nationalism. *Contributions to Indian Sociology, 53*(1), 133–157. https://doi.org/10.1177/0069966718813588

Sawyer, K., Thoroughgood, C., & Webster, J. (2016). Queering the gender binary: Understanding transgender workplace experiences. In T. Köllen (Ed.), *Sexual orientation and transgender issues in organizations: Global perspectives on LGBT workforce diversity* (pp. 21–42). Springer.

Scharrón-del Río, M. R., & Aja, A. A. (2020). Latinx: Inclusive language as liberation praxis. *Journal of Latinx Psychology, 8*(1), 7–20. https://doi.org/10.1037/lat0000140

Schilt, K. (2006). Just one of the guys? How transmen make gender visible at work. *Gender & Society, 20*(4), 465–490. https://doi.org/10.1177/0891243206288077

Schilt, K., & Connell, C. (2007). Do workplace gender transitions make gender trouble? *Gender, Work, and Organization, 14*(6), 596–618. https://doi.org/10.1111/j.1468-0432.2007.00373.x

Schilt, K., & Wiswall, M. (2008). Before and after: Gender transitions, human capital, and workplace experiences. *The B.E. Journal of Economic Analysis & Policy, 8*(1). https://doi.org/10.2202/1935-1682.1862

Scrappy Jew [@scrappyjew]. (2019, June 15). *On duty @HamiltonPolice in uniform at @hamiltompride in @gageparkhamont told me that they wouldn't stop a fight between fascist and Pride patrons* [Tweet]. Twitter. https://twitter.com/scrappyJew/status/1140008358780506112

Sears, A. (2016). Situating sexuality in social reproduction. *Historical Materialism, 24*(2), 138–163. https://doi.org/10.1163/1569206X-12341474

Seattle Police Foundation. (2021). *Safe place.* https://www.seattlepolicefoundation.org/foundation-impact/community-partnership-programs/safe-place

Sellers, M. D. (2018). Absent inclusion polices: Problems facing homeless transgender youth. *Public Integrity, 20*(6), 625–639. https://doi.org/10.1080/10999922.2018.1446629

Sentencing Project. (2022). *State-by-state data.* https://www.sentencingproject.org/the-facts/#map

Serano, J. (2007). *Whipping girl: A transsexual woman on sexism and the scapegoating of femininity.* Seal Press.

Sewell, A. A., & Jefferson, K. A. (2016). Collateral damage: The health effects of invasive police encounters in New York City. *Journal of Urban Health, 93*(Suppl. 1), 42–67.

Shabazz, R. (2014). "Walls turned sideways are bridges": Carceral scripts and the transformation of the prison space. *ACME, an International E-journal for Critical Geographies, 13*(3), 581–594.

Shah, G. (2009). The impact of economic globalization on work and family collectivism in India. *Journal of Indian Business Research, 1*(2/3), 95–118. https://doi.org/10.1108/17554190911005318

Shelton, J., Poirier, J. M., Wheeler, C., & Abramovich, A. (2017). Reversing erasure of youth and young adults who are LGBTQ and access homelessness services: Asking about sexual orientation, gender identity, and pronouns. *Child Welfare, 96*(2), 1–28.

Silvestri, M. (2017). Police culture and gender: Revisiting the "cult of masculinity." *Policing, 11*(3), 289–300. https://doi.org/10.1093/police/paw052

Simula, B. L. (2019). Pleasure, power, and pain: A review of the literature on the experiences of BDSM participants. *Sociology Compass, 13*(3), e12668. https://doi.org/10.1111/soc4.12668

Sinclair, J. A., Love, M., & Gutiérrez-Vera, M. (2021). Federalism, defunding the police, and democratic values: A functional accountability framework for analyzing police reform proposals. *Publius, 51*(3), 484–511.

Singh, A. A., Boyd, C. J., & Whitman, J. S. (2010). Counseling competency with transgender and intersex persons. In A. Erickson Cornish (Ed.), *Handbook of multicultural counseling competencies* (pp. 415–441). John Wiley & Sons.

Sklansky, D. A. (2005). Not your father's police department: Making sense of the new demographics of law enforcement. *Journal of Criminal Law & Criminology, 96*(3), 1209–1243.

Snapp, S. D., Hoenig, J. M., Fields, A., & Russell, S. T. (2015). Messy, butch, and queer: LGBTQ youth and the school-to-prison pipeline. *Journal of Adolescent Research, 30*(1), 57–82. https://doi.org/10.1177/0743558414557625

Snorton, C. R. (2017). *Black on both sides: A racial history of trans identity.* University of Minnesota Press. https://doi.org/10.5749/j.ctt1pwt7dz

Somerville, E., & Dixon, H. (2021, June 8). Police forces threatened with legal action over links to Stonewall. *The Telegraph.* https://www.telegraph.co.uk/news/2021/06/08/exclusive-police-forces-threatened-legal-action-links-stonewall/

Soss, J., & Weaver, V. (2017). Police are our government: Politics, political science, and the policing of race-class subjugated communities. *Annual Review of Political Science, 20*(1), 565–591. https://doi.org/10.1146/annurev-polisci-060415-093825

Sowa, J. E., & Selden, S. C. (2003). Administrative discretion and active representation: An expansion of the theory of representative bureaucracy. *Public Administration Review, 63*(6), 700–710. https://doi.org/10.1111/1540-6210.00333

Spinelli, E. (2006). Human sexuality: Existential challenges for psychotherapy. *Psychotherapy Section Review, 40,* 17–29.

Starheim, R. P. (2019, July). *Women in policing: Breaking barriers and blazing a path.* National Institute of Justice. https://nij.ojp.gov/library /publications /women-policing-breaking-barriers-and-blazing-path

State and Local Backgrounders. (2020). *Criminal justice expenditures: Police, corrections, and courts.* Urban Institute. https://www.urban.org/policy -centers/cross-center-initiatives/state-and-local-finance-initiative/state -and-local-backgrounders/criminal-justice-police-corrections-courts -expenditures

Stein, A., & Plummer, K. (1994). "I can't even think straight": "Queer" theory and the missing sexual revolution in sociology. *Sociological Theory, 12*(2), 178–187. https://doi.org/10.2307/201863

Stewart-Winter, T. (2015). Queer law and order: Sex, criminality, and policing in the late twentieth-century United States. *Journal of American History* [Bloomington, IN], *102*(1), 61–72. https://doi.org/10.1093/jahist/jav283

Stotzer, R. L. (2014). Law enforcement and criminal justice personnel interactions with transgender people in the United States: A literature review. *Aggression and Violent Behavior, 19*(3), 263–277. https://doi.org/10.1016 /j.avb.2014.04.012

Strauss, A. L. (1987). *Qualitative analysis for social scientists.* Cambridge University Press. https://doi.org/10.1017/CB09780511557842

Stryker, S. (2008). Transgender history, homonormativity, and disciplinarity. *Radical History Review* (no. 100), 145–157.

Stryker, S. (2017, April 8). *What transpires now: Transgender history and the future we need* [Keynote address]. 28th annual John Wesley Powell Student Research Conference, Illinois Wesleyan University. https:// digitalcommons.iwu.edu/jwprc/2017/keynote/1

Stulberg, L. M. (2018). *LGBTQ social movements.* Polity Press.

Stychin, C., & Herman, D. (Eds.). (2000). *Sexuality in the legal arena.* A & C Black.

Swan, A. A. (2016). Masculine, feminine, or androgynous: The influence of gender identity on job satisfaction among female police officers. *Women & Criminal Justice, 26*(1), 1–19. https://doi.org/10.1080/08974454.2015 .1067175

Taylor, T. O., Wilcox, M. M., & Monceaux, C. P. (2020). Race and sexual orientation: An intersectional analysis and confirmatory factor analysis of the Perceptions of Police Scale. *Psychology of Sexual Orientation and Gender Diversity, 7*(3), 253–264. https://doi.org/10.1037/sgd0000392

Taylor, T. W. (1896). The conception of morality in jurisprudence. *Philosophical Review, 5*(1), 36–50. https://doi.org/10.2307/2176104

Tellis, A. (2012). Disrupting the dinner table: Re-thinking the "queer movement" in contemporary India. *Jindal Global Law Review, 4*(1), 142–156.

Terrill, W., & Reisig, M. D. (2003). Neighborhood context and police use of force. *Journal of Research in Crime and Delinquency, 40*(3), 291–321. https://doi.org/10.1177/0022427803253800

Theobald, N. A., & Haider-Markel, D. P. (2009). Race, bureaucracy, and symbolic representation: Interactions between citizens and police. *Journal of Public Administration Research and Theory, 19*(2), 409–426. https://doi.org/10.1093/jopart/mun006

Thorne, B. (1993). *Gender play: Girls and boys in school.* Open University Press.

Thumala, A., Goold, B., & Loader, I. (2011). A tainted trade? Moral ambivalence and legitimation work in the private security industry. *British Journal of Sociology, 62*(2), 283–303. https://doi.org/10.1111/j.1468-4446.2011.01365.x

Toesland, F. (2021, September 25). *Police departments across U.S. are mandating LGBTQ training.* NBC News. https://www.nbcnews.com/nbc-out/out-news/police-departments-us-are-mandating-lgbtq-training-rcna2250

Tomassilli, J. C., Golub, S. A., Bimbi, D. S., & Parsons, J. T. (2009). Behind closed doors: An exploration of kinky sexual behaviors in urban lesbian and bisexual women. *Journal of Sex Research, 46*(5), 438–445. https://doi.org/10.1080/00224490902754202

Tomsen, S. (2009). *Violence, prejudice and sexuality.* Routledge.

The Tower. (2019, June 21). *Starting yesterday evening and into today Hamilton Police Services (HPS) have begun to harass* [Group post]. Facebook. https://www.facebook.com/thetowerhamilton/posts/2834984806528595

Transgender Persons (Protection of Rights) Act (2019). Pub. L. No. 40 of 2019.

Turley, E. L. (2016). "Like nothing I've ever felt before": Understanding consensual BDSM as embodied experience. *Psychology and Sexuality, 7*(2), 149–162. https://doi.org/10.1080/19419899.2015.1135181

Turley, E. L. (2022). "I feel so much better in myself": Exploring meaningful non-erotic outcomes of BDSM participation. *Sexualities, 27*(1–2). https://doi.org/10.1177/13634607211056879

Turley, E. L., & Butt, T. (2015). BDSM—bondage and discipline; dominance and submission; sadism and masochism. In C. Richards & M. J. Barker (Eds.), *The Palgrave handbook of the psychology of sexuality and gender* (pp. 24–41). Palgrave Macmillan.

Turley, E. L., King, N., & Monro, S. (2018). "You want to be swept up in it all": Illuminating the erotic in BDSM. *Psychology and Sexuality, 9*(2), 148–160. https://doi.org/10.1080/19419899.2018.1448297

Uniform Crime Report. (2018). *Full-time law enforcement employees* [Table 74]. 2018 crime in the United States. Criminal Justice Information Services Division, FBI. https://web.archive.org/web/20191007230146/https://ucr.fbi.gov/crime-in-the-u.s/2018/crime-in-the-u.s.-2018/tables/table-74

United We Dream. (2019, February). *The truth about ICE & CBP: A comprehensive analysis of the devastating human impact of the deportation force by the immigrant youth and families who know it best.* https://unitedwedream.org/wp-content/uploads/2019/02/TheTruthICECBP-02052019-v3.pdf.

Valcore, J. L., & Dodge, M. (2019). How hate crime legislation shapes gay and lesbian target groups: An analysis of social construction, law, and policy. *Criminal Justice Policy Review, 30*(2), 293–315. https://doi.org/10.1177/0887403416651924

Valcore, J. L., Fradella, H. F., Guadalupe-Diaz, X., Ball, M. J., Dwyer, A., DeJong, C., Walker, A., Wodda, A., & Worthen, M. G., (2021). Building an intersectional and trans-inclusive criminology: Responding to the emergence of "gender critical" perspectives in feminist criminology. *Critical Criminology, 29*, 687–706.

Valcore, J. L., & Pfeffer, R. (2018). Systemic error: Measuring gender in criminological research. *Criminal Justice Studies, 31*(4), 333–351. https://doi.org/10.1080/1478601X.2018.1499022

Valdes, F. (2005). Legal reform and social justice: An introduction to LatCrit theory, praxis and community. *Griffith Law Review, 14*(2), 148–173. https://doi.org/10.1080/10383441.2005.10854554

Valentine, V. (2015). *Non-binary people's experiences in the UK.* Scottish Trans Alliance. https://www.scottishtrans.org/wp-content/uploads/2016/11/Non-binary-report.pdf

Vanita, R., & Kidwai, S. (2002). Same-sex love in India: Readings from literature and history. *International Journal of Sociology of the Family, 30*(1), 91–93.

Vitale, A. S. (2017). *The end of policing.* Verso.

Waite, S. (2021). Should I stay or should I go? Employment discrimination and workplace harassment against transgender and other minority employees in Canada's federal public service. *Journal of Homosexuality, 68*(11), 1833–1859. https://doi.org/10.1080/00918369.2020.1712140

Walker, A., Sexton, L., Valcore, J. L., Sumner, J., & Wodda, A. (2018). Transgender and nonbinary individuals. In C. Roberson (Ed.), *Routledge handbook of social, economic and criminal justice* (pp. 220–233). Routledge.

Walker, A., Valcore, J., Evans, B., & Stephens, A. (2021). Experiences of trans scholars in criminology and criminal justice. *Critical Criminology, 29*(1), 37–56. https://doi.org/10.1007/s10612-021-09561-5

Warner, M. (1993). *Fear of a queer planet: Queer politics and social theory.* University of Minnesota Press.

Watson, H. G. (2020, August 10). The anatomy of a city with a hate problem. *Xtra Magazine.* https://xtramagazine.com/power/hamilton-ontario-hate-problem-city-177031?fbclid=IwAR3_-P300P52xteSurxWk1szYZbbPQPoJmJT02S66b0AlKqdXvKVS6dnk00

Watson, K. (2005). Queer theory. *Group Analysis, 38*(1), 67–81.

Weait, M. (2007). Sadomasochism and the law. In D. Langdridge & M. Barker (Eds.), *Safe, sane and consensual contemporary perspectives on sadomasochism* (pp. 63–84). Palgrave Macmillan.

Weaver, V., Prowse, G., & Piston, S. (2019). Too much knowledge, too little power: An assessment of political knowledge in highly policed communities. *Journal of Politics, 81*(3), 1153–1166. https://doi.org/10.1086/703538

Weiss, M. (2011). *Techniques of pleasure: BDSM and the circuits of sexuality.* Duke University Press. https://doi.org/10.1515/9780822394914

Weiss, M. D. (2006). Mainstreaming kink: The politics of BDSM representation in U.S. popular media. *Journal of Homosexuality, 50*(2–3), 103–132. https://doi.org/10.1300/J082v50n02_06

West, C., & Zimmerman, D. H. (1987). Doing gender. *Gender & Society, 1*(2), 125–151. https://doi.org/10.1177/0891243287001002002

Westbrook, L., & Schilt, K. (2014). Doing gender, determining gender: Transgender people, gender panics, and the maintenance of the sex/gender /sexuality system. *Gender & Society, 28*(1), 32–57. https://doi.org/10.1177 /0891243213503203

Westmarland, L. (2001). *Gender and policing: Sex, power and police culture.* Willan.

Wilkins, V. M., & Williams, B. N. (2008). Black or blue: Racial profiling and representative bureaucracy. *Public Administration Review, 68*(4), 654–664.

Williams, D. J., Thomas, J. N., & Prior, E. E. (2015). Moving full-speed ahead in the wrong direction? A critical examination of US sex-offender policy from a positive sexuality model. *Critical Criminology, 23*(3), 277–294. https://doi.org/10.1007/s10612-015-9270-y

Williams, D. J., Thomas, J. N., Prior, E. E., & Christensen, M. C. (2014). From "SSC" and "RACK" to the "4Cs": Introducing a new framework for negotiating BDSM participation. *Electronic Journal of Human Sexuality, 17*(5), 1–10.

Williams, M. L., & Robinson, A. L. (2004). Problems and prospects with policing the lesbian, gay and bisexual community in Wales. *Policing and Society, 14*(3), 213–232. https://doi.org/10.1080/1043946042000241811

Wismeijer, A. A. J., & van Assen, M. A. L. M. (2013). Psychological characteristics of BDSM practitioners. *Journal of Sexual Medicine, 10*(8), 1943–1952. https://doi.org/10.1111/jsm.12192

Wolff, K. B., & Cokely, C. L. (2007). "To protect and to serve?" An exploration of police conduct in relation to the gay, lesbian, bisexual, and transgender community. *Sexuality & Culture, 11*(2), 1–23. https://doi.org/10.1007 /s12119-007-9000-z

*Women encouraged to join Navajo Nation Police Force.* (2017, February 20). KNAU News Talk–Arizona Public Radio. https://www.knau.org/knau -and-arizona-news/2017-02-20/women-encouraged-to-join-navajo -nation-police-force

Woods, J. B. (2014). Queer contestations and the future of a critical "queer" criminology. *Critical Criminology, 22*(1), 5–19. https://doi.org/10.1007 /s10612-013-9222-3

Woods, J. B. (2017). LGBT identity and crime. *California Law Review, 105*(3), 667–733. https://doi.org/10.15779/Z389W08Z24

Woods, J. B., Galvan, F. H., Bazargan, M., Herman, J. L., & Chen, Y. T. (2013). Latina transgender women's interactions with law enforcement in Los Angeles County. *Policing, 7*(4), 379–391. https://doi.org/10.1093/police /pat025

Worden, R. E. (1990). A badge and a baccalaureate: Policies, hypotheses, and further evidence. *Justice Quarterly, 7*(3), 565–592. https://doi.org/10.1080 /07418829000090731

World Health Organization. (2017). *Violence against women.* https://www .who.int/news-room/factsheets/detail/violence-against-women.

Wright, J. E., & Headley, A. M. (2020). Police use of force interactions: Is race relevant or gender germane? *American Review of Public Administration, 50*(8), 851–864. https://doi.org/10.1177/0275074020919908

Wright, S. (2006). Discrimination of SM-identified individuals. *Journal of Homosexuality, 50*(2–3), 217–231. https://doi.org/10.1300/J082v50n02_10

Wright, S. (2018). De-pathologization of consensual BDSM. *Journal of Sexual Medicine, 15*(5), 622–624.

Zempi, I. (2020). "Looking back, I wouldn't join up again": The lived experiences of police officers as victims of bias and prejudice perpetrated by fellow staff within an English police force. *Police Practice & Research, 21*(1), 33–48. https://doi.org/10.1080/15614263.2018.1525381

# Index

*Italicized page numbers indicate figures.*

Abdi, Abdirahman, 54
Abdi, Chevranna, 39–40
abnormality, concept of, 104, 147
abolishment/defunding of police,
    calls for, 31–32, 54, 170
Aboriginal and Torres Strait
    Islanders, 8
accountability systems, self-reliant, 32
Acker, J., 128
activist movements, 16, 20, 26–27, 32
affinity groups, 46, 55n7
AIDS Coalition to Unleash Power
    (ACT UP), 32
Aja, A. A., 24
Allport, Gordon, 137–38
anti-police sentiment, 41, 54, 71, 197
assigned female/male at birth, 8, 62,
    179
Atkinson, P., 120
Australia, 8, 19, 111, 147, 166

Ball, M. J., 21, 147, 165, 167
bathrooms, sex-segregated, 181, 188,
    196
Bayerl, P. S., 118
BDSM: communication guidelines
    for professionals, 111–12; conflated
    with intimate partner violence,
    102, 110–12; consenting adults, 4,
    110–11; crime in context of, 108;
    differences between heterosexual
    and LGBTQ+ people, 100,
    102; kinkphobia, 101, 108–10;
    mainstream media depictions of,
    103–5; Operation Spanner, 105;
    organized communities, 104, 108–9;
    overview of, 101–2; pathologization
    of, 100, 103–6, 112; police inability
    to distinguish between consent and
    abuse, 4, 100; safety systems, 104,
    110

LGBTQ+ people of color, 24, 198. *See also* Black people; Latinx LGBTQ+ communities

LGBTQ+ police officers, 1–5, 84; banned from Pride events, 79; femininity looked down on, 128–29; liaison officers, 136, 147, 166–69; more barriers for gay men than lesbians, 148, 152–53; "real" policing/police, 82–83, 154–55; stereotyped as "unfit" to serve, 146–47, 152, 173, 182, 185; transgender work experiences and identity formation in occupational settings, 116–17; and transitioning, 115–30; visibility and intra-conflict within LGBTQ+ policing community, 125–27. *See also* gay male police officers in United Kingdom; identities, LGBTQ+; lesbian police officers; transgender police officers; transitioning police officers

liaison programs, 1, 6, 9, 77; in Australia, 166; community liaisons, 164–65; definition of liaison officer, 163–64; family liaison officers, 164–65; and genderqueer officers, 188; LGBTQ+ liaison officers, 136, 147, 166–69; officer preference not to be visibly aligned with, 147; queering LGBTQ+ liaisons and its implications, 170–73; queer theory applied to, 162–63, 169–74; sequestering of, 81, 83–84; in U.S. South, 95, 97, 98; as "window dressing," 165

Lipman, Nancy, 135, 137

Loftus, B., 149

Loku, Andrew, 54

Lutsky, N., 128–29

Macpherson report (United Kingdom), 149

Mallory, C., 89

manuals, police, 95–97

*Mapping the Void: Two-Spirit and LGBTQ+ Experiences in Hamilton*, 39, 40–41

marginalized communities and people, 3–4, 23; acknowledged in some police departments, 77; and lesbian police officers, 139, 144; and LGBTQ+ police officers, 5; massive elimination of, 33; perceptions of police, 165–66; and police department structure, 76, 82, 108; police protection of as conditional, 38, 41, 52–53; underrepresented in policing, 163

masculinity: attributed to gay men, 102; cis-masculinity, performance of, 129; critical perspectives on, 156–57; hegemonic, 107, 117–18, 133, 144, 170, 174, 179–80; hypermasculinity, 5, 9, 108, 117, 124, 130, 145–48, 153–56, 161, 199; lesbian, 129; in police organizational culture, 5, 9, 108, 117–19, 128–30; as synonymous with police work, 153–54; transgender, 129

massive elimination, 33

Maxwell, Kevin, 159

Maynard, Robyn, 39, 40

McGuffey, Charmaine, 141–42, 144

McLean, C., 150

McNichols, J., 139

mental health outcomes, 28, 62, 66, 75, 142

Mercer, E., 165

Messerschmidt, J.W., 117

Metropolitan Police Service (London, United Kingdom), 149, 150, 159

Miles-Johnson, T., 125
Millennials, 178
Miller, S. L., 154
Moore, 54
moral agents, police as, 13, 16, 22, 134, 167
Moretti, John Mark, 47
Moser, C., 106, 111
Moton, Lauren, 143
Municipal Equality Index (Human Rights Campaign), 87, 90–91
murders/shootings by police, 39, 54, 89, 165
Myers, K. A., 154

National Association for the Advancement of Colored People, 7–8
National Center for Transgender Equality, 19, 29; ID Document Center, 87, 90–91
National Coalition of Anti-Violence Programs (United States), 19
National Conference of State Legislatures, 89
National Institute of Justice report, 142
National LGBT+ Police Network (United Kingdom), 149
National LGBTQ Task Force, 29
National Police Chiefs' Council (United Kingdom), 146
National Standard for Workforce Data (United Kingdom), 146
National Transgender Discrimination Survey (NTDS), 27–28, 31, 61
Native American/Indigenous persons, 3
Navajo, or Diné, Nation Police Department, 193–94
Navarro, Ray, 32
Neil, Jeff, 142

Nestlé, Indigenous activism against, 42–43
New South Wales Police Force, 166
New York Police Department, 33
nonbinary people, 4, 9, 178; elevated risk of police attention for, 64; police harassment of, 59–61; presentation management by, 59–72; and sex-segregated public bathrooms, 181, 188, 196; terms used by, 63. *See also* gender-nonconforming people; genderqueer police officers; presentation management; transgender people
"normality," queer theory challenges to, 159, 169
normalizing strategies, 152
norms: international, 20; police as moral agents, 13, 16, 22, 134, 167; police enforcement of, 13–14, 62. *See also* cisgender normativity; "deviants" (norm violators); heteronormativity
North Shore, 42, 49, 55n6

Office of the Correctional Investigator (Canada), 8
O'Neill, M., 165, 166
Operation Spanner (UK), 105
organizational culture, 2, 199; binary ideologies within policing, 118–19, 125, 127–30; gender androgyny or nonconforming gender not accepted in, 119; and gendered work assignments, 117–18; masculinity/hypermasculinity in, 5, 9, 108, 117–18, 128–30, 145, 147, 153–56; positive shifts in, 139; post-transition experiences, 121–22; sex-segregated characteristics, 6; theoretical concepts of gender and identity

within, 117–19. *See also* four-frame model of organizational dynamics; police departments; public service agencies; transitioning police officers; young people, LGBTQ+

outing, by police, 39, 89; of LGBTQ+ colleagues, 141–42, 184, 189

over- and under-policing, 27, 107, 112, 148–49, 162

Paddick, Brian, 151

Palmer, N. A., 90

Panter, Heather, 119, 121, 176–77

pathologization, 112; of BDSM, 100, 103–6; of sexual and gender minorities, 106

Pfeffer, C. A., 68

pink-washing, 2

police: banned from Pride events, 3, 33, 37, 43–47, 50–54, 79, 162–63; gendering of occupation, 157; great physical strength not required, 139–40; Hamilton, Ontario, 37–38; homophobia and transphobia in, 101, 106–8, 133–34; as moral agents, 13, 16, 22, 134, 167; movements to abolish, 31–32, 54, 170; murders/ shootings by, 39, 54, 89, 165; neutrality as foil for supporting white supremacists, 49; norms enforced by, 13–14, 62; order maintenance and social control by, 60–61; queer notion of, 14; safety compromised by, 43–44; secondary victimization by, 9, 51–52, 108; slavery enforced by in United States, 26, 76; teams, 181, 184–85, 189. *See also* gay male police officers in United Kingdom; genderqueer police officers; law enforcement personnel (LEP); lesbian police officers; LGBTQ+ police officers;

police violence; transgender police officers

police departments: efficiency, effectiveness, economy, and equity, 77–78; factions within, 80–81, 84; heteronormativity in, 108, 123–24, 147–48, 151–52, 160–61; hypermasculinity in, 5, 9, 108, 117, 124, 130, 145–47, 153–56. *See also* organizational culture

police harassment, 1, 59–61, 89, 107, 162; of colleagues, 5, 141–42, 179–80, 184–85, 189–91; deadnaming, 39, 175; for gender presentation, 59–61, 64–66, 189–90; racialized, 70. *See also* police violence

police violence, 2, 77; hierarchical and exclusionary, 82; in India, 16–18; toward Latinx LGBTQ+ communities, 26–30; in United States, 19, 23. *See also* police harassment

political frame, 80–81, 83

positive actions and interactions, 1–2, 4

power: and political frame, 80–81; queering, 170

Praat, A. C., 153

preachers, homo/transphobic, 37–38, 40–43, 47–50. *See also* white supremacists

presentation management, 4, 59–72, 107; automatic process of, 67; "disorder," policing of, 60–61, 71; experiences of profiling and harassment, 64–66; by gay male police officers, 152; harassment for gender presentation, 59–61; identification documents and mismatch with presentation, 65–66; by lesbians, 140–41; literature review, 60–62; profiling for alleged

societal acceptance of LGBTQ+ people, 76–77
sodomy laws, 107; India, 15–16; overturned by *Lawrence v. Texas*, 89
SOGIE (sexual orientation, gender identity and expression), 163
solitary confinement, as a form of torture, 29
South, U.S., 4, 86–99; anti-transgender laws, 87; cities, 87, 91; city reforms, 95–97; LGBTQ+ policing reforms in, 89–90; policing and LGBTQ+ communities, 88–89; policing LGBTQ+ bodies, 90; stand-your-ground or self-defense laws, 89, 97; state criminal law and policies, 91–92, *92*; stigmatization of LGBTQ+ people, 86–87
spectacle, 18–19
State of Equality Index (Human Rights Campaign), 87, 90–91
"stealth" presentation, 67, 90
stigma, 15, 86, 107; and BDSM, 103, 105, 109–10; internalized, 134; and transgender policing, 122–23
Stonewall charity (United Kingdom), 150
Stonewall riot, 2, 27, 77
Stonewall Top 100 Employers list, 150
Strauss, A. L., 120
Street Transvestite Action Revolutionaries, 27, 32
structural frame, 75–78, 81–84
"survival consciousness," 147
Swan, A. A., 141
Sydney Mardi Gras arrests, 2
symbolism, 81–82

Taylor, Breonna, 54
TD Canada Trust, 43

teams, police, 184–85, 189; mixed-gender double-crewing, 181
Teena, Brandon, 1, 89, 98
"three piece" rule, 60
Tower (anarchist social space, Hamilton), 39, 44
*Transexual Phenomenon, The* (Benjamin), 27
*Transgender Cops: The Intersection of Gender and Sexuality Expectations in Police Cultures* (Panter), 119–20, 130
transgender men, 119, 123–29; and male privilege, 123–24
transgender people, 4, 9; anti-transgender laws, 87; disappearance and murder rates, 2; occupational challenges while transitioning, 116–17; police harassment of, 59–61; presentation management by, 59–72; repeated arrests of, 64; sex work as only option for, 29; terms used by, 63; in United States, 19; "walking while trans," 29, 61–62, 89, 170. *See also* nonbinary people
Transgender Persons (Protection of Rights) Act (India), 20–21
transgender police officers, 5; cisgender LGB police bias toward, 125–27; harassment of by colleagues, 175–76, 187; and searches, 189–90. *See also* transitioning police officers
Transgender Survey of 2015, 178
"transgender" umbrella, 178
transgender women: of color, 39–40, 61, 69, 89; and documentation, 90; high levels of harassment and violence by police, 61–65, 90; Latinx, 28–31, 61; as police officers, 122–30. *See also* hijras

transitioning police officers, 115–30; changes in occupational socialization within policing, 127–29; experiences in occupational settings, 116–17; (transgender) visibility, transitioning, and identity with policing, 121–25. *See also* identities, LGBTQ+; LGBTQ+ police officers; organizational culture; transgender police officers

transphobia, 20, 25, 40, 65, 125; in police, 101, 106–8

trauma-informed models, 36

Trump, Donald, 49

Tuffin, K. F., 153

Two-Spirit, queer, and transgender people: community solidarity, 49–50; defense provided by, 37–38. *See also* Indigenous communities; LGBTQ+ community members

uniforms, police, 180–81, 190–91, 195

unions, 81

United Kingdom: anti-transgender movement, 150; BDSM laws, 105; Equality Act of 2010, 149; Gender Identity Certificate, 189; Hampshire Constabulary investigation, 155; Macpherson report, 149; policing policy and reform context, 148–51; racism in policing practices, 149. *See also* gay male police officers in United Kingdom

United States: activist movements, 26–27, 32; BDSM laws, 105–6; civil rights movement, 26; colonialism, 23; criminalization of same-sex/same-gender/queer relations, 26; detention centers, 28–29, 33–34, 36; history of police violence toward BIPOC and Latinx communities, 26–30; immigration to,

25–26, 28–29, 33–34, 36; interacting systems of white supremacy, white nationalism, and policing, 24, 26, 31; police violence in, 19, 23; slavery enforced by police in, 26, 76. *See also* Latinx LGBTQ+ communities; white supremacy

Vanderweide, Chris, 47

Vanguard, 27, 32

victim-blaming by police, 19, 51–52, 108

Vitale, A. S., 170

vulnerabilities, 5–6

vulnerable people, police treatment of, 199

walking while trans, 29, 61–62, 89, 170

Wallis, Terri, 41

Ward 23 (Chicago), 136

Warehouse Spa and Bath (Hamilton), 39–40

Watson, HG, 40

West, C., 116

Western values, 192

white privilege, 139, 154, 157

white supremacists: aggressiveness of, 44–45, 47; Charlottesville, Virginia, rally, 49; enabled by police neglect, 48; Hamilton, Ontario, 37, 42; at Pride Hamilton, 37–38, 43–51; searches by Black and/or queer officers, 189–90. *See also* preachers, homo/transphobic

white supremacy, 3, 23; in Hamilton, Ontario, 37, 42, 43–51. *See also* United States

Williams, D. J., 146, 153

women: cisgender police officers, 118; positive contributions to policing, 132; shunned from police professions, 134. *See also* lesbian police officers

# PERSPECTIVES
## ON CRIME AND JUSTICE

Open, inclusive, and broad in focus, the series covers scholarship on a wide range of crime and justice issues, including the exploration of understudied subjects relating to crime, its causes, and attendant social responses. Of particular interest are works that examine emerging topics or shed new light on more richly studied subjects. Volumes in the series explore emerging forms of deviance and crime, critical perspectives on crime and justice, international and transnational considerations of and responses to crime, innovative crime reduction strategies, and alternate forms of response by the community and justice system to disorder, delinquency, and criminality. Both single-authored studies and collections of original edited content are welcome.

## Series Editor

Joseph A. Schafer is a professor of criminology and criminal justice at St. Louis University. His research considers issues of police behavior, police organizations, and citizen perceptions of crime. He is the author, coauthor, or coeditor of several books, including *Effective Leadership in Policing: Successful Traits and Habits* and *Contemporary Research on Police Organizations*, and he has written more than fifty scholarly journal articles and more than two dozen book chapters and essays.